The Fur Trade
of the
American West
1807-1840

The Fur Trade of the American West
1807-1840

A Geographical Synthesis

David J. Wishart

UNIVERSITY OF NEBRASKA PRESS
Lincoln/London

Library of Congress Cataloging in Publication Data

Wishart, David J.   1946–
    The fur trade of the American West, 1807–40

    Bibliography: p. 219
    Includes index.
    1. Fur trade — The West — History. 2. The West —
History — To 1848. I. Title.
F592.W78   978'.02   78-62915
ISBN 0-8032-4705-2

Contents

List of Illustrations

Acknowledgements

Preface   9

1. The Geographical Setting   13

2. The Upper Missouri Fur Trade: Strategy   41

3. The Upper Missouri Fur Trade: Annual Cycle of
   Operations   79

4. The Rocky Mountain Trapping System: Strategy   115

5. The Rocky Mountain Trapping System:
   Annual Cycle of Operations   175

6. The Fur Trade of the West: Assessment   205

Bibliography   219

Index   231

Illustrations

Figures

1. Louisiana, from the 1804 Arrowsmith and Lewis Atlas 15
2. Native American and Euro-American Boundaries,
   circa 1830   16
3. The Physical Setting   24
4. Drouillard's Map of the Yellowstone Country, 1808   43
5. The Upper Missouri Fur Trade, 1807–20   44
6. The Upper Missouri Fur Trade, 1820–6   49
7. The Upper Missouri Fur Trade, 1826–40   55
8. Spatial Organisation of the Upper Missouri Fur Trade   80
9. Plan of Fort Pierre   89
10. The Annual Cycle of Operations on the Upper
    Missouri, circa 1835   93
11. Transportation Routes to Market, circa 1835   108
12. The Pacific Fur Company, 1810–13   118
13. The Rocky Mountain Trapping system, 1822–6   123
14. David Burr's Map of the United States 1839   134
15. The Rocky Mountain Trapping System, 1826–30   135
16. The Rocky Mountain Trapping System, 1830–4   144
17. Bonneville's Map of the Central Rockies   153
18. The Rocky Mountain Trapping System, 1834–40   164
19. The Spatial Organisation of the Rocky Mountain
    Trapping System   176
20. The Annual Cycle of Operations in the Rocky
    Mountains, circa 1830   177
21. Rendezvous and Winter Sites   186

Tables

1. Stream Gradients and Beaver Habitats   28
2. The State of the Fur Trade on the Missouri
   River in 1819   47
3. Fur Production at the Trading Posts:
   A Fragmentary Record, 1828–43   58
4. The Operation of the Credit System: The Crazy
   Bear, Assiniboine Chief   94
5. Fur Returns at Astoria, 1812–13   120
6. 'Amount of Property Lost by the firm of
   Smith, Jackson and Sublette, from depredations
   of different tribes of Indians from July 1826
   to July 1830'   138
7. Nathaniel Wyeth's Estimates of Beaver Production
   in the Rocky Mountains and Northern Great Plains,
   1832 and 1833   147
8. Estimated Costs of Sending a Supply Train
   to the Central Rockies in 1833   195
9. Trading Rates at Fort Hall, 1834   199

Plates

1. Fort Pierre on the Missouri
   (Carl Bodmer, 1840)   57
2. Fort Union on the Missouri
   (Carl Bodmer, 1841)   60
3. Fort Laramie, or Sublettes Fort, near the
   Nebraska or Platte River (Alfred Jacob Miller, 1837)   63
4. The Steamer *Yellowstone* on 19 April 1833
   (Carl Bodmer, 1840)   84
5. Setting Traps for Beaver (Alfred Jacob Miller,
   1837)   180

Acknowledgements

I would like to express my appreciation to the individuals and institutions whose support facilitated the writing of this book. I owe thanks to the staff of the Missouri Historical Society for their expertise and hospitality and to the Nebraska State Historical Society for gathering scattered source materials in one convenient location. I am also grateful to the Woodrow Wilson Foundation for the Dissertation Fellowship which got me started on this topic and to the University of Nebraska for small grants of time and money which allowed me to finish it. Thanks are also due to Timothy Keelan for his interpretative cartography work and to Kent Heerman who directed the reproduction of the maps. Ms Audria Shumard did an impeccable job of typing the manuscript. I owe a particular debt to Dr Leslie Hewes for his sound advice and quiet authority in the area of historical geography. Finally, but first of all, I give special thanks to Carole who encouraged me to be serious about my work without taking myself too seriously.

To my father and the memory of my mother

Preface

The American fur trade of the Trans-Missouri West is a well studied subject. This is understandable, for there has been a persistent intellectual fascination with the American confrontation with the wilderness since the Romantic movement of the eighteenth and nineteenth centuries.[1] This historical literature constitutes a rich collection of professional and popular works, and some scholars have devoted lifetimes of meticulous research to the subject.

The historical emphasis, however, has generally been more on personality than on place, more on the detailed study of parts of the fur trade than on the general characteristics of the whole.[2] There is a need for a new synthesis which adopts an interdisciplinary approach and focuses on the interrelationships between the biological, physical, and cultural environments of the fur trade. That is the objective of this study. The fur trade is viewed as a spatial system, and the 'guiding ideas' are what D.W. Meinig has termed strategy and ecology — man's organisation of area and man's relationships with the other parts of the ecosystem.[3]

The first trappers and traders approached the Trans-Missouri West with an unsophisticated knowledge of its geographic content. Their initial attempts to devise methods of exploiting the fur resources of the northern Great Plains and Rocky Mountains were, therefore, experiments — preludes to the emergence of successful production systems in the mid-1820s. As information concerning the details of the land

and its native inhabitants accumulated, the basis for decision-making became more assured and less a matter of trial and error.

In the mid-1820s, after twenty years of experimentation, the fur trade of the Trans-Missouri West crystallised into a 'steady state' and functioned for almost a decade without substantial change in areal organisation. Two production systems emerged, each with a distinctive strategy. The Rocky Mountain Trapping System was based on beaver pelts, the Euro-American trapper, the rendezvous trade nexus, and the Platte overland supply route. The main product of the Upper Missouri Fur Trade, on the other hand, was bison robes, procured and processed by Native Americans, exchanged at the trading posts for manufactured products, and moved to St Louis by water transportation. At St Louis the production systems joined and the robes, skins and furs were fed into a trade network that was of national and international extent. A condition of dynamic equilibrium was maintained until the mid-1830s when, dislocated by major changes in its parts, the system was retrenched and a new strategy for the fur trade was formulated.[4]

This study is a geographic synthesis, and no attempt is made to write a definitive historical narrative. Attention is first directed to the geographical setting of the fur trade. Then the two production subsystems will be analysed, first their macrogeographic structures, then the details of man's intimate relations with the environment. Finally an assessment will be made of the fur trade as a stage of frontier occupance, which for almost forty years at the beginning of the nineteenth century was the primary form of Euro-American activity in the Trans-Missouri West.

Notes

1. R. Nash, *Wilderness and the American Mind* (New Haven and London: Yale University Press, 1973).
2. Notable exceptions are H.M. Chittenden, *The American Fur Trade of the Far West* (New York: F.P. Harper, 1902); P.C. Phillips, *The Fur Trade* (Norman: University of Oklahoma Press, 1961); J.E. Sunder, *The Fur Trade on the Upper Missouri, 1840—1865* (Norman: University of Oklahoma Press, 1965); and L.R. Hafen, *The Mountain Men and*

the Fur Trade of the Far West (Glendale, California: Arthur H. Clarke Co., 1965), vol. 1, pp. 20—176.

3. D.W. Meinig, *The Great Columbia Plain: A Historical Geography, 1805—1910* (Seattle and London: University of Washington Press, 1968), xii.

4. For further information on the concepts of ecosystem and systems analysis see D.R. Stoddart, 'Organism and Ecosystem as Geographical Models', in R.J. Chorley and P. Haggett (eds.), *Integrated Models in Geography* (London: Methuen, 1970), pp. 511—48; H.C. Brookfield, 'On the Environment as Perceived', in C. Board, R.J. Chorley, P. Haggett, and D.R. Stoddart (eds.), *Progress in Geography* (London: Edward Arnold, 1969), vol. 1, pp. 51—80; R.J. Berkhofer, Jr, *A Behavioral Approach to Historical Analysis* (New York: The Free Press, 1969), pp. 169—210; and L. Von Bertalanffy, *General System Theory* (New York: George Braziller, 1968).

1 The Geographical Setting

The Geostrategic Context

On 30 April 1803, quite unexpectedly, the transfer of Louisiana from France to the United States was transacted, and overnight the young nation more than doubled its land-holdings. The Louisiana Purchase, described by one historian as a 'precocious and despotic act on the part of a very young and rather insecure state',[1] terminated the era of Spanish and French control of New Orleans and secured the American grip on the fertile Mississippi valley. When the French minister Talleyrand was asked to define the content and bounds of Louisiana he evasively replied, 'You have made a noble bargain, make the most of it.'[2] In time the United States would follow this advice, and within a century the plains and prairies of the Louisiana Purchase would be transformed into the most important agricultural region in the world. In the early nineteenth century, however, Louisiana Territory was viewed by the American government more as a reserve to be held for some indefinite future development than as an area suitable for immediate settlement.

A century and a half of Spanish, French and British exploration had furnished only a skeleton of information on Louisiana; even the boundaries of the cession were obscure. The 'true northern boundary', according to Thomas Jefferson, followed the 'northern water line' to the Lake of the Woods, then traced the forty-ninth parallel to the crest of the Rocky

13

Mountains.[3] The location and form of those 'Shining Mountains' was a matter of conjecture in 1803, and contemporary cartographers often placed them too far to the west (Figure 1).

The southern boundary of Louisiana was not clarified until the Adams—Onis Treaty was negotiated with Spain on 22 February 1819. Under the terms of this treaty Spain ceded her claim to Oregon, sold Florida to the United States, and in turn was guaranteed in her possession of Texas which would serve as a bulwark for Mexico. The boundary of Louisiana followed the Sabine River to the thirty-second parallel, thence north to the Red River and the one hundredth line of longitude, north again to the Arkansas which was traced to its source, north to the forty-second parallel, then west to the Pacific (Figure 2). American and British fur trappers, remote from the seats of political power, would pay scant attention to these undemarcated boundaries.

Jefferson admitted that the United States was given 'no claim in right of Louisiana'[4] to the land west of the Rocky Mountains, but this did not dim his vision of an American empire extending to the Pacific. A rather tenuous claim to Oregon was formulated upon Captain Robert Gray's discovery of the mouth of the Columbia in 1792, the Lewis and Clark exploration of 1804 to 1806, and the Pacific Fur Company's trading settlement at Astoria from 1811 to 1813.

With Spain eliminated from Oregon, the United States was left with only Russia and Britain as contenders for that distant country. Russia withdrew her claim on 5 April 1824, relinquishing all rights of settlement in the territory south of 50° 40' north. The British challenge was more tenacious. On 20 October 1818, having failed to reach a satisfactory agreement on the location of the northern boundary, Britain and the United States arranged a joint occupance of Oregon for ten years. This agreement was extended in 1828 for an indefinite period of time. The settlement favoured the British, for the Hudson's Bay Company was securely established on the Columbia. As long as the fur trade was the medium for rivalry British control of Oregon was never seriously threatened.

In 1803 American plans for the occupance of Louisiana Territory were nebulous, and the lack of specific geographic

Figure 1: Louisiana, from the 1804 Arrowsmith and Lewis Atlas

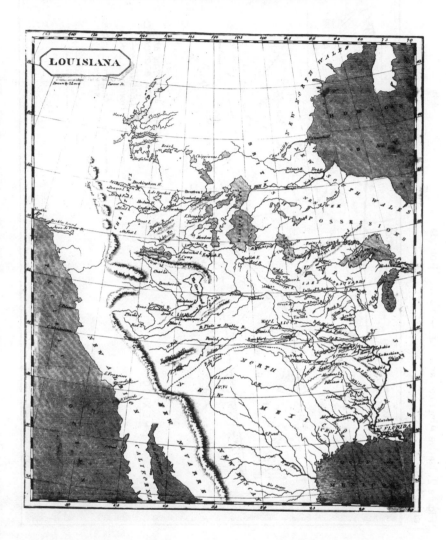

Figure 2: Native American and Euro-American Boundaries circa 1830

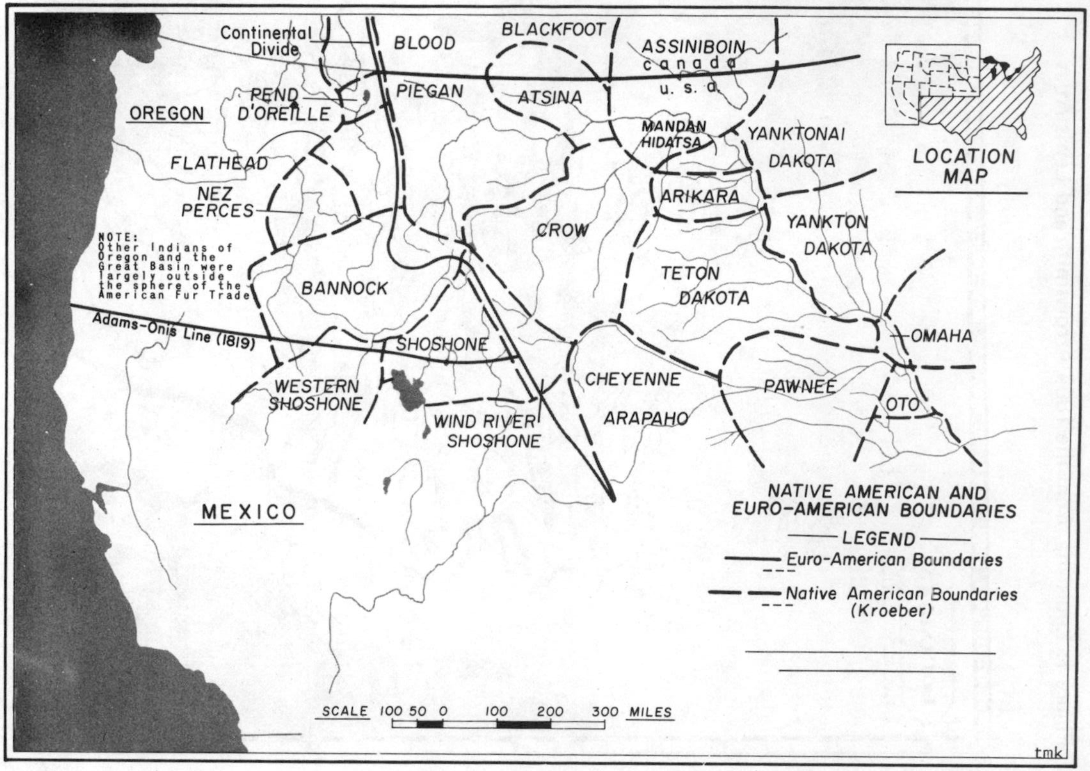

Continental Divide
BLOOD
BLACKFOOT
ASSINIBOIN
canada
u. s. a.
PIEGAN
ATSINA
PEND D'OREILLE
OREGON
MANDAN HIDATSA
YANKTONAI DAKOTA
LOCATION MAP
FLATHEAD
NEZ PERCES
ARIKARA
CROW
YANKTON DAKOTA
NOTE: Other Indians of Oregon and the Great Basin were largely outside the sphere of the American Fur Trade
BANNOCK
TETON DAKOTA
Adams-Onis Line (1819)
SHOSHONE
OMAHA
CHEYENNE
WESTERN SHOSHONE
PAWNEE
OTO
WIND RIVER SHOSHONE
ARAPAHO
MEXICO
NATIVE AMERICAN AND EURO-AMERICAN BOUNDARIES
LEGEND
Euro-American Boundaries
Native American Boundaries (Kroeber)
SCALE 100 50 0 100 200 300 MILES
tmk

information on the area further confused the issue. Two contradictory environmental images of Louisiana were expressed in the literature of the day. Spanish explorers had implanted the notion in some American minds that much of Louisiana was a desert, and this image was substantiated by the reports of the expeditions of Zebulon Pike and Stephen Long, published in 1810 and 1823 respectively.[5] The dominant intellectual view, however, was that of a 'garden' — a salubrious, fertile agricultural Utopia that would eventually provide the agrarian base for the American republic.[6] The politicians felt free to sponsor the image which fitted best their geopolitical designs.

Jefferson's Federalist opponents, critical of his policy of agrarian expansionism, disparaged his edenic portrayal of Louisiana. Since colonial times there had been a fear, based on the philosophy of environmentalism, that Euro-Americans would revert to savagism if they were allowed to scatter into the wilderness.[7] Thomas Griffin of Virginia expressed this fear to the House of Representatives on 17 October 1803, opining that 'this Eden of the New World would prove a cemetery for the bodies of our citizens'.[8]

In the same debate Gaylord Griswold of Connecticut warned that:

the vast and unmanageable extent which the acquisition of Louisiana will give the United States, the consequent dispersion of our population and the destruction of that balance which it is so important to maintain between the Eastern and Western states threatens at no very distant day the subversion of our union.[9]

The need to keep a state's population within surveyable limits had been an axiom of political theory since the time of Aristotle, and the Federalist arguments greatly influenced Jefferson's policy toward Louisiana. He believed that, for the first half of the nineteenth century at least, Louisiana could most suitably be occupied by Indians and fur traders rather than by farmers.[10]

In his message to Congress in 1803 Jefferson stated his intentions 'to transplant our Indians into it [Louisiana] constituting them a marechaussee (a mounted patrol) to prevent emigrants from crossing the river until we shall have filled up all the vacant country on this side'.[11] Louisiana would serve as a massive reservation for Native Americans, particularly for those eastern Indians who were blocking the progress of the westward surge of Euro-American settlement. Louisiana would also dam that flow of settlement, condense the nation's population, and prevent any 'Balkanisation' of the United States.

Nevertheless, Thomas Jefferson, as the 'intellectual father of the American advance to the Pacific',[12] was not willing to leave the Trans-Missouri West to the British, who had already extended their sphere of trading operations onto the northern Great Plains. Jefferson hoped to encourage American fur traders to move into Louisiana. The fur trade would constitute the first stage of a progressive settlement of the American West.

Across the entire sweep of North America the fur trade had been the cutting edge of the frontier process. Furs were of low bulk and high value and they could, therefore, bear transportation costs over extended distances. Moreover, the overhead costs of production were low wherever the Native American was willing to act as primary producer. The fur trader was able to coexist with the native inhabitants. Traders generally laid no claim to Indian lands or minds but worked within the framework of the existing Indian system to encourage the production of furs. Some authorities, like Edwin Denig, the head trader at Fort Union from 1837 to 1855, even thought that the fur trade acted as a 'civilising' agent by introducing the Indians to the concepts of private property and regular work. Finally, and most vitally, fur traders and trappers would explore the West and so pave the way to eventual American political dominàtion.

A primary purpose of the Lewis and Clark expedition was to determine the suitability of the Trans-Missouri West for the fur trade. President Jefferson instructed Meriwether Lewis to make note of fur-bearing animals, to ascertain the attitudes of the native occupants to the fur trade, and, most fundamentally, to establish the 'most direct and practicable water communication across the continent, for the purposes of commerce'.[13] This route would serve as an artery for the fur trade, a trade route far more efficient than any the British could establish to the north.

The transcontinental route proved more difficult than established geographical lore had suggested — the Rocky Mountains did not terminate at the forty-sixth or forty-seventh parallel allowing an easy traverse from the Missouri to the Columbia. But Lewis and Clark left no doubts that the Trans-Missouri West offered rich prospects for the fur trade. Bison herds were so massive that the explorers often feared for the safety of their camps, and at the headwaters of the Missouri where the Great Plains interpenetrate with the Rocky Mountains, Lewis and Clark found an area 'richer in beaver and otter than any country on earth'.[14]

Lewis and Clark also discovered that many of the Indian societies of the Trans-Missouri West were receptive to Euro-Americans and to the American fur trade. The Mandan, for example, were described by the explorers as the 'most friendly, well disposed Indians inhabiting the Missouri', and the Pawnee were praised as 'friendly and hospitable to all white persons'. Even the Teton Dakota, condemned by Lewis as a 'lawless, savage, and rapacious race', promised a valuable trade 'if ever they were reduced to order'.[15]

The native societies which Lewis and Clark and the fur traders encountered were, however, suffering from the stress that often accompanies rapid cultural change. The American fur trade would accelerate this rate of change and would in turn be greatly affected by the growing tension and conflict which the Indians of the Trans-Missouri West experienced in the first half of the nineteenth century.

The major cause of the instability on the northern Great Plains was the rapid in-migration of Indians from the upper Midwest during the waning decades of the eighteenth century. The seven bands of the Teton Dakota, the Cheyenne, the Arapahoe (and their offshoot, the Atsina), and the Crow were forced under pressure from the Cree, Assiniboine, and Ojibwa to migrate across the Missouri River. There on the densely populated bison range of the western Great Plains, the migrants made a remarkable transition to equestrian nomadism (Figure 2).

During the same time period there was also a progressive southward movement of Indians from the grassland and parkland belts of Canada. The Piegan band of Blackfoot led this migration south after 1750, following the bison herds and seeking horses from the Flathead of northern Montana. They were followed by the Blood and Blackfoot bands, and at the beginning of the American fur trade these closely-related Blackfoot groups frequented the territory between the Marias River and the Three Forks of the Missouri. The Cree and Assiniboine also moved south toward the Missouri during the last decades of the eighteenth century as they responded to changes in livelihood and habitat incurred by contact with the Hudson's Bay Company.

The incursion of the Teton Dakota drove a wedge between the indigenous horticultural groups of the eastern Great Plains. The Arikara were isolated from their fellow Caddoan-speakers, the Pawnee, who inhabited villages on the Loup Fork of the Platte, and the Mandan and Hidatsa were separated from the other Siouan horticulturalists, the Omaha and Ponca, who lived in villages in eastern Nebraska (Figure 2).

A fundamental tension developed between the equestrian nomads and the horticulturalists as each group of peoples attempted to adapt to rapidly changing conditions.[16] At the beginning of the nineteenth century, according to Mishkin,

> the horticultural village peoples ... were hesitantly sur-rendering their settled economy in favor of horse hunting and were busily engaged in raiding the western tribes to obtain sufficient horses to take up the nomadic life. They in turn were being pressed and robbed of their grain resources by the nomads.[17]

The acquisition of the horse swayed the balance of power in favour of the nomads, increasing their mobility and facili-tating large-scale bison hunting. The village Indians, however, were tied to their horticulture (both culturally and econo-mically) and were unable to take full advantage of this new 'tool'. The equestrian nomads became alternatively symbiotic and parasitic in their relationships with the horticulturalists. Thus Lewis and Clark described the Arikara as 'tenants at will' to the Teton Dakota,[18] and Chardon's journal of events at Fort Clark from 1834 to 1839 indicates that the Mandan and Hidatsa were constantly threatened by Yankton, Yanktonai, and Assiniboine attack.[19] Throughout the period of the American fur trade, and partially as a result of the impact of that trade, there was a progressive disintegration of village life on the Missouri River. The nomadic peoples, on the other hand, were able to adopt a more independent stance toward the fur trade and they experienced a flowering of their power and culture during the first half of the nineteenth century.

The impact of the horse on the Indians of the Rocky Mountains was also immense. The horse diffused northward from the Spanish settlements at Santa Fe after 1600 and reached the Nez Perce and Flathead by 1720.[20] The greater mobility that the horse allowed extended the spheres of trading and raiding, and the annual expeditions of the Flathead, Nez Perce, and Shoshonian peoples eastward to the bison range brought increasing contact with the plains cultures.

The horse was incorporated into a trading system that had flourished for centuries. Lewis and Clark, asked by Jefferson to discover each tribe's 'Trafik with other nations in what it consists of and where carried on',[21] found an extensive trade network which linked the Indians of the South-West with those of the northern Rocky Mountains and Great Plains through the Shoshoni rendezvous and the Mandan, Hidatsa and Arikara villages. In the aboriginal stage this trade consisted of non-durable goods — an exchange of bison hunters' meat and leather products for the horticulturalists' corn, squash, and tobacco.[22] Gradually during the eighteenth century, European trade goods from Canada and horses from the Spanish settlements filtered into the system. The American fur trade affected this trade by increasing the supply of European manufactured goods and by encouraging specialisation in the production of robes and furs by the Indians. Yet as Ewers points out, the aboriginal trade characteristics persisted alongside the fur trade well into the nineteenth century.[23]

It is important to specify these characteristics of the Indian occupance at the onset of a study of the American fur trade of the Trans-Missouri West. The fur trade was superimposed upon and incorporated into the existing Native American cultural and economic systems. This was less the case in the Rocky Mountains, where the Indian was largely by-passed in the fur production chain, but on the northern

Great Plains the Indian was the producer and a primary influence on the patterns of the American fur trade. On the upper Missouri the American trader was, in a sense, no more than a manager in a production system where the Indian furnished the labour.

The Lewis and Clark expedition acted as a catalyst for the American fur trade of the West. Before 1806 the St Louis fur trade was confined to the lower reaches of the Missouri River, where a small number of French, Spanish and American traders obtained robes and pelts from the Otoe, Osage, Kansas, Ponca, and Omaha Indians. But even before the triumphant return of Lewis and Clark to St Louis on 23 September 1806, American traders were moving up the Missouri River to the Mandan villages, penetrating an area that had been exclusively the trading domain of the North West Company.

From 1804 to 1840 trappers and traders spread a thin veneer of Euro-American occupance over the Trans-Missouri West. The main theatre of operations was the Great Plains north of the Platte[24] and the adjacent central and northern Rocky Mountains, but American trappers occasionally probed to California and to the mouth of the Columbia, exploring and searching for furs. By 1840, according to the traveller Frederick Ruxton, the initial Euro-American exploration and exploitation of the West had been accomplished:

> Not a hole or corner but has been ransacked by these hardy men. From the Mississippi to the mouth of the Colorado of the West, from the frozen regions of the north to the Gila in Mexico, the beaver hunter has set his traps in every creek and stream. All this vast country, but for the daring and enterprise of these men would be even now a Terra Incognita to geographers.[25]

The Face of the Land

The northern Great Plains and adjacent Rocky Mountains is an area of great diversity and a difficult environment for human occupance. The winters are cold in the extreme, especially at high altitudes and on the exposed plains, summers are debilitatingly hot, and the Great Plains are plagued by periodic drought. Even the native inhabitants, with their thorough knowledge of the total environment, often suffered famine in the harsh lands of the Trans-Missouri West.[26]

By necessity the trappers and traders developed an intricate knowledge of the shape and character of the land — their lives and livelihood depended upon that knowledge. The hazy details of the Trans-Missouri West were gradually brought into sharp focus by men like Jedediah Smith and William Ashley and also by the many anonymous trappers who left no written records of their lives, but who passed on their knowledge by word of mouth. These trappers, Bernard DeVoto wrote, 'went about the blank spaces of the map like men going to the barn'.[27]

Geomorphologists recognise a number of distinctive physiographic provinces in the area that served as the hinterland for the St Louis fur trade.[28] (Figure 3).

The northern Great Plains province is composed mainly of the glaciated and unglaciated sections of the Missouri Plateau. This plateau, drained by the Missouri River and its tributaries, is characterised in several areas by highly dissected terrain. These mesas, buttes and badlands hindered lateral movement between the Missouri River and the Rocky Mountains, but the Missouri River system gave a unity to the plateau and formed a lattice and artery for the fur trade on the northern Great Plains.

South of the Pine Ridge Escarpment, which marks the northern edge of the High Plains, the land has been fluted into thousands of square miles of sand dunes. The Sandhills of Nebraska were largely by-passed by trappers and traders who travelled along the White River to the north[29] or, more importantly, across the Platte alluvial plain to the south. The Platte overland route became the most important arterial for the Rocky Mountain Trapping System and the most vital routeway in the settlement of the Trans-Missouri West. Travellers and trappers crossing this route noted the uncompromising flatness of the terrain and incorrectly deduced from this atypical swath that all of the Great Plains was flat and monotonous.[30]

On the western flank of the Missouri Plateau the Great

Figure 3: The Physical Setting

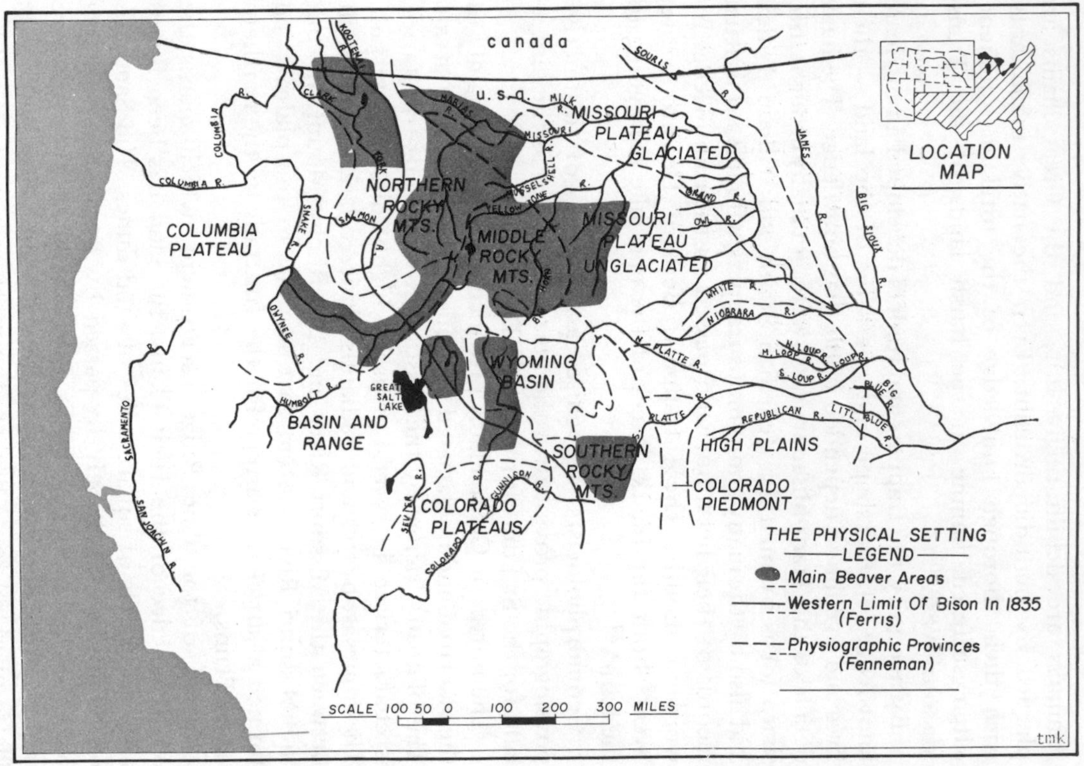

THE PHYSICAL SETTING
LEGEND

● Main Beaver Areas

▬▬ Western Limit Of Bison In 1835
(Ferris)

- - - Physiographic Provinces
(Fenneman)

SCALE
100 50 0   100   200   300 MILES

LOCATION
MAP

Plains interpenetrate with the Rocky Mountains. Outliers of the Rocky Mountains — the Black Hills, Big Belt, Little Belt and Crazy Mountains — stand as islands on the Great Plains, adding more topographic diversity to the province. In this cis-Rocky Mountain zone the Upper Missouri Fur Trade and the Rocky Mountain Trapping System overlapped and competed for the richest reserves of furs in the western United States.

The Rocky Mountains and the Great Plains merge together in the Wyoming Basin, a massive embayment extending west to Utah. The Platte route traversed this arid basin through South Pass to the Green River. South Pass, a wide depression to the south of the Wind River Mountains, afforded easy access to important trapping grounds on the Green, Bear and Snake rivers and to the down-faulted valleys of Jackson Hole and Pierre's Hole, which straddle the sides of the Tetons. South Pass was the gateway to the central Rockies which became the core of the Rocky Mountain Trapping System in the mid-1820s.

The Central Rocky Mountain province is characterised by north—south trending ranges which alternate with parallel alluvial valleys. In these valleys of the Bear, upper Snake and Green rivers, in 1824 and 1825, William Ashley and his trappers found the vast reserves of beaver which would draw more than 1000 trappers to the Rocky Mountains in the following decade. The valleys facilitated movement northward to the rich trapping grounds at the headwaters of the Yellowstone and Missouri, and they were the most popular winter sites for the mountain bison, the Indians and the trappers. The valley of the upper Green River, central to the main trapping grounds, richly stocked with game and grass, and within easy reach of South Pass, was of particular importance. The rendezvous (the annual trade fair) was most commonly held on the upper Green, which may be considered as the primary focus of the Rocky Mountain Trapping System.

The Southern Rocky Mountain province stretches from the Laramie Mountains (called, confusingly, the Black Hills by the trappers because their cedars presented a dark vista) to northern New Mexico. The Colorado Front Range, extending for 185 miles from the Arkansas River to the Laramie Mountains, is a formidable barrier to movement, and trappers were deflected to the north or the south of the range. From the south and south-east trappers worked the Southern Rockies from bases at Taos and Bent's Fort. Only in the 1830s, when the beaver reserves had been depleted in the central Rockies, did St Louis-based trappers penetrate the intermontane basins of the Colorado mountains (North Park, Middle Park and South Park) on a large scale.

The Northern Rocky Mountains form the least unified and most rugged of all the physiographic provinces of the United States. The western portion of the province is dominated by the knot of the Idaho Batholith, a 16,000 square mile maze of peaks. Rivers such as the Salmon and the Clearwater are incised into the granite of the Batholith. In places their valleys widen into small alluvial basins which were favoured wintering sites for the trappers. Southward, reaching to the incised canyon of the Snake River, is an expanse of lava plains sparsely covered with sagebrush. The trappers avoided these Snake River Plains because they offered little in the way of beaver or game.

The eastern section of the North Rocky Mountain province, occupying much of western Montana, is an area of high ranges separated by rivers which flow in glacially-deepened trenches northward to join the Columbia and northeastward to the headwaters of the Missouri. These trenches were lines of movement for both American and British trapping parties, the latter operating out of Flathead Post. East—west movement was difficult (as Lewis and Clark discovered), but the headwaters of the Missouri and Yellowstone could be reached from the upper Snake by the well-established Indian trail that passed through Jackson Hole, and from the Salmon River via Lemhi Pass.

The American trappers occasionally extended their operations down the Snake River, but the Columbia Plain was the domain of the Hudson's Bay Company. The American trappers tried repeatedly but in vain to loosen the British grip on the Pacific Northwest. Southwestward the trappers were repulsed by the arid wastes of the Great Basin, or 'Starvation Country' as it was called. Jedediah Smith and Joseph Walker did lead parties across this basin and range country to California, but the paucity of fur-bearing and food-providing animals made operations difficult and unprofitable. In general the Rocky Mountain Trapping System was restricted on the west by the equally formidable barriers of the British and the desert.

It would be erroneous, of course, to suggest that the strategy of the fur trade was determined by the physical environment; man has always used his ingenuity in defiance of such limitations. Yet the traders and trappers, limited in technology and therefore in practical options, formulated their strategies within a rather rigidly defined context. The supply trains, for example, crossed the Great Plains in summer, because that was the only season when a large expedition could make the traverse. Trapping operations were concentrated in fall and spring, because ice-covered streams hampered winter trapping and in summer the beaver's pelt was thin and relatively worthless. As a final example, it might be noted that the fortunes of the Upper Missouri Fur Trade depended to a great extent on the migrations of the bison herds, which in turn were greatly influenced by climatic variations.

Beaver Ecology

The beaver pelt was the most important raw material of the Rocky Mountain Trapping System and until 1834 the most valuable product of the entire fur trade of the Trans-Missouri West. The pelt was demanded in the markets of Europe and eastern North America not for the dark brown fur but for the barbed, fibrous underhair which was 'pounded, mashed, stiffened, and rolled' to make felting material for hats.[31]

The beaver is a strict monogamist who mates in February and produces two to four cubs in late May or early June. The gestation period lasts for about 100 days. After two and a half years the beaver grows to a mature weight of thirty to sixty pounds. The family unit is organised as a colony, consisting of the male and female and their progeny. When the cubs are fully grown they are driven from the parental colony. After a brief period of mobility they establish their own colony, often in close proximity to their parents' lodge.

Seton described the ideal habitat of the beaver as 'sluggish streams and small lakes with clay banks that are well wooded with aspen and willow'.[32] Streams that flow in constricted valleys, where floods are a hazard, and streams with steep gradients are avoided (Table 1). Rocky Mountain meadows,

Table 1: Stream Gradients and Beaver Habitats

Stream Gradient	Suitability for Beaver
0%—6%	Excellent
7%—12%	Good
12%—15%	Questionable
more than 15%	Unsuitable

Source: Colorado Game, Fish, and Parks Department, *The Beaver in Colorado.*
Its Biology, Ecology, Management and Economics (Technical Bulletin, No. 17,
1964), p. 19.

for example, are ideal habitats. These 'beaver meadows' are
often formed where a moraine or dyke restricts stream
erosion and levels the grade of the stream. In such locations
the beaver constructs a lodge of branches cemented together with mud, or a den hollowed out of the bankside and
with underwater access. The beaver is therefore, an important
physiographic agent. The dams regulate the flow of the stream,
aggrade the valleys, and result in the deposition of rich
silt.[33]

One of the main determinants of beaver distribution is the
availability of preferred food sources, particularly the aspen
tree. In studies conducted in the Superior National Forest it
was found that aspen is the main food of the beaver and that
birch, elder, willow and cottonwood are also of importance.[34]
Conifers are not eaten by the beaver, although they are used
in lodge construction, but aquatic plants — sedge, cattail roots
and water lilies — are utilised for food, especially in the
summer season.

The altitudinal range of the beaver in the Rocky Mountains
is great and coincides with the distribution of the aspen tree.
In Colorado, for example, beaver are found at altitudes above
10,500 feet.[35] On the Great Plains beaver inhabit slow-flowing
streams with clay or alluvium banks (which facilitate den
construction) and utilise cottonwood and willow for food. In
both the mountain and plains habitats, the food sources are
found close to the streams: the aspen, for example, rarely
grows more than 100 feet from water. The beaver is, therefore,
a rather stationary mammal with little need to stray far from
the home pond.

In the early nineteenth century beaver were distributed widely throughout the northern Great Plains and the Rocky Mountains. In certain favoured areas beaver populations were particularly dense. These areas became poles of attraction for trappers operating from the rendezvous and from the trading posts on the upper Missouri (Figure 3).

The most celebrated of all the trapping grounds was Blackfoot country, with its core area at the Three Forks of the Missouri. It was in this area that Lewis and Clark first noted the vast quantities of beaver and otter that drew trappers to the upper Missouri after 1806. William Ashley, writing in 1829, estimated that the Blackfoot trade was 'more valuable than one half of all the other tribes' in the Trans-Missouri West.[36] The Blackfoot, however, repulsed any American attempts to tap these furs, choosing instead to channel their furs north to the Hudson's Bay Company posts in Canada. Blackfoot country remained a virtual preserve of fur-bearing animals until the 1830s.

The land of the Crow, centred on the Bighorn Valley and including the Rosebud, Powder and Tongue rivers, was also richly stocked with beaver. According to trappers' lore, beaver were so plentiful in 'Absaroka' that they could be taken from the streams with clubs. 'Crow Beaver' was considered to be superior to 'Missouri Beaver' and as good as the best 'Mountain Beaver'. This was not only because of the high natural quality of the pelt, but also because of the superior processing skill of the Crow women. The trapper Michael Immel, brought before a St Louis court on 25 June 1821 in connection with a theft of furs, explained the superiority of 'Crow Beaver':

Question by Mr Bates — In what regions is the Crow Beaver procured?

Answer — Along the foot of the Rocky Mountains, or the headwaters of the Yellowstone and Arkansas and occasionally on the Columbia.

Question by same — What constitutes the differences

between Crow Beaver and the
ordinary Missouri Beaver?

Answer   — The difference is very great, and
the fur much longer and thicker
on the skin — the Missouri
Beaver is just taken in the rough
state — and no pains taken to
press it . . . the Crow Beaver is
scraped and rub'd with pains to
make it pliable and fit for
transportation.[37]

Crow country was trapped by mountain men and by the
Crow thoroughout the period 1807 to 1840.

The northern, central, and southern Rocky Mountains
were also well endowed with beaver. In the northern Rockies,
for example, the focus of trapping operations was at Flathead
Lake where the Hudson's Bay Company maintained their
trading post. The streams of the Lewis and Bitteroot Ranges
and the tributaries of Clark's Fork of the Columbia were
worked consistently during the late 1820s and 1830s by both
British and American trappers.

The initial focus of the American trappers, however, was
the central Rockies, where in 1825 William Ashley found
numerous 'small streams issuing from the mountains bordered
with a thick growth of small willows and richly stocked with
beaver'.[38] A modern survey of beaver populations on the
upper Snake gives an idea of the carrying capacity of these
streams: 83 beaver colonies were counted on 46 miles of
Willow Creek, 48 colonies on 87 miles of the Blackfoot
River, and smaller but significant numbers were counted on
the Portneuf, Teton and Bear rivers. Altogether, 309 colonies
were located on 1,593 stream miles of the upper Snake and
its tributaries.[39]

The sedentariness of the beaver, which made trapping easy,
and the relatively low rate of natural increase (when compared,
for example, to the muskrat) leaves the beaver vulnerable to
depletion. The Rocky Mountain Trapping System operated
against a background of a rapidly diminishing resource base.
This was partially caused by natural fluctuations in beaver

populations, but mostly it was a result of unbridled exploitation by British and American trappers.

Populations of fur-bearing animals fluctuate in cycles as a result of changes in the natural environment and the regular occurrence of epizootics (wildlife epidemics). In the mid-1830s for example, in the Cumberland Department of the Hudson's Bay Company, low water levels resulted in an epizootic (probably tularemia) which destroyed thousands of mus-krats.[40] Beaver are also subject to such cycles. A mild winter produces a high rate of survival among beaver cubs, and the resulting increase in population density facilitates the diffusion of diseases. It is impossible to chart the details of these natural beaver cycles for the Rocky Mountains in the early nineteenth century, although Cowan has used Hudson's Bay Company records to identify population fluctuations of several fur-bearers in the Pacific Northwest from 1825 to 1857.[41] It is conceivable that the decline of beaver in the Rocky Mountains and the northern Great Plains in the 1820s and 1830s was partially a result of changes in the biological environment operating quite independently of man's intervention. Beaver populations would not rebound quickly from such losses because of their relatively low rate of natural increase and because of persistent and indiscriminate trapping by the British and Americans.

It is probable, however, that the depletion of beaver and other small fur-bearers in the early nineteenth century was caused primarily by the advent of Euro-Americans, armed with the steel trap. The American trappers personified the prevalent frontier attitude toward the natural environment, an attitude that emphasised short-term exploitation rather than long-term sustained yield.[42]

The irrationality of this exploitative attitude was pointed out in 1827 by William Ashley who, having already made his own substantial fortune in the Rocky Mountains, then argued that fur production should be placed upon a sustained yield basis:

> after trapping beaver, where they were considered plenty, until they became so diminished in numbers, as not to justify the hunter's continuing his operations in the same place, leaving the streams undisturbed for five or six years,

they will, at the expiration of that time be found as numerous as when first trapped.[43]

Such restraint and planning was inconceivable to the frontier mind. The fur companies competed ruthlessly in a race to derive the maximum economic gain in the shortest possible time.

In Canada, by contrast, Governor George Simpson of the Hudson's Bay Company introduced comprehensive conservation policies into the fur trade after 1821.[44] Edwin Denig, head trader at Fort Union on the upper Missouri, explained Simpson's quota system:

> They allow the Indian to trap certain streams at stated seasons and prohibit the successive hunting of any place for two or three years. The country in which that animal (the beaver) abounds is parcelled out into hunting portions which are worked in rotation each third year leaving them the intervening two years to accumulate.[45]

These enlightened policies were difficult to enforce and they did not apply to the disputed territories along the forty-ninth parallel and to the west of the continental divide. The British encouraged the Piegan to trap without restraint the headwaters of the Missouri and to trade the furs in the Saskatchewan District of the Hudson's Bay Company.[46] *The Missouri Advocate and St Louis Enquirer* protested in 1825 that the 'riches which this company are carrying out of the United States is immense'.[47] In Ashley's estimation, the Hudson's Bay Company trapped 85,000 beaver, worth $60,000, on the American side of the Rocky Mountains in the mid-1820s.[48] While this may be an exaggeration, designed to turn public opinion against the British presence in Oregon, the policy of the Hudson's Bay Company along the Snake River was certainly one of blatant over-exploitation. This was stated concisely by Governor Simpson in October 1824, when he described the Snake River country as 'a rich preserve of Beaver . . which for political reasons we should endeavour to destroy as soon as possible'.[49] The British wanted to garner the furs before the Americans arrived in force. This would create a 'fur desert', a buffer zone to protect the Pacific Northwest from American penetration.

The end product of the British and American attitudes toward the environment was a devastated resource base. As early as 1831, according to the trader William Gordon, beaver were 'extirpated' on the northern Great Plains.[50] In the Rocky Mountains the relentless competition of the late 1820s and early 1830s destroyed the beaver reserves, first in the accessible areas of the central Rockies, then progressively outward from this core into the southern and northern Rockies. No other factor (even the collapse of the market after 1834) had a greater influence on the areal strategy and eventual decline of the Rocky Mountain Trapping System than this blind destruction of the fur-bearing animals.

Bison Ecology

The resource base of the Upper Missouri Fur Trade was more resilient than that of the Rocky Mountain Trapping System. A variety of furs and skins was produced on the northern Great Plains, but by 1830 the emphasis was clearly on the bison robe. The bison was also killed for its bones and fat (which was used in the manufacture of tallow), and bison meat was the staple food of the fur trade. At Fort Union, for example, the traders consumed the meat of 600—800 bison annually.[51]

Seaton estimated that the Great Plains had a carrying capacity for forty million bison.[52] According to Edwin Denig, the bison ranged 'from the Platte to the Saskatchewan and from the Red River to the Rocky Mountains'.[53] Throughout this vast area bison were found in great quantities, an abundant resource for the fur trade and the native inhabitants.

The migration patterns of the bison largely determined both the robe production and the food supply of the Upper Missouri Fur Trade. Ethologists traditionally believed that the bison migrated in large herds following well-defined seasonal patterns, moving south in winter to seek milder conditions and returning in spring and early summer to re-occupy the refurbished northern pastures. This theory has been somewhat discredited. The current consensus is that the migrations were random movements of small, loosely, knit bands.[54]

The literature of the Canadian and American fur trades fails to settle this issue. Moodie and Ray, drawing largely from Hudson's Bay Company records, concluded that the bison migrations in the Canadian plains followed regular seasonal and geographic patterns.[55] Conversely, Edwin Denig, basing his conclusions on two decades of observation at Fort Union, opined that the movements of the bison were unpredictable and erratic: 'A trading post in a new country may have but few buffalo the first and second years and innumerable herds for the third, or vice versa. There is no rule for this. The bison migrate and return.'[56]

The journals of the trading posts on the upper Missouri suggest that the local movements of the bison herds were closely related to seasonal climatic conditions. During mild winters the herds remained on the open plains, but when the winter was severe the herds congregated in the river valleys seeking shelter and forage. In December of 1830, for example, Daniel Lamont, the head trader at Fort Tecumseh, informed his employer, Pierre Chouteau, Jr, that the prospects for robe production were poor because the season was mild and there were no bison herds within reach of the post. The winter worsened in the early months of 1831 and the herds sought shelter in the Missouri Valley. In April Lamont was able to report an excellent return of robes because 'cattle' had been 'in the greatest abundance'.[57]

As robe production mounted in the 1820s and 1830s some contemporary observers warned of the impending depletion of the herds. In 1834, the traveller William Marshall Anderson was told by Lucien Fontenelle, an experienced trapper, that the 'diminution of the buffalo' was 'very considerable'.[58] Denig, however, believed that the herds were larger in 1850 than in the first few decades of the nineteenth century. Denig conceded that pressure on the bison herds from encroaching settlement was concentrating the herds and may have given a false impression of increased numbers. Yet he was able to demonstrate that in 1850 the bison's natural rate of increase exceeded any depletion by hunting. Only winter robes from cows and young bulls, Denig explained, were sufficiently thick and pliable to be of use to the traders. Even the Indians who killed the bison perennially for a plethora of uses scratched 'merely the outskirts of these large herds'.[59]

The extensive range of the bison, which observers saw only in fragments, and the erratic nature of the bison's movements made generalisation on the subject of depletion difficult. There is, however, no substantial evidence to show that the fur trade on the northern Great Plains before 1840 faced the problem of a dwindling resource base, except in eastern Nebraska which was on the fringe of the bison range.

The Rocky Mountain bison, on the other hand, was quickly depleted during the fur trade era. Before the seventeenth century the mountain bison ranged over much of the Trans-Rocky Mountain West.[60] It is possible that the mountain bison had crossed from the Great Plains in historic times, driven by the pressure of Indian hunting.[61] Joe Meek, a veteran trapper, believed that there was a seasonal movement of bison herds from the Great Plains to the Rocky Mountains crossing the continental divide near the headwaters of the Snake and Green rivers.[62] Whatever the case, Tom Fitzpatrick (one of the most famous trappers) recalled that in 1824:

> buffalo were spread in immense numbers over the Green River and Bear River valleys, and through all the country lying between the Colorado or Green River of the Gulf of California and Lewis' Fork of the Columbia, the meridian of Fort Hall then forming the western limit of their range.[63]

The range was subsequently eroded by the Indians and the trappers. The mountain bison was not in demand for its robe, which was too bulky to be transported by land to St Louis, but bison meat was the main form of sustenance for the trappers. Fitzpatrick noted that 'about the year 1834 or 1835 they began to diminish very rapidly and continued to decrease until 1838 or 1840'.[64] By 1844, according to the explorer Fremont, the bison herds were no longer found 'west of the Three Forks of the Missouri or the plains of the Yellowstone'.[65] The Rocky Mountain Trapping System decayed not only because its main fur-bearer, the beaver, was depleted but also because the main source of provisionment, the mountain bison, was destroyed.

Other Sources of Furs

The beaver and bison were by far the most important fur-bearing animals in the fur trade of the Trans-Missouri West to 1840. However, the trappers and traders collected all the skins and furs, bones and fat that were available — anything that had commercial value, was easily exploitable, and could be marketed through the established system. Muskrat, otter, deer, mink, martens, sable, weasels, racoons, bears, wolves, various types of foxes, even swans, were killed for their furs or skins. Their value was set against a beaver standard in the Rocky Mountains and against a robe standard on the upper Missouri. So an otter skin might be valued at 'one skin made beaver' (both pelts selling for $3 or $4 each), and two red fox furs were the equivalent of one bison robe.

Next to beaver the muskrat was the most widely trapped mammal. The range and habitat of the muskrat are quite similar to those of the beaver. Dense populations occur in marshy areas, wherever the muskrats' preferred foods (roots and the lower stalks of cattails) are found. Muskrat populations fluctuate widely because the mammal lives in shallow water and is more susceptible to changes in water level than the beaver. However, population losses are quickly replenished because the muskrat reproduces at an early age and rears five litters annually, often with as many as eleven cubs a litter. The muskrat pelt was easily taken and prepared by the trappers, but it was worth only six to twenty cents in the early nineteenth century. Muskrat were trapped, therefore, almost as a by-product of the beaver trade.

The river otter occupies the same environmental niche as the beaver and the muskrat. The otter was distributed widely throughout the Rocky Mountains and the northern Great Plains, but densities were low. The rich dark brown guard hairs and silky underfur of the otter gave the pelt a high value. Moreover, the otter is mobile during the winter breeding season and could be taken using a standard beaver trap. This extended fur production throughout the winter, a season that was otherwise slack in the Rocky Mountain Trapping System.

Deerskins were possibly the second most valuable product of both the Upper Missouri Fur Trade (particularly after the exhaustion of the beaver reserves) and the Rocky Mountain Trapping System. The skins were highly demanded in the markets of Europe and eastern North America, where they brought fifteen cents a pound in the 1820s and 1830s. Mule, blacktail and whitetail deer were most commonly taken by the trappers, and the richest hunting area was the Rocky Mountain–High Plains border where the two production systems overlapped.

The geographical base (including the physical, biological, and cultural environments) was the foundation for the fur trade of the Trans-Missouri West. The traders and trappers built their production system on this foundation, improvising, modifying and intensifying their methods of exploitation until the superstructure became too heavy for the base and large areas of operations were abandoned.

Notes

1. R.F. Nichols, 'The Louisiana Purchase: Challenge and Stimulous to American Democracy', *The Louisiana Historical Quarterly*, vol. 38 (1955), p. 2.

2. B. Hermann, *The Louisana Purchase* (Washington, DC: Government Printing Office, 1898), p. 33.

3. T. Jefferson to J. Melish, 31 December 1816, in H.A. Washington (ed.), *The Writings of Thomas Jefferson* (Washington, DC: Taylor and Maury, 1854), pp. 51–2.

4. Washington, *The Writings of Thomas Jefferson*, pp. 51–2.

5. There is an extensive literature in history and historical geography on the myth and reality of the 'Great American Desert'. See, for example, T.L. Alford, 'The West as a Desert in American Thought prior to Long's 1819–20 Expedition', *Journal of the West*, vol. 8 (1969), pp. 515–25. Also, G.M. Lewis, 'Three Centuries of Desert Concepts in the Cis-Rocky Mountain West', *Journal of the West*, vol. 4 (1965), pp. 457–68, or any of Lewis' perceptive articles on this subject. Some scholars believe that the importance of the desert image has been exaggerated. See M.J. Bowden, 'The Perception of the Western Interior of the United States, 1800–1870: A problem in Historical Geosophy', *Proceedings*, Association of American Geographers, vol. 1 (1969), pp. 16–21. The rank and file of the fur trade were probably too involved in their work to give much thought to such esoteric matters.

6. L. Allen, 'Geographical Knowledge and American Images of Louisiana', *The Western Historical Quarterly*, vol. 2 (1971), pp. 151–70. Also by the same author, *Passage Through the Garden: Lewis and Clark and the Image of the American Northwest* (Urbana: University of Illinois Press, 1975).

7. This theme is explored in Nash, *Wilderness and the American Mind;* and R.H. Pearce, *Savagism and Civilization, a Study of the Indian and the American Mind* (Baltimore: John Hopkins Press, 1967).

8. *Annals of the Congress of the United States,* Eighth Congress, Second Session, 1803 (Washington, DC: Gales and Seaton, 1852), p. 443.

9. *Annals of Congress,* p. 443.

10. H.N. Smith, *Virgin Land: The American West as Symbol and Myth* (New York: Vintage Books, 1950), pp. 16—19.

11. *Annals of Congress,* p. 1064.

12. Smith, *Virgin Land,* p. 16.

13. 'Jefferson's Instructions to Lewis', 20 June 1803, in R.G. Thwaites (ed.), *Original Journals of the Lewis and Clark Expedition, 1804—1806* (New York: Dodd, Mead and Co., 1905), vol. 7, pp. 247—52.

14. Thwaites, *Original Journals,* vol. 7, p. 335.

15. Thwaites, *Original Journals,* vol. 6, pp. 86, 90, 98.

16. P. Holder, *The Hoe and the Horse on the Plains* (Lincoln: University of Nebraska Press, 1970).

17. B. Mishkin, *Rank and Warfare among the Plains Indians* (New York: Monographs of the American Ethnological Society, 1940), p. 57.

18. Thwaites, *Original Journals,* vol. 6, pp. 80—1.

19. A.H. Abel (ed.), *Chardon's Journal at Fort Clark, 1834—9* (Pierre, South Dakota: State Historical Society, 1932).

20. F. Haines, 'The Northward Spread of Horses among the Plains Indians', *American Anthropologist,* vol. 40 (1938), pp. 429—37.

21. Thwaites, *Original Journals,* vol. 6, p. 89.

22. J.C. Ewers, 'The Indian Trade of the Upper Missouri before Lewis and Clark: An Interpretation', *Bulletin, Missouri Historical Society,* vol. 10 (1954), pp. 429—46.

23. Ewers, 'Indian Trade of the Upper Missouri', p. 435.

24. The Platte was recognised as the dividing line between the upper and lower Missouri, as the traveller Brackenridge pointed out: 'the river Platte is regarded by navigators of the Missouri as a point of as much importance as the equinoctial line amongst mariners . . . From this we enter what is called the Upper Missouri.' H. Brackenridge, *Journal of a Voyage up the Missouri in 1811,* in R.G. Thwaites (ed.), *Early Western Travels* (Cleveland: Arthur H. Clark Co., 1904), vol. 5, p. 226.

25. C.M. Porter and L.R. Hafen, *Ruxton of the Rockies* (Norman: University of Oklahoma Press, 1950), p. 228.

26. J.C. Ewers, 'The Nomadic Plains Indians' Image of their Environment'. Paper presented at the Images of the Plains Conference, held in Lincoln, Nebraska, 30 April—1 May 1973.

27. B. DeVoto, *Across the Wide Missouri* (Boston: Houghton Mifflin Co., 1947), p. 5.

28. Information on the physiography of this area is taken from N.M. Fenneman, *Physiography of Western United States* (New York: McGraw Hill, 1931); and W.D. Thornbury, *Regional Geomorphology of the United States* (New York: John Wiley and Sons, 1965).

29. C.E. Hanson, Jr, 'The Fort Pierre—Fort Laramie Trail', *Museum of the Fur Trade Quarterly,* vol. 1 (1965), pp. 3—7.

30. G.M. Lewis, 'The Great Plains and Its Image of Flatness', *Journal of the West,* vol. 6 (1967), pp. 11—26.

31. J.L. Clayton, 'The Growth and Significance of the American Fur Trade', in *Aspects of the Fur Trade: Selected Papers of the 1965 North American Fur Trade Conference* (St Paul: Minnesota Historical Society, 1967), pp. 62–72. In this sense, as Clayton points out, the fur trade might more appropriately be called a fibre trade.

32. E.T. Seton, *Life Histories of Northern Animals* (New York: Constable and Co., 1910), vol. 1, p. 453.

33. W.J. Hamilton, *American Mammals* (New York and London: McGraw Hill, 1939), pp. 312–14.

34. A.E. Shaler, 'Beaver Food Utilization Studies', *Journal of Wildlife Management*, vol. 2 (1938), pp. 215–22.

35. E.R. Warren and E.R. Hall, 'A New Sub-Species of Beaver from Colorado', *Journal of Mammalology*, vol. 20 (1939), pp. 358–67.

36. W.H. Ashley to T.H. Benton, 11 January 1829, in D.L. Morgan (ed.), *The West of William H. Ashley* (Denver: The Old West Publishing Co., 1964), pp. 183–6.

37. 'Deposition and Interrogation of Michael E. Immel, June 25, 1821', *Bulletin of Missouri Historical Society*, vol. 4 (1948), pp. 78–81.

38. W.H. Ashley, *Diary* (St Louis: Missouri Historical Society).

39. *Utah Fur-Bearers Management Recommendations and Harvest Report* (Boise: Utah Department of Fish and Game, 1953–4).

40. A.J. Ray, 'Some Conservation Schemes of the Hudson's Bay Company, 1821–50: An Examination of Resource Management in the Fur Trade', *Journal of Historical Geography*, vol. 1 (1975), pp. 49–68. It is possible that wildlife diseases, such as tularemia and pseudotuberculosis, were transmitted to the Indians and were an important factor in the decline of native populations. See C. Martin, 'Wildlife Diseases as a Factor in the Depopulation of the North American Indian', *The Western Historical Quarterly*, vol. 7 (1976), pp. 47–62.

41. J.M. Cowan, 'The Fur Trade and the Fur Cycle: 1825–1857', *British Columbia Historical Quarterly*, vol. 2 (1938), pp. 19–30. The beaver was so heavily trapped that it is difficult to distinguish natural cycles.

42. The need to re-examine frontier settlement from an ecological perspective rather than from the traditional point of view of glorious American expansion is forcibly argued in C.O. Sauer, 'Theme of Plant and Animal Destruction in Economic History', *The Co Evolution Quarterly*, No. 10 (1976), pp. 48–51. This article was first published in *The Journal of Farm Economics*, vol. 20 (1938), pp. 765–75. See also W.R. Jacobs, 'The Indian and the Frontier in American History — A Need for Revision', *The Western Historical Quarterly*, vol. 4 (1973), pp. 43–56.

43. Morgan, *The West of William H. Ashley*, pp. 177–8. Ashley was correct in this assessment. In 1957, for example, a massive tularemia epizootic destroyed large numbers of beaver in Colorado. Within a few years beaver populations had rebounded to pre-epizootic levels. R.R. Lechleitner, *Wild Mammals of Colorado* (Boulder: Pruett Publishing Co., 1969), p. 125.

44. Ray, 'Conservation Schemes of the Hudson's Bay Company',

pp. 49—68.

45. J.C. Ewers (ed.), *Five Indian Tribes of the Upper Missouri* (Norman: University of Oklahoma Press, 1961), p. 121.

46. Ray, 'Conservation Schemes of the Hudson's Bay Company', p. 57.

47. *Missouri Advocate and St Louis Enquirer*, 8 October 1825.

48. *Missouri Observor*, 31 October 1827.

49. F. Merk (ed.), *Fur Trade and Empire: George Simpson's Journal, 1824—1825* (Cambridge, Mass.: Belnap Press, 1968), p. 46.

50. W. Gordon to H.L. Cass, 3 October 1831. *Fur Trade Envelope* (St Louis: Missouri Historical Society).

51. Prince Maximilian of Wied Neuweid, *Travels in the Interior of North America, 1832—34*, in R.G. Thwaites (ed.), *Early Western Travels* (Cleveland: Arthur H. Clark, 1904—7), vol. 22, p. 382.

52. Seton, *Life Histories of Northern Animals*, vol. 1, p. 259.

53. J.N.B. Hewitt (ed.), *Indian Tribes of the Upper Missouri*, Forty-Sixth Annual Report of the Bureau of American Ethnology, 1928—9 (Washington, DC: Government Printing Office, 1930), p. 462.

54. F.G. Roe, *The North American Buffalo* (Toronto: University of Toronto Press, 1951).

55. D.W. Moodie and A.J. Ray, 'Buffalo Migrations in the Canadian Plains', *Plains Anthropologist*, vol. 21 (1976), pp. 45—54.

56. Hewitt, *Indian Tribes*, p. 463.

57. D. Lamont to P. Chouteau Jr, 30 December, 1830; and D. Lamont to P. Chouteau Jr, 4 April, 1831. *Fort Tecumseh and Fort Pierre Letterbooks, Chouteau Collection* (St Louis: Missouri Historical Society).

58. D.L. Morgan and E.T. Harris (eds.), *The Rocky Mountain Journals of William Marshall Anderson* (San Marino: The Huntington Library, 1967), p. 178.

59. Hewitt, *Indian Tribes*, p. 462.

60. G.M. Christman, 'The Mountain Bison', *American West*, vol. 8 (1971), pp. 44—7.

61. This is proposed in W.B. Davis, *The Recent Mammals of Idaho* (Caldwell, Idaho: Caxton Printers, 1939).

62. F.F. Victor (ed.) *The River of the West* (Hartford, Connecticut: R.W. Bliss and Co., 1870), p. 90.

63. D. Jackson and M.L. Spence (eds.), *The Expeditions of John Charles Fremont* (Urbana: University of Illinois Press, 1970), vol. 1, pp. 490—1.

64. Jackson and Spence, *John Charles Fremont*, p. 491.

65. Jackson and Spence, *John Charles Fremont*, p. 491.

2 The Upper Missouri Fur Trade: Strategy

The fur trade was established on the upper Missouri almost two decades before the emergence of the Rocky Mountain Trapping System. The northern Great Plains were relatively accessible from St Louis via the Missouri River. Moreover, the traditional strategy of the American fur trade could be applied there: the Indians produced the furs, which were then exchanged for manufactured products at the trading posts. The Upper Missouri Fur Trade was, therefore, largely an Indian trade.

Experimental Strategies, 1807–26

Before the transfer of Upper Louisiana to the United States on 10 March 1804, the trade area of the St Louis fur trade was limited, as Thomas Biddle explained in 1819:

> The history of this trade under the Spanish and French Colonial governments would be a recital of the expeditions of vagrant hunters and traders who never ventured up the river beyond a few miles of this place [Council Bluffs].[1]

Traders such as Jacques Clamorgan, Bernard Pratte, Benito Vasquez, Jean Cabanne, and August Chouteau were licensed to trade with the Osage, Omaha, Ponca, and Pawnee during the late eighteenth century and the first few years of the

41

nineteenth century. Clamorgan expanded the sphere of exploration and trading to the Mandan villages in the 1790s, and Regis Louisel built a trading post at Cedar Island in 1802 to serve the Dakota trade. It was Manuel Lisa, however, who provided the spark that initiated large-scale trading on the upper Missouri.[2]

Lisa, an enigmatic man, had served his apprenticeship in the Osage trade and in a number of business ventures in Missouri. He was impetuous, ambitious, and talented: 'I go a great distance,' he wrote, 'while some are considering whether they will start today or tomorrow. I impose upon myself great privations.'[3]

Lisa initially envisaged a cis-Rocky Mountain trading empire that would link the fur trade of the upper Missouri with the Santa Fe trade. He may have been working under the mistaken impression that Santa Fe was only a few days' ride from the upper Missouri, a geographical error that appears on George Drouillard's map of 1808 (Figure 4).[4] The Santa Fe venture was shelved in 1807 (although probably not forgotten), and Lisa directed his attention to the upper Missouri.

In the spring of 1807 Lisa organised an expedition of fifty to sixty men who ascended the Missouri and built a trading post, Fort Raymond, at the confluence of the Yellowstone and Bighorn rivers (Figure 5). While profitable trading was being conducted with the Crow, Lisa's trappers worked the small tributaries of the Yellowstone, Bighorn, Powder, and Tongue rivers and accumulated a large quantity of furs. Encouraged by this success, Lisa returned to St Louis to mount a larger expedition.

In the winter of 1808–9 the Missouri Fur Company was formed with the backing of most of the important merchants in St Louis. Lisa's strategy, described by Thomas Biddle in 1819, was the prototype for the Upper Missouri Fur Trade until the American Fur Company took control in the mid-1820s:

> The objectives of this company appear to have been to monopolize the trade among the lower tribes of the Missouri, who understand the art of trapping, and to send a large party to the headwaters of the Missouri capable of defending and trapping beaver themselves.[5]

Figure 4: Drouillard's Map of the Yellowstone Country, 1808

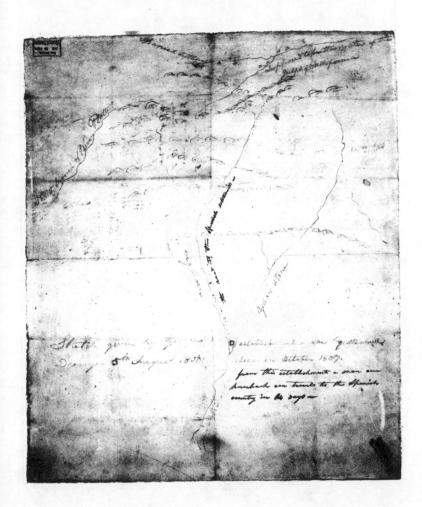

Library of Congress.

Lisa saw the need to placate the Missouri River Indians (from the Mandan villages down to the Council Bluffs) by building trading posts and distributing gifts. This would keep the river route open and allow access to the Three Forks of the

Figure 5: The Upper Missouri Fur Trade, 1807-20

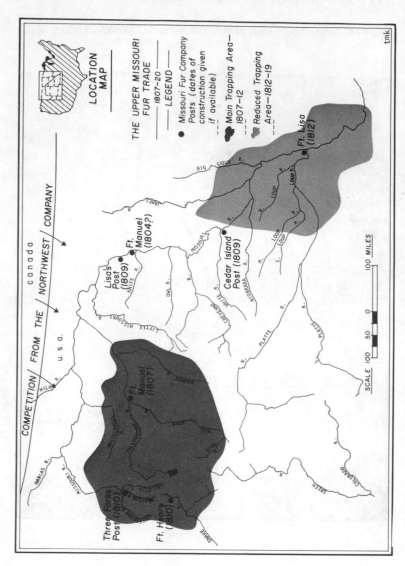

Missouri, where the greatest profits (and risks) lay.

The second expedition of the Missouri Fur Company, comprising 160 men, left St Louis in the spring of 1809. Trading posts were built at the Council Bluffs (for the Omaha, Oto, Iowa, and Pawnee), at Cedar Island (for the Teton and Yankton Dakota), and at the Arikara and Mandan—Hidatsa villages (Figure 5). These posts would serve all the trading Indians of the upper Missouri, while Fort Raymond would be a centre for the Crow trade and a base for trapping expeditions into Blackfoot country.

Ever since the return of Lewis and Clark the furs of Blackfoot country had been a major objective for American trappers. The Blackfoot, however, would not trade with the Americans, nor would they allow American trappers to hunt in their territory. The Americans, with some justification, accused the British of stoking this Blackfoot animosity, but the problem was rooted in the initial cultural contact between the Blackfoot and the Americans: a member of the Lewis and Clark expedition had killed two Piegan, and Blackfoot—American relations were jaundiced from their inception. American trappers repeatedly attempted to work the head-waters of the Missouri despite Blackfoot opposition. It was not until 1831, however, when an uneasy peace was established with the Piegan, that Americans could reap the furs of Blackfoot country on a large scale. Even then the Blackfoot would permit only traders, not trappers, on their turf.

In the spring of 1810, while Lisa was in St Louis attempting to secure backing for another expedition, John Colter (a veteran of the Lewis and Clark expedition) and Alexander Henry led a party of 32 men to the Three Forks of the Missouri. There, on a narrow neck of land between the Jefferson and Madison rivers, the trappers built a fort. This was a direct affront to the Blackfoot. The British had managed to maintain tolerably good relations with the Blackfoot only by staying outside the Blackfoot hunting grounds and encouraging those Indians to travel to the posts on the Saskatchewan to trade. Moreover, Lisa had further alienated the Blackfoot by trading with the Crow, the traditional enemies of the Blackfoot. The American trapping operations were thwarted by constant Blackfoot harassment. When the Three Forks post was abandoned in the summer of 1810, 30 packs of beaver had been accumulated,[6] and 20 men, including Drouillard, had been killed.

The dangers of trapping Blackfoot country prompted Reuben Lewis, a partner in the Missouri Fur Company, to suggest to his brother Meriwether that American efforts should be directed instead to the Columbia and the central Rocky Mountains.[7] This was possibly what Alexander Henry had in mind when he led his men over the continental divide to winter quarters on the upper Snake. By the spring of 1811 Henry's men had collected 40 packs of beaver which were transported down the Yellowstone to the Mandan villages where Lisa was waiting.

The first Missouri Fur Company was dissolved in January 1812. Although the company had made a small profit, it had by no means fulfilled Lisa's expectations. The existence of a rich reserve of beaver on the upper Missouri had been proven, and trade had been established with all the horticultural groups and with the Teton Dakota and Crow. However, the problem of obtaining long-term credit at St Louis, the difficulties of transportation and communication over extended distances, the overhead costs incurred by lavish gift-giving and, most of all, the adamant opposition of the Blackfoot frustrated Lisa's schemes. Nevertheless, a new Missouri Fur Company was formed in 1812 with a capital of $50,000, a considerable increase in backing.[8]

A small expedition was dispatched in May of 1812 to collect the furs from the trading posts and to dispense trappers to the Rocky Mountains. The new company was formed at an inopportune time. The market price for beaver was declining — pelts were worth only $2.50 a pound in St Louis in 1812 compared to the standard price of $4. The war with Great Britain, declared in June 1812, blocked the New Orleans route to the east coast markets, and British agents fermented the Indians of the upper Missouri against the American traders. Lisa was forced to abandon his plans to trap Blackfoot country, but in his new capacity as Sub-Agent for Indian Affairs he continued to trade with the Missouri River Indians, and, in the process, to tie them to the American cause. Fort Lisa at the Council Bluffs became the focal point of a retrenched trading area from 1812 to 1819 (Figure 5). Lisa continued to organise expeditions for the upper Missouri

Table 2: The State of the Fur Trade on the Missouri River in 1819

The following statement exhibits the trade of this river, viz: The Company (i.e. Missouri Fur Company) consists of Messes Lisa, Pilcher, Perkins, Wood, Carsen, Williams and Tenonee . . . they trade with the Ottoes, Missourias, Ioways, the Mahas, Pawnees, Piankeshaws, and Sioux, their principal trading establishment is near this place Fort Lisa.

	Capital:	$17,000
Serres and Francis Chouteau Osage and Kansas nations — trading post mouth of Kansas:		$4,000
LeQuare, Chouteau and Bros. Osage and Kansas nations — post on Osage		$16,000
US Factory at Fort Osage		
Roberdeau and Pepin Ottoes, Ioways, Missourias, Pawnees, Mahas, Piankeshaws, Sioux (partners with Chouteau) prnc. est. Nashantotollana		$12,000
Pratt and Vasquez — same as above post nr. Mahas village		$7,000
Broseau and De Lorian Sioux and Arikara		$7,000

Source: Letter, T. Biddle to Col. H. Atkinson, *Indian Trade Papers.*

until his death in 1820, but in Biddle's estimation the St Louis fur trade was of 'little importance from a pecuniary point of view' at that date (Table 2).[9]

The period from 1820 to 1824 was a time of transition in the fur trade of the Trans-Missouri West. One era had ended with the death of Lisa, another era would begin when William Ashley instituted the Rocky Mountain Trapping System and when the American Fur Company extended its operations onto the upper Missouri. The intervening years were characterised by strenuous competition between a number of trading companies which were jostling for control of the fur trade on the Missouri River and competing for the furs of Blackfoot country.

The financial panic of 1819, which disarranged the nation's economy, gave a new impetus to the fur trade.[10] St Louis was forced to fall back upon a frontier-type economy and the fur trade (which would be entered with a relatively small amount of capital) was an integral part of that economy. By 1822 at least five major trading companies were contesting for the furs of the northern Great Plains and Rocky Mountains. In that year Benjamin O'Fallon, Indian agent at Fort Atkinson, wrote to Ramsey Crooks of the American Fur Company that 'it remains for the enterprize of individuals to contend for the wealth of the upper country'.[11]

The Missouri Fur Company continued to operate after Lisa's death under the capable leadership of Joshua Pilcher and Thomas Hempstead.[12] The new leaders adopted Lisa's strategy absolutely. The trading post system on the upper Missouri was reactivated and included a new post, Fort Recovery, built in the fall of 1820 just above the mouth of the White River (Figure 6). The main goal, however, remained the furs of Blackfoot country. In the fall of 1821 Michael Immell and Robert Jones were sent into the field with 180 trappers. They built Fort Benton at the junction of the Yellowstone and Bighorn rivers and commenced to trade with the Crow and to make preparations for trapping northwestward into the heart of Blackfoot country. There is even an indication that Pilcher intended to extend his trading and trapping empire to Oregon — to build a 'chain of posts from the western limits of the state of Missouri, across the country, to the Pacific Ocean'.[13]

The new Missouri Fur Company encountered the same obstacles as its predecessors. Their suppliers and agents — Stone, Bostwick and Company of Boston — proved to be both unreliable and unscrupulous. By controlling the credit of the Missouri Fur Company Stone, Bostwick and Company had power of life and death over the traders. The death blow, however, was wielded by the Blackfoot. On 17 May 1823 a trapping party led by Immell and Jones was attacked by the Blackfoot. Jones, Immell and five trappers were killed, four others were wounded, and traps, pelts, and horses were stolen. Faced with this loss, with the problems of credit and supply, and with burgeoning competition on the Missouri River,[14] Pilcher abandoned all his trading posts except the one at Bellevue, which became the focus of a reduced trade area. In the fall of 1824 the Missouri Fur Company was dissolved.[15]

From 1820 onward the Missouri Fur Company had encountered strong competition on the lower reaches of the

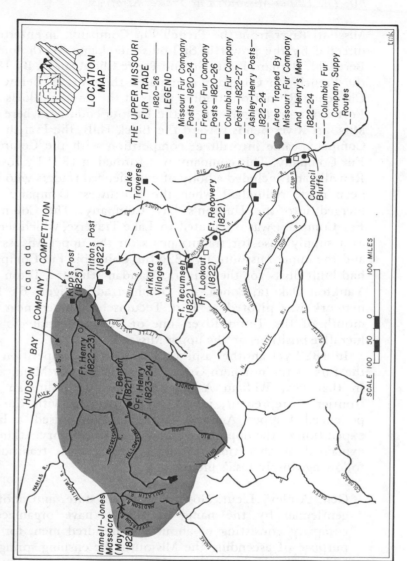

Figure 6: The Upper Missouri Fur Trade, 1820–6

Missouri River from the French Fur Company, an enterprise directed by the powerful St Louis merchants, Bartholomew Berthold, Bernard Pratte Sr, and Pierre Chouteau Jr. By 1826 the French Fur Company dominated the fur trade below the Cheyenne River from trading posts at the Council Bluffs and Fort Lookout (Figure 6). In the Dakota country, where the Missouri River bends toward the Black Hills, the French Fur Company came into direct competition with the Columbia Fur Company. This company was formed in 1821 by Joseph Renville and included a body of experienced traders who had been made redundant when the Northwest Company was merged into the Hudson's Bay Company. The Columbia Fur Company was orientated to Lake Traverse, which served as a supply base for trading posts on the upper Mississippi and the upper Missouri. By 1826 the Columbia Fur Company had built posts for the Arikara, Mandan–Hidatsa, Teton and Yankton Dakota, Ponca, and Omaha trades (Figure 6). This network was pivoted at Fort Tecumseh, situated near the mouth of the Teton River, one of the most strategic and lucrative positions on the upper Missouri.

In 1822 yet another aspirant entered the competition for the furs of the northern Great Plains and Rocky Mountains. In that year William Ashley, the Missouri politician and frontier entrepreneur, joined in partnership with the experienced trapper Andrew Henry and organised a large expedition to the upper Missouri. As General Henry Atkinson explained at that time, Ashley's strategy was traditional, following closely Lisa's model:

> Gen. Ashley, Lieut. Governor of this state, and another gentleman by the name of Henry, have organized a company consisting of about one hundred men, for the purpose of ascending the Missouri, the ensuing spring, as high as the Yellowstone to hunt and trap and trade with the Indian Tribes inhabiting that part of the country.[16]

The primary objective was again Blackfoot country, where the headwaters of the Missouri and Yellowstone cut into the front of the northern Rocky Mountains. Ashley may even have intended to penetrate the Rocky Mountains proper, beyond the continental divide to the Snake and Columbia rivers. The method of approach was, however, the customary Missouri River route, and trading with the Indians of the northern Great Plains was an important part of Ashley's strategy.

After some initial success (Henry established a base for trapping at the junction of the Yellowstone and Missouri rivers in 1822) Ashley's plans disintegrated. In April 1832 the two keelboats that Ashley was taking to the mouth of the Yellowstone were attacked by the Arikara and 14 of his men were killed.

The Arikara had always been regarded with suspicion and contempt by the American traders.[17] In the 1830s Francis Chardon personified this American attitude and referred to the Arikara in his journal as the 'Horrid Tribe'.[18] Yet the Arikara had welcomed the French and Spanish traders during the second half of the eighteenth century, appreciating the gifts and trade goods which they brought. The traders, however, also brought smallpox and other diseases which decimated the Arikara population in the 1770s and 1780s.[19] When an Arikara chief died while on a mission to Washington, DC the Arikara's attitude toward the American traders became particularly aggressive. Subsequently, according to the trapper Zenas Leonard, Arikara children were ingrained from an early age with a hatred of Euro-Americans.[20] Moreover, by establishing direct contact with the western hunting groups of the Great Plains, the American traders threatened the Arikaras' traditional role as middlemen in the fur trade. The Arikara became particularly assertive in their demands for gifts from American traders passing by their villages and this only served to reinforce the traders' opinion that the Arikara were a treacherous people. As the flow of American traders increased after 1807 the Arikara, reacting from fear and insecurity, struck out at these visitors who threatened their way of life. The culmination of these conflicts was the attack on Ashley's party and the savage retaliative campaign under the command of Colonel Henry Leavenworth, which devastated the Arikara villages and left those Indians more hostile (and afraid) than ever.[21]

The Arikara attack prompted Ashley to change his strategy and to divert his attention from the upper Missouri to the central Rocky Mountains. Ashley shifted his emphasis from trading to trapping and in the fall of 1823 he dispatched his leading trappers, Jedediah Smith, Tom Fitzpatrick, and William Sublette from Fort Lookout on a direct lateral route to the Rocky Mountains. A decade later, the merchant-trader Nathaniel Wyeth described this transition in Ashley's strategy, a transition which would result in the establishment of the Rocky Mountain Trapping System:

> His first attempts were predicated upon the possibility of trading furs from the Indians in the interior for goods. In this he was not successful, and in the event become much reduced in means, and credit, but in the course of this business perceived that there was plenty of Beaver in the country to which he had resorted to trade, but great difficulty to induce the Indians to catch it. After many tyrals [sic] of trading voyages he converted his trading parties into trapping parties.[22]

The demise of the Missouri Fur Company and the diversion of Ashley's energies from the northern Great Plains to the central Rocky Mountains created an opportunity for the American Fur Company to channel its massive resources into the Upper Missouri Fur Trade. Overcoming the reluctance of the cautious Jacob Astor, Ramsey Crooks eased the American Fur Company into the St Louis fur trade. The initial steps were hesitantly taken, for Crooks realised that although the potential profits were great so too were the risks. In 1821 an arrangement was made with Berthold and Chouteau to supply their goods for the following year. A year later the American Fur Company created a Western Department, absorbed Stone, Bostwick and Company (thus securing a foothold in St Louis), and prepared to contend for the furs of the upper Missouri.[23]

By 1823 only the French Fur Company and the Columbia Fur Company blocked the Western Department's drive to gain control of the Upper Missouri Fur Trade. The American Fur Company generally eliminated opponents in one of two ways: by negotiation, which invariably led to the incorporation of the rival company, or by outpricing the opposition and taking short-term losses in order to achieve long-term victory. The French and Columbia fur companies were eliminated in the former manner.

In December 1826 Ramsey Crooks placed the affairs of the Western Department in the hands of Berthold, Chouteau, and Pratte (known at that time as Bernard Pratte and Company), and so the French Fur Company was remodelled as a unit of the American Fur Company. In July of the following year an agreement was reached with the Columbia Fur Company which, in effect, left the American Fur Company in a position of virtual monopoly on the upper Missouri. The Columbia Fur Company agreed to withdraw from the Great Lakes fur trade where it had been challenging the Northern Department of the American Fur Company. On the upper Missouri the Columbia Fur Company was incorporated into the American Fur Company as the Upper Missouri Outfit, with jurisdiction above the mouth of the Big Sioux River. By 1827, therefore, the American Fur Company had acquired a string of trading posts on the upper Missouri and the services of a group of experienced traders. The foundation had been laid for a production system that would endure until the 1860s.

The Upper Missouri Fur Trade Under the American Fur Company, 1826–40

The American Fur Company, ever conservative, at first concentrated on the Indian trade. Entry into the Rocky Mountain Trapping System was postponed until the fur trade on the upper Missouri was secured. The 'Company', as it was called, inherited an embryonic trading empire which stretched from the mouth of the White Earth River down to the Council Bluffs. James Kipp of the Columbia Fur Company had built the White Earth River post in winter of 1825 – 6 to serve the Assiniboine trade. Kipp was also responsible for establishing the trading posts at the Mandan and Hidatsa villages in 1822 and 1823. The most prized acquisition of the Upper Missouri Outfit was Fort Tecumseh, built by the Columbia Fur Company in 1822 just above the mouth of the Teton River. Between the White and Niobrara rivers, near the old Missouri Fur Company post, Fort Recovery, the Upper Missouri Outfit gained possession of Fort Lookout (or Fort Kiowa) from the French Fur Company.

Where the Missouri River bends eastward and receives the Niobrara, James, Vermillion, and Big Sioux rivers the American Fur Company acquired the Ponca, Vermillion, and Big Sioux posts. Finally, on the stretch of river known as the Council Bluffs, above the confluence of the Platte and Missouri rivers, the Western Department maintained Cabanne's Post from 1826 to 1833 and, later, Sarpy's Post at Bellevue. By 1827, therefore, all the horticultural groups of the Missouri valley plus the Teton and Yankton Dakota and the Assiniboine were served by American Fur Company trading posts.

In the course of the next seven years, building from this foundation, the American Fur Company established a hierarchy of trading posts throughout the northern Great Plains (Figure 7). At the top of the hierarchy were the three major depots — Fort Union, Fort Tecumseh (rebuilt in June 1832 as Fort Pierre), and Fort William (later Fort Laramie). These depots served as control points for the fur trade: decision-making centres, collection foci for the furs from dependent regional posts, and major trading centres in their own right. At the next, lower level of the hierarchy were the fixed regional posts, built to serve, and often at the request of, the Indians. The depots and regional posts spawned numerous temporary trading posts each winter: 'loghouses or block-houses', Prince Maximilian called them, 'quickly erected and as quickly abandoned'.[24] These trading posts were, in effect, central places for the exchange of goods and services and, by 1835, all of the Indian groups of the northern Great Plains had access to such a centre.

Fort Tecumseh, situated where the Missouri River bends towards the rich bison range at the eastern foot of the Black Hills, was, next to Fort Union, the most important trading post in the entire system. Fort Tecumseh received the lucrative trade of the Teton and Yankton Dakota. This was generally a reliable trade. However, among the equestrian nomads a great deal of power was vested in the tribal leader and, as Denig explained, 'the conduct of all and every band of Indians takes its nature from the chief'.[25] There were, therefore, significant variations in attitudes (and, therefore, productivity) between the different bands of the Dakota. The Oglala band, for example, was praised by Denig as

Figure 7: The Upper Missouri Fur Trade, 1826–40

LOCATION MAP

THE UPPER MISSOURI
FUR TRADE
1826–40

LEGEND

——— American Fur Company
■ Major Depots
■ Regional Posts
□ Temporary Posts
Main Opposition Posts
● Sublette And Cambell
▲ Bent And St. Vrain
Journey Of
Steamboat Omega–1843
—— Upriver–10 Day
Isochromes
- - - - Downstream–5 Day
Isochromes

Canada
HUDSON BAY COMPANY COMPETITION
U. S. A.

Ft. William (1833)
Ft. Assinibone (1834)
Ft. Union (1829)
Ft. McKenzie (1834)
Ft. Clark (1831)
Ft. Cass (1833)
Arikara Post
Forks of Cheyenne
Ft. Pierre (1832)
James River Post
Vermillion Post
Ponca Post
Big Sioux Post
Pawnee Post
Council Bluffs Posts
Ft. Laramie (1834)
Ft. St. Vrain (1837)
to Bent's Fort

Competition From Rendezvous Based Trappers

MARIAS R.
MISSOURI R.
MILK R.
MUSSELSHELL R.
YELLOWSTONE R.
POWDER R.
BIG HORN R.
WIND R.
JEFFERSON R.
MADISON R.
SNAKE R.
GREEN R.
COLORADO R.
PLATTE R.
N. PLATTE R.
S. PLATTE R.
LOUP R.
N. LOUP R.
S. LOUP R.
NIOBRARA R.
WHITE R.
OWL R.
CHEYENNE R.
LITTLE MISSOURI R.
LITTLE MO. R.
JAMES R.
BIG SIOUX R.

49

SCALE 100 50 0 100 MILES

tmk

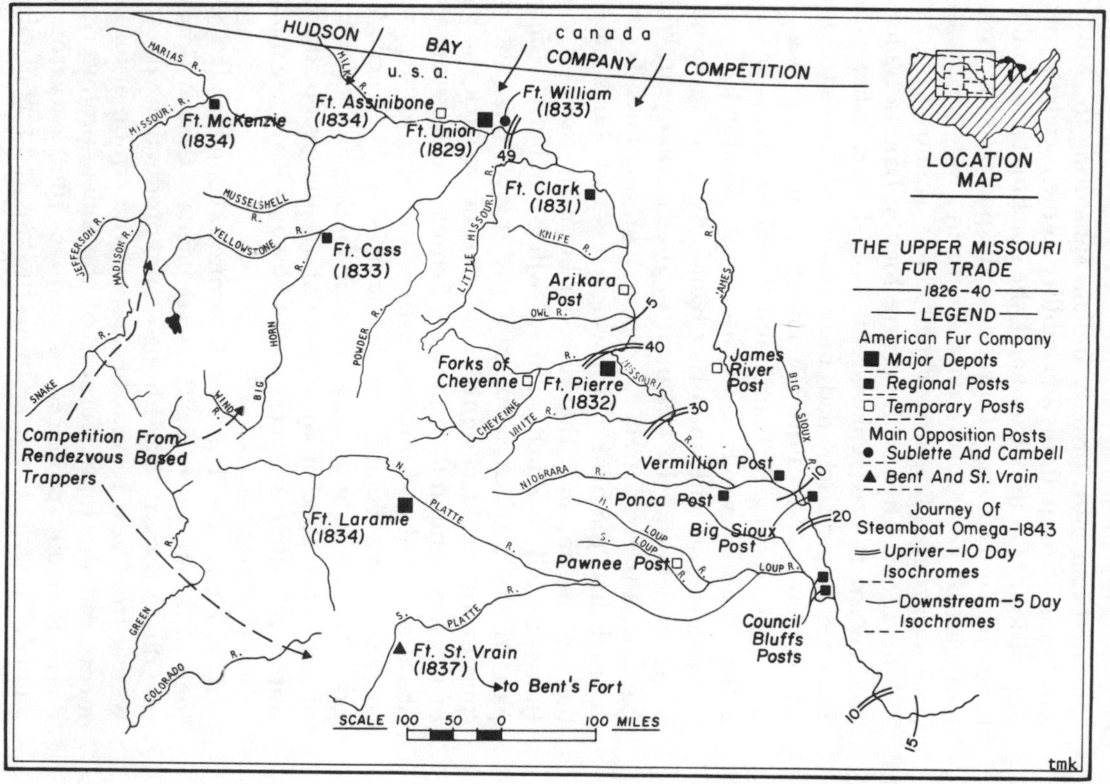

'The best and most orderly Indians inhabiting the Missouri', and Denig attributed this amenability to their leader's friendly disposition.[26] On the other hand, the Blackfoot and Yanktonai bands of the Dakota, who roamed the plains to the west and northeast of Fort Tecumseh respectively, were hostile to the American traders because of their chiefs' animosity.

Fort Tecumseh was the centre for the Dakota trade until 1832 when it was replaced by Fort Pierre. Whereas Fort Tecumseh's situation had been excellent, its site proved unsatisfactory. At Fort Tecumseh, 'The river was wide . . . and crossing difficult', and 'for three and four days at a time the high winds, low waters and quicksands closed all communication with the other bank'. By 1830 the post was being eroded into the Missouri. In June of that year, William Laidlaw, the head trader, recorded in the Fort Tecumseh Journal that 'the bank upon which this fort stands has been daily caving in since the Missouri began to rise — if it continues to fall in much soon we will be obliged to move a part of the fort'. A week later the traders were forced to 'pull down the Blacksmith's shop and move back the picots of the fort', and in the following February a two-storey store was dismantled and built back from the river in preparation for the spring flood.[27] The lesson was well learned. When Fort Pierre was built on a site three miles above the mouth of the Teton River it was placed above the level of the flood waters yet with easy access to the Missouri River for transportation (Plate 1).

Fort Pierre was described by Prince Maximilian in 1833 as 'one of the most considerable settlements of the Fur Company on the Missouri'.[28] Although fur production fluctuated widely from year to year because of the erratic bison movements and the capriciousness of the Indian producers, Fort Pierre generally produced more than 1000 packs of robes annually as well as large amounts of skins and furs (Table 3).

The American Fur Company realised that they needed a major depot in the upper country to act as a counterpart to Fort Tecumseh. In 1829 Kenneth McKenzie was sent by Pierre Chouteau Jr to establish a post at the mouth of the Yellowstone, the gateway to the northern Rocky Mountains.[29] Fort Union was erected 'where the chief of the band of Rocks had desired him [McKenzie] to build', on a 'beautiful

Plate 1: Fort Pierre on the Missouri (Bodmer, 1840)

Northern Natural Gas Company Collection, Joslyn Art Museum, Omaha, Nebraska.

site, abounding in the best of timber above, below, and opposite the fort, and with all kinds of game'.[30] (Plate 2). The post would receive the trade of the Assiniboine, Cree, and Chippewa and, as its name suggests, act as a bridgehead to join the Rocky Mountain Trapping System to the Upper Missouri Fur Trade. McKenzie urged Chouteau to launch a drive to the mountains as early as 1827, but it was not until 1830 that Chouteau felt secure enough on the upper Missouri to challenge the Rocky Mountain Fur Company.

Fort Union was 'the principal and handsomest trading post on the Missouri River'.[31] Not only was the post a lucrative trading centre in its own right, but it served as an entrepot for furs produced in the Crow and Blackfoot lands. In 1835, for example, McKenzie wrote to Ramsey Crooks that he would 'be satisfied if this post equals last year from whence there were shipped 4100 lbs. Beaver Skins, 1970 packs

Table 3: Fur Production at the Trading Posts:

Post	Year	Production	
Fort McKenzie	1834–5	9000 robes 1020 beaver 40 otters 2000 muskrats 180 wolves	200 red foxes 1500 prairie dogs 19 bears 390 buffalo tongues
	1836–7	1000 packs of robes	
Fort Assiniboine*	1834–5	179 red foxes 1646 prairie dogs 74 badgers 269 muskrats 89 white wolves 196 white hares 5 swanskins	4200 robes 37 dressed cowskins 450 salted tongues 3500 lb powdered buffalo meat 3000 lb dried buffalo meat
Fort Union	1833–4 1834–5	430 packs of robes 1970 packs of robes 4100 lb beaver 4000 fox skins 9000 muskrats	
	1836–7	1150 packs of robes	
Fort Cass	1834–5	450 packs of robes 1200 lb beaver	
	1836–7	450–500 packs of robes	
Fort Clark	1835–6	313 packs of robes 4 packs of beaver (100 pelts each)	

Sources: Fort Union Letterbooks, *Chouteau Collection*; Fort Tecumseh and Fort Pierre Letterbooks and Journal, *Chouteau Collection*; Abel, *Chardon's Journal*; Coues, *Forty Years a Fur Trader*. Note: Unless stated otherwise, a pack of bison

Robes, 4000 fox skins, 9000 rats etc.'[32] Or again, in 1837, Edwin Denig (then a clerk at Fort Union) wrote that there had been an excellent trade at the post, with '900 packs in the warehouse' and another 250 packs waiting to be traded. Denig added that he anticipated a further 450 to 500 packs from the Crow and 1,000 packs from the Blackfoot before the season was concluded.[33] Fort Union became the pivot of the American Fur Company's trading system on the Upper Missouri, and its importance was compounded after

A Fragmentary Record, 1828–43

Post	Year	Production
		1 pack of beaver (42 pelts)
		1 pack of wolfskins (48 skins)
		1 pack of red foxes (102 skins)
		1 mixed pack, containing:
		82 gray foxes
		4 badgers
		7 hares
		6 red foxes
		85 muskrats
		2 minks
	1836–7	3200 robes
		436 beaver
	1837–8	2870 robes
		404 beaver
Fort Tecumseh	1829–30	2000 packs of robes
Fort Pierre	1831–2	1300 packs of robes
Forks of the Cheyenne*	1829–30	4360 robes
Yankton Post	1831–2	120–130 packs of robes
Cabanne's Post	1827–28	26–28 packs of beaver
		56–58 packs of oppossum
		3 packs of otter
		400 packs of robes
Pawnee Villages*	1829–30	7–8 packs of beaver
		203 packs of robes
Fort Laramie	1843–4	1000 packs of robes

robes contained ten robes, a pack of beaver 80 to 100 pelts, and a pack of otter or oppossum about 60 skins. The asterisk denotes temporary posts.
*Temporary posts.

1832 when it became the head of steamboat navigation on the river.

The American Fur Company's hold on the upper Missouri was secured in the early 1830s with the establishment of three important regional posts: Fort Clark, at the Mandan–Hidatsa villages, Fort Cass, in Crow country, and, finally, a Blackfoot post, Fort Piegan (later Fort McKenzie).

The Mandan and Hidatsa villages, one of the main hubs of the aboriginal trade system, was perhaps the most persistent

Plate 2: Fort Union on the Missouri (Bodmer, 1841)

Northern Natural Gas Company Collection, Joslyn Art Museum, Omaha, Nebraska.

trading site in the fur trade of the Trans-Missouri West. In 1831 the American Fur Company built Fort Clark at the villages to replace Kipp's old post. The Mandan and Hidatsa were willing producers and traders, although they had abandoned extended bison hunts during the late nineteenth century because of the danger of enemy raids on their depopulated villages.[34] For extended periods during the 1830s the Mandan were unable to leave their villages to hunt because of the threat of Yankton, Yanktonai, and Assiniboine attack.[35] Nevertheless, until the devastating smallpox epidemic of 1837 the Mandan and Hidatsa traded about 300 packs of robes annually at Fort Clark and, in addition, a variety of skins and small furs.

In the late eighteenth century and during the 1820s, when they were without a trading post, the Crow bartered their robes and furs at the Mandan and Hidatsa villages. In doing so they were incorporating the fur trade into the existing aboriginal trade network. The Crow obtained horses, Spanish riding equipment, and horn bows from the Flathead, Shoshone, and Nez Perce in exchange for European manufactured products — metal knives, arrowheads and awls, brass kettles, and second-hand guns. These goods the Crow acquired in turn at the Mandan—Hidatsa and Arikara villages, where they were traded for dried meat, skin lodges, and other fine leather products created by the Crow women. It was in the interest of the village Indians to retain their middleman role between the American traders and the Crow, but Lisa had demonstrated to the Crow the advantages of direct trade.

In 1832, therefore, the Crow requested a trading post in their lands to relieve them of the onerous task of carrying their furs to Fort Union or Fort Clark. The Upper Missouri Outfit responded by building Fort Cass at the junction of the Yellowstone and Bighorn rivers. The post was only moderately successful, returning an average of 400 to 500 packs of robes annually and smaller amounts of the high quality Crow beaver. Robe production was often curtailed while the Crow and Blackfoot were embroiled in horseraiding skirmishes. Moreover, the Crow absorbed the fur trade into this horseraiding complex, and the frequent loss of horses, furs, and equipment added significantly to the overhead costs of trading and trapping in 'Absaroka'. In 1834, Kenneth McKenzie, irritated by the sporadic nature of their trade, warned the Crow that 'the permanency of any establishment in their country depends entirely on themselves'.[36] The traders would defer to Indian custom and demands only as long as it was profitable to do so. Despite these problems, the American Fur Company maintained a trading post in Crow country until the 1860s.[37]

In 1830 the Upper Missouri Outfit realised one of the original goals of the St Louis fur trade when Kenneth McKenzie negotiated a treaty with the Piegan band of Blackfoot using the old trapper Jacob Berger as a go-between.[38] The following year McKenzie sent Kipp to build a post, Fort Piegan, deep in Blackfoot country at the mouth of the Marias River. In 1833 the Blackfoot post was moved six miles and renamed Fort McKenzie.

In the summer of 1833, according to Prince Maximilian,

Fort McKenzie had a complement of only twenty-seven men.[39] Nevertheless, Fort McKenzie was the most productive single trading site on the upper Missouri. In the mid-1830s the Blackfoot traded almost 1000 packs of robes and a wealth of skins, small furs, and animal by-products each year at Fort McKenzie. Even after the treaty, however, relations with the Blackfoot were precariously balanced, and any attempt by the Americans to trap the streams of Blackfoot country was opposed violently. In 1833, Jacob Astor advised Chouteau to suspend trapping operations at the headwaters of the Missouri:

> The Indians are now too well aware of the value of the furred animals in their country to allow us to hunt them peaceably, and I apprehend a lofs (sic) of our trade with the Blackfeet will be a natural consequence of our coming into collision with them as we must do if we persevere in the present system of trapping.[40]

By 1833, however, Chouteau had committed the American Fur Company to the Rocky Mountain Trapping system, and Blackfoot country was one of the few remaining areas with large quantities of beaver. Trapping continued, but so too did trading at Fort McKenzie. By 1841 that post was returning 21,000 robes annually, and to a great extent Fort McKenzie was the key to the continuing success of the American Fur Company on the upper Missouri.[41]

By 1833, therefore, the American Fur Company had established a series of fixed posts which served as trading centres for the equestrian nomads of the western plains and as bridgeheads for the company's drive into the Rocky Mountains. In 1835, the acquisition of a third major depot, Fort William, completed the American Fur Company's trading network on the northern Great Plains (Plate 3).

Fort William was built by the veteran mountain trappers and suppliers William Sublette and Robert Campbell in June of 1834. The post was located at the mouth of Laramie's Fork on the North Platte in the lee of the Laramie Range. There the ancient Indian trail along the Rocky Mountain front crossed the road to South Pass, the Green River, Oregon and California. Fort William was a symbol of the

Plate 3: Fort Laramie, or Sublette's Fort, near the Nebraska or
Platte River (Miller, 1837)

Northern Natural Gas Company Collection, Joslyn Art Museum, Omaha,
Nebraska.

growing convergence of the two production systems of the
fur trade of the Trans-Missouri West. The Cheyenne, Arapahoe,
and the Oglala band of the Teton Dakota traded there and
the supply trains from Missouri paused at Fort William
before crossing the arid, sagebrush-covered basins to the
Green River rendezvous.

In 1835, Sublette and Campbell sold Fort William to
Fontenelle, Fitzpatrick and Company, the field representatives of the American Fur Company in the Rocky Mountains.
The post was rebuilt on the same site and named Fort John
in 1840, but it was popularly known as Fort Laramie. By
1840, Fort Laramie was producing an average of 1000 packs
of robes annually, as well as a large quantity of skins and

small furs that were traded from the bands of trappers who remained in the Rocky Mountains after the collapse of the rendezvous system.

The basic strategy of the American Fur Company on the northern Great Plains was to work within the limits of the existing patterns of Indian occupance to encourage the production of furs and robes. This necessitated, as Pierre Chouteau explained to the Secretary of War in 1831, a flexible trading system:

> The fur trade labors under disadvantages from the location of their posts being continued at the same place from year to year the Indians changing their hunting grounds each year the trader should be allowed to follow them and erect his post where the Indian hunted.[42]

So the pattern emerged by 1830 whereby a small group of traders would be dispatched from the fixed posts each fall with a supply of trade goods. They would build a trading hut in a location central to the hunting range of an Indian band, or they would simply set up trading quarters in the lodge of a tribal leader. Cabanne's Post, for example, maintained winter posts at the Pawnee villages, at the Otoe, Omaha and Ponca camps, and in various locations for the Dakota trade.[43]

The locations of these posts were specified by the Indians. In 1831, for example, William Laidlaw enumerated the temporary posts that had been requested at Fort Pierre for the following year:

> The Ogallalas have requested a post at or about the mouth of the Eau qui Court . . . the Cheyennes have also requested a post somewhere between the forks of the Cheyenne and the Brules wanted a post higher up than the Forks of the White River.[44]

Normally these demands were met, for it was in the traders' interest to conciliate the robe producers. Occasionally, however, a location did not make economic sense. Robert Campbell, a trader at Fort William (a rival post established adjacent to Fort Union by Sublette and Campbell in 1833—4), refused to establish a temporary post for the Cree on the Souris River because the only fur he could expect was muskrat, and transportation was all by land and therefore expensive.[45]

In 1833 some 500 men were employed by the American Fur Company at the trading posts on the upper Missouri.[46] The main depots each housed from fifty to 100 men and stored as much as $100,000 worth of trade goods,[47] the regional posts, according to William Gordon, kept from $15,000 to $20,000 worth of trade goods on hand and employed 15 to 20 men, and each temporary post was operated by three to six men and stored trade goods to the value of $500 to $3000.[48] This trading system was successful, and the Western Department and Upper Missouri Outfit became increasingly important segments of the American Fur Company's massive fur empire.[49]

Stresses and Competition

During the 1830s the American Fur Company's position in the Upper Missouri Fur Trade was jeopardised by changes in parts of the ecosystem. The American Fur Company was also challenged by contenders who, with little investment and, consequently, little to lose, employed desperate (and often illegal) tactics in their attempts to obtain a share of the Upper Missouri Fur Trade.

The proliferation of trading posts on the upper Missouri in the 1820s and 1830s and the associated intensification of trapping and hunting activities placed great stress on the resource base. At Fort Union, in 1833, Prince Maximilian was told that 'wild beast and other animals whose skins are valuable in the fur trade' had 'diminished greatly in number' along the Missouri River.[50] This depletion was also noted by Edwin Denig who recalled that beaver used to be found in great abundance 'on the upper Missouri, but in the 1830s they had become very rare, having been trapped and dug out by the Indians and the fur trappers residing with them'.[51]

The beaver was saved from total extirpation along the Missouri only because the demand for pelts in the European market was drastically curtailed after 1833. The market price fell so low in the late 1830s that it was no longer profitable to trap beaver, and within a decade their numbers were replenished by natural increases. In 1854, Denig observed that beaver were again 'tolerably plentiful in all of the small streams and in the Missouri and Yellowstone'.[52]

With the exhaustion of the beaver reserves on the upper Missouri the emphasis shifted fully to the robe trade which, in William Gordon's estimation, was in 'flourishing condition' in 1831.[53] The bison herds were large enough, and the rate of natural increase high enough, to withstand sustained exploitation without any noticeable depletion. However, the herds shifted geographically under pressure from the fur trade: during the 1830s there was a progressive movement of the herds westward and northwestward away from the Missouri River until, by the 1840s, the country to the east of that river had been totally abandoned by the bison.[54]

The developing scarcity of the bison and small fur-bearers was reflected in the falling productivity of the trading posts on the lower reaches of the Missouri, below Fort Pierre (Table 3). By 1830 this area had been within the sphere of Euro-American trading operations for a century and its resource base and its native inhabitants were feeling the damaging effects of this contact. As early as 1825 Cabanne complained to Chouteau that 'these posts are not what they were', and he argued that the Omaha, Ponca, and Yankton trades should be channelled into one centralised post because their dwindling returns did not justify the overhead costs of separate posts.[55] This amalgamation did not take place, and in 1831 the Ponca Post was still 'the most miserable post on the Missouri', according to Chouteau.[56] It was fortunate for the American Fur Company that the expansion of operations at the headwaters of the Missouri came in time to offset the falling production of the posts lower down the river.

The traders attributed the flagging production of the lower posts not only to the depletion of the fur-bearers, but also to the laziness and discontent of the Indian producers.[57] Perhaps the traders were too close to the situation to understand that the village communities, caught between the threatening forces of the equestrian nomads on one side and the Euro-American traders on the other, were suffering from the stress of rapid cultural change. Deluged by new tools, devastated by epidemics of measles, influenza, venereal disease, and smallpox, and torn between the traditional horticultural way of life and the new way of equestrian nomadism, the village cultures were fractured, if not broken. By 1830, according to Indian Agent John Dougherty, the village Indians were suffering from famine for six months of every year;[58] by 1833, the Ponca were so reduced by famine, war, and disease that they had abandoned their permanent villages and were living a semi-nomadic life in tents.[59] The fur trader was, to a great extent, the propagator of these changes, and the fur trade subsequently was greatly affected by the derangement of Indian life.

The most immediate damaging impact of the fur trade on the Indians was the transmittal of smallpox and other exogenous diseases. The fur trade was the carrier of smallpox through the northern Great Plains in the 1790s and on a number of occasions in the early nineteenth century. Each wave of smallpox destroyed large numbers of Indians and altered the ways of life of the survivors. This, in turn, had drastic repercussions on the system of the upper Missouri fur trade which relied heavily on native labour.

In 1837 the American Fur Company steamboat, the *St Peters*, carried smallpox upriver on the annual supply journey to Fort Union. By mid-July the Mandan and Hidatsa villages had been stricken and smallpox diffused rapidly to the nearby Arikara settlements. In August a Mandan war party grappled with a band of Teton Dakota and passed on the epidemic. Despite the obvious consequences, the steamboat completed the journey to Fort Union. There an attempt had been made to innoculate the resident Indians and to warn the Assiniboine to keep their distance from the post. This effort failed because the Assiniboine thought that the traders were trying to dupe them of their presents and trade goods. The Assiniboine contracted smallpox and as they attempted to flee its effects, they diffused the disease through the prairie provinces of Canada.[60] By November the Cree were striken, although to a lesser extent than the Assiniboine. The Blackfoot received the disease from two directions: the Blood

Indians contracted smallpox at Edmonton House and diffused it through the Piegan, Atsina, and Blackfoot proper, and from Fort Union the virus was carried directly to Fort McKenzie with the trade goods. There the trader Alexander Culbertson tried in vain to prevent the Piegan and Blood from examining the trade goods, but included was a crucial cache of arms which they were to use in their annual forays against the Crow and Flathead. The Indians insisted. Smallpox raged among the Blackfoot all autumn and only the Mandan fared worse. Fortunately, information diffused to the Crow camp faster than smallpox and they fled the environs of Fort Cass and so avoided the effects. The diffusion continued in a southerly direction. An Oglala war party skirmished with some Pawnee in late 1837 and the Pawnee warriors carried captives and smallpox back to their camp.

Possibly one quarter of the Pawnee died — they got off relatively lightly because, like the Atsina, they had been partially immunised by earlier, milder epidemics. At the Mandan villages the disease was still virulent in the spring of 1838 with an average of eight to ten deaths each day:[61] only twenty-three male adults, forty adult women, and sixty to seventy children survived. The Commissioner of Indian Affairs estimated that, of the six tribes most seriously affected (Mandan, Hidatsa, Arikara, Dakota, Assiniboine, and Blackfoot), at least 17,200 died.[62]

By refusing to jettison a year's supplies by burning or quarantining the steamboat, the American Fur Company not only brought havoc to the Indians but damaged its own trade for years to come.[63] As Jacob Halsey, a clerk at Fort Pierre, callously remarked, 'our most profitable Indians have died'.[64]

The epidemic changed the entire balance of power on the northern Great Plains and greatly affected the Indians' attitudes toward the fur trade. The Assiniboine, reduced from 1000 to 400 lodges within a year, attributed the disease to the Great Spirit rather than the traders.[65] The Blackfoot regarded the epidemic as retribution for their traditional hostility toward the Americans, and they were never such a serious threat to the traders again. The Mandan directly blamed Francis Chardon and his fellow traders for the disaster and their attitude changed to one of aggression against the Americans. In an impassioned speech delivered on

30 July 1837, Chief 4 Bears urged the Mandan to 'rise all together and leave not one of them [the traders] alive'.[66] The Mandan had neither the strength nor the spirit to carry out this threat. For the Mandan and the other village communities, 'the fur trade began with the promise of a bright future and grew into a curse or incubus which assisted in the destruction of the Indians'.[67]

In the long run, the indiscriminate use of alcohol in the fur trade may have damaged the Indian societites as seriously as the smallpox epidemics. Many contemporary observers believed that the 'philosophy of rum' determined Indian trading patterns, debased Indian character, decimated Indian populations, and vitiated the 'benefits of civilization' that the fur trade was supposed to bring.[68] There can be no doubt that alcohol was an integral part of the trading process on the upper Missouri in the 1820s and 1830s. In certain areas, especially during times of competition, alcohol was the most important trade good, as Thomas Biddle suggested in 1819: 'so violent is the attachment for it that he who gives most is sure to obtain the furs, while should any attempt be made to trade without it he is sure to lose ground to an antagonist'.[69]

It is possible that the extent and evils of alcohol use in the fur trade before 1840 have been exaggerated. There is no record in Chardon's rather candid journal, for example, that alcohol was dispensed at Fort Clark. Moreover, it is worth noting that the Crow and Arikara largely refrained from the use of alcohol during the fur trade period. Temperance leagues had proliferated in the United States in the 1820s, and many observers of the fur trade considered themselves moral crusaders against alcohol. These observers generally saw the Indians only at the trading posts, where group drinking was an important part of the trading process. It would be easy to assume that such behaviour characterised Indian lifestyles year-round. Given the problems of transporting a bulky product over extended distances to the Indian camps, this is a dubious assumption. Denig believed that alcohol was an incentive which increased the Indians' willingness to work and so raised his standard of living,[70] but considering Denig's fondness for drink this is probably as biased an opinion as those of the travellers and missionaries who came looking for alcohol's devastations.

During the early nineteenth century the Federal Government progressively tightened its legal control over the Indian trade.[71] The licence system was supposed to winnow out any undesirable traders, and Indian agents were empowered to prevent the importation of alcohol into Indian country. The American Fur Company generally supported these laws, although it did not always observe them. The Company was interested in a steady, year-by-year trade and realised that an excessive use of alcohol in the fur trade would eventually debilitate the Indian producers. However, when a total prohibition was placed on the use of alcohol in the fur trade in 1832, the American Fur Company found itself in a difficult position, unable to compete successfully within the Hudson's Bay Company (which allowed the discretionary use of alcohol in the trade along the international boundary),[72] and easy prey for the unlicensed traders who dispensed alcohol liberally in a frantic effort to make short-term profits.

In 1832 Chouteau wrote to Astor complaining that 'the late law prohibiting the carrying of liquor to our trading establishments will do us an incalculable injury at all our posts above the mouth of the Yellowstone'.[73] During the early 1830s the Hudson's Bay Company made a concerted effort to draw the trade of the Cree and Assiniboine northward to the posts on the Qu'Appelle River. Without the lure of alcohol the American Fur Company could do little to resist this competition. From Fort Union, McKenzie wrote to Cabanne in 1835: 'nothing short of almost profuse liberality on my part will induce them to make peltries, "no liquor no trade" is the prevailing sentiment with the Assiniboine'.[74] Consequently, McKenzie attempted to evade the importation law by establishing a whisky still at Fort Union, using Mandan corn as raw material. This ingenious, but illegal ploy was short-lived.

Despite the law of 1832 the fur traders continued to import alcohol into Indian country, often carrying the kegs overland to avoid inspection stations on the Missouri River at Westport, Fort Leavenworth, and the Council Bluffs. It is clear from Larpenteur's journal of events at Fort Union and Campbell's diary at the adjacent Fort William that alcohol continued to be a major ingredient of the Cree and Assiniboine trades. Even in the 1850s Denig was obliged to deal alcohol to the

Cree or else lose their trade to the British.[75]

The small trading companies and unlicensed traders who periodically challenged the American Fur Company on the upper Missouri did not hesitate to break the importation laws. They were less conspicuous than the American Fur Company and they had less to lose. For example, when McKenzie tried to ship alcohol upriver in the spring of 1833 he was stopped at Fort Leavenworth and his small cache of liquor was confiscated. That same year, however, William Sublette and Robert Campbell managed to smuggle 100 kegs of alcohol past Fort Leavenworth and into Indian country. This alcohol would be used in an attempt to wrest control of the Upper Missouri Fur Trade from the American Fur Company.

Sublette and Campbell, both accomplished Rocky Mountain trappers, joined in partnership in the fall of 1832 and prepared to challenge the American Fur Company on the northern Great Plains. The partners travelled to the east coast that winter and purchased their supplies on credit from Wolfe, Spies, and Clark of New York.[76] On the return journey Sublette bought two keelboats in Pittsburgh and arranged for them to be towed to St Louis in preparation for an expedition to the upper Missouri.

Sublette and Campbell received their trading licence on 15 April 1833, which allowed them to trade for a year and a half at 33 places in Indian country. Campbell departed overland for the Green River rendezvous, where he traded successfully for the furs of the independent trappers. Sublette accompanied the keelboats upriver, erecting trading houses adjacent to most of the fixed posts that the American Fur Company maintained on the upper Missouri (Figure 7). The two partners were reunited at the mouth of the Yellowstone, Campbell having shipped his furs and equipment down the Bighorn River on bullboats. There, about one and a half miles below the mouth of the Yellowstone and three miles from Fort Union, they built Fort William in the late summer of 1833 and went into direct competition with the Upper Missouri Outfit.

The strategy of Sublette and Campbell is representative of the tactics generally employed by the opponents of the American Fur Company. The number of suitable trading sites was fixed — by Indian dictates, transportation considerations and, simply, by tradition — and the American Fur Company kept a post at each of these locations. The opposing company, therefore, generally went into direct 'storefront competition' with the American Fur Company posts and attempted to capture the trade of the local Indians by offering high prices for their furs and by dispensing alcohol freely. The American Fur Company generally responded by matching the high prices and by taking short-term losses in order to achieve long-term victory. Invariably the American Fur Company, with its greater financial resources, prevailed and bought out the opponents or else arranged a suitable division of trade areas.

Campbell kept up strong competition at Fort William throughout the winter of 1833—4. His success was limited, however, and the Indians continued to trade their furs at Fort Union. In the first year of trading Fort William returned only 100 packs of robes, five packs of beaver, six packs of wolf skins, and one of rabbit and fox skins. In that same year 430 packs of robes were traded at Fort Union.[77]

Yet the tenacious competition mounted by Sublette and Campbell had its rewards. In the summer of 1834 an agreement was reached whereby Sublette and Campbell agreed to relinquish their trade and posts on the upper Missouri and in return the American Fur Company agreed to withdraw from the Rocky Mountain Trapping System for a year.[78] Sublette and Campbell had opposed the American Fur Company at an opportune time, for McKenzie's attempts to evade the alcohol restrictions had placed the Company's licence in jeopardy. It is not inconceivable that Sublette and Campbell had planned from the beginning to force the American Fur Company from the Rocky Mountain Trapping System by challenging them on their home ground. Whatever the case, this division of trade territory — likened at the time to the Partition of Poland — gave Sublette and Campbell virtual control over the Rocky Mountain Trapping System, but only in the short run.

More localised, but still a major threat, was the competition that developed along the South Platte in the second half of the 1830s. While The American Fur Company was still embroiled with Sublette and Campbell, a powerful competitor appeared on the western Great Plains. The threat was antici-

pated by William Laidlaw who, in January 1834, warned
Chouteau that 'Charles Bent has built a Fort on the Arkansas
and if judiciously carried on it cannot fail to be very injurious
to the fur trade in this part of the country'.[79] Bent and his
partner Ceran St Vrain intended to capture the robe trade of
the Cheyenne, Arapahoe, and Teton Dakota and to extract
what little wealth remained from the Rocky Mountain Trapping System.[80] They were given permission to build trading
posts in a number of locations in Colorado and Wyoming,
and in 1837 they established Fort Lookout (Fort St Vrain)
on the South Platte.

By 1837, the Colorado Piedmont was lined with a chain of
trading posts[81] (Figure 7). Just to the south of Fort Lookout
was Fort Vasquez, where Andrew Sublette and Louis Vasquez
had been operating since 1835. Then, in the summer of 1836,
an independent trader named Lancaster Lupton built a post,
Fort Lupton, just to the north of the future site of Denver.
All of these outfits vied for the trade of the Cheyenne,
Arapahoe, and Teton Dakota — the same trade that supported
Fort William, the Western Department's depot on the North
Platte. The American Fur Company responded aggressively
in the spring of 1837 by sending Henry Fraeb and Peter
Sarpy to build Fort Jackson in the midst of the opposition
posts.

In 1837, however, the American Fur Company was reeling
from the loss of trade caused by the impact of the smallpox
epidemic on the upper Missouri and was in no position to
engage in a trade war. Consequently, when Bent and St Vrain
suggested a cartel in the summer of 1838, Chouteau was most
receptive. The two companies divided the trade area of the
western Great Plains: Chouteau agreed to restrict his company's trade to the region above the South Platte, and Bent and
St Vrain promised to avoid the North Platte. Thereafter,
except for some minor frictions, relationships between these
two dominant companies were cordial, and the smaller
companies were unable to compete, and folded.

The focus of competition shifted in the early 1840s to the
North Platte and to the upper Missouri. In 1841, Lancaster
Lupton built Fort Platte adjacent to Fort Laramie and went
into direct competition for the Indian trade of the western
Great Plains. At the same time the American Fur Company

was confronted with vehement opposition on the upper Missouri from the firm of Ebbetts, Cutting, and Kelsey, otherwise known as the Union Fur Company. The common denominator in all of this competition was alcohol, which was used in unprecedented quantities to tempt the Indians from the American Fur Company posts. Chouteau, realising that the fur trade could collapse under the weight of such competition, came out in full support of enforcing the 1832 law against alcohol. He was instrumental in securing the appointment of Andrew Drips as an 'agent to reside in the Indian Country for the purpose of suppressing the whiskey'.[82] Drips was sympathetic toward the American Fur Company who gained a powerful ally to be used against future competitors on the upper Missouri.

Despite these challenges and stresses, the American Fur Company's hold on the Upper Missouri Fur Trade remained firm. The Company had the financial resources, political sway, and effective leadership to overcome any opposition. Its production system was efficient, the resource base sound for a few more years, and the market for bison robes was consistently good. The structure of the Upper Missouri Fur Trade, established in the late 1820s, remained essentially unchanged until after 1860, when the northern Great Plains were opened for settlement and the bison herds were wantonly exterminated.

Notes

1. T.Biddle to Col. H. Atkinson, 1819, *Indian Trade Papers* (St Louis: Missouri Historical Society).
2. Unless noted otherwise, the information on Manuel Lisa is taken from R.E. Oglesby, *Manuel Lisa and the Opening of the Missouri Fur Trade* (Norman: University of Oklahoma Press, 1963); and W.B. Douglas, 'Manuel Lisa', *Missouri Historical Society Collections*, vol. 3 (1911), pp. 233–68 and 367–406.
3. M. Lisa to W. Clark, 1 July 1817, in Douglas, 'Manuel Lisa', p. 382.
4. George Drouillard had been to the Pacific with Lewis and Clark. He stayed on the upper Missouri as one of Lisa's trappers. His two maps of the northern Great Plains, drawn in 1808 by William Clark under Drouillard's supervision, show the areas trapped by Lisa's men. On the first map the Bighorn River is designated 'the road to the Spanish settlements' and near Lisa's Post is written 'from this establishment a

man on horseback can travel to the Spanish country in 14 days'. C.I. Wheat, *Mapping the Transmississippi West, 1540—1861* (San Francisco: The Institute of Historical Cartography, 1958), vol. 2, pp. 51—6.

5. Biddle to Atkinson, 1819, *Indian Trade Papers.*

6. A pack of beaver normally contained 70—100 pelts, a pack of robes 10 skins, and a pack of otter or opossum about 60 skins.

7. R. Lewis to M. Lewis, 21 April 1810, in Oglesby, *Manuel Lisa*, pp. 95—6.

8. The business side of the St Louis fur trade is extremely complex. A few merchants (most notably, the Chouteau family) had financial resources and were, therefore, involved in most of the trading ventures. Alliances were, however, transitory and it was not uncommon to find opposing companies with the same suppliers and backers. See R.E. Oglesby, 'The Fur Trade as Business', in J.F. McDermott (ed.), *The Frontier Re-examined* (Urbana: University of Illinois Press, 1967), pp. 111—27.

9. Biddle to Atkinson, 1819, *Indian Trade Papers.*

10. Oglesby, 'The Fur Trade as Business', pp. 116—18.

11. B. O'Fallon to R. Crooks, 10 July 1822, *Chouteau Collection* (St Louis: Missouri Historical Society).

12. The best source on Joshua Pilcher and the Missouri Fur Company after Lisa's death is J. Sunder, *Joshua Pilcher* (Norman: University of Oklahoma Press, 1968).

13. 'Joshua Pilcher's Report', 1 December 1831, in Sunder, *Joshua Pilcher*, p. 33.

14. As a result of this competition, keelboats were in great demand but short supply at St Louis, and reliable traders and trappers were difficult (and costly) to obtain.

15. It is worth noting that, whereas the fur companies were extremely transitory, the traders and trappers persisted in their livelihood. The empolyees of the defunct Missouri Fur Company, for example — Pilcher, William Henry Vanderburgh, Andrew Drips, Lucien Fontenelle, and Charles Bent, to mention only a few names — continued to play important roles in the fur trade of the Trans—Missouri West.

16. H. Atkinson to J.C. Calhoun, 25 January 1822, in Morgan, *The West of William H. Ashley*, p. 1.

17. L.O. Saum, *The Fur Trader and the Indian* (Seattle and London: University of Washington Press, 1965), pp. 47, 55—6. To a great extent the traders judged the Indians according to their productivity, and the Arikara were not proficient trappers.

18. Abel, *Chardon's Journal*, p. 110.

19. P. Holder, 'The Fur Trade as Seen from the Indian Point of View', in McDermott, *The Frontier Re-examined*, pp. 129—39.

20. J.C. Ewers (ed.), *Zenas Leonard: Fur Trapper* (Norman: University of Oklahoma Press, 1959), p. 57.

21. For details of the Arikara campaign see D.L. Morgan, *Jedediah Smith and the Opening of the West* (Lincoln: University of Nebraska Press), pp. 42—77.

22. F.J. Young (ed.), 'The Correspondence and Journals of Captain

76 The Upper Missouri Fur Trade: Strategy

Nathaniel J. Wyeth, 1831—6', *Sources of the History of Oregon* (Eugene: University Press, 1899), vol. 1, pp. 73—4.

23. For a full understanding of the business machinations, deals and counterdeals in the St Louis fur trade from 1820 to 1823, see Oglesby, 'The Fur Trade as Business'.

24. Maximilian, *Travels in the Interior*, vol. 23, p. 92.

25. Ewers, *Five Indian Tribes*, p. 23.

26. Ewers, *Five Indian Tribes*, p. 21. The Teton Dakota were not bound to the American Fur Trade until the 1820s. Before that time they would deal only with the French traders from St Louis, who respected their customs and were willing to adopt Indian life-styles. See G.E. Hyde, *Red Cloud's Folk* (Norman: University of Oklahoma Press, 1937), pp. 34—5.

27. Fort Tecumseh Journal, 10 June 1830, 17 June 1830, 23 February 1831. *Chouteau Collection*.

28. Maximilian, *Travels in the Interior*, vol. 22, pp. 317—18.

29. Kenneth McKenzie was a veteran of the Columbia Fur Company. A gentleman, trader, and frontier diplomat, McKenzie was head of the Upper Missouri Outfit from 1827 to 1834. Pierre Chouteau Jr was the active head of the American Fur Company's interests in St Louis. When J.J. Astor retired from the fur trade in 1834, the trade of the Trans-Mississippi West fell into the hands of Pratte, Chouteau and Company. When Bernard Pratte retired in 1838, Pierre Chouteau became the head of the American Fur Company's interests on the upper Missouri and in the Rocky Mountains, a position he held until his death in 1865.

30. E. Coues (ed.), *Forty Years a Fur Trader on the Upper Missouri: The Personal Narrative of Charles Larpenteur*, 1833—72 (New York: Francis P. Harper, 1898), vol. 1, p. 109.

31. 'Denig's Description of Fort Union', in M.R. Audubon and E. Coues (eds.), *Audubon and His Journals* (New York: Charles Scribner's Sons, 1897), vol. 2, p. 180.

32. K. McKenzie to R. Crooks, 10 December 1835, *Fort Union Letterbooks, Chouteau Collection*.

33. E. Denig to J. Halsey, 25 March 1837, *Fort Union Letterbooks, Chouteau Collection*.

34. Holder, *The Hoe and the Horse*, p. 71.

35. Abel, *Chardon's Journal*, p. 105.

36. K. McKenzie to S. Tullock, 8 January 1834, *Fort Union Letterbooks, Chouteau Collection*.

37. Fort Cass' successors were Fort Van Buren (1835—43), Fort Alexander (1843—50), and Fort Sarpy (1850—60).

38. Berger had long traded among the Blackfoot for the British.

39. Maximilian, *Travels in the Interior*, vol. 23, p. 92.

40. J. Astor to P. Chouteau Jr, 17 April 1833, *Fort Tecumseh and Fort Pierre Letterbooks, Chouteau Collection*.

41. J.E. Sunder, *The Fur Trade on the Upper Missouri, 1840—65*, (Norman: University of Oklahoma Press, 1965), p. 60.

42. P. Chouteau Jr, to L. Cass, 3 October 1831, *Fort Tecumseh and Fort Pierre Letterbooks, Chouteau Collection*.

43. J. Dougherty to L. Cass, 19 November 1831, *Fur Trade Envelope*.
44. W. Laidlaw to H.F. Bean, September 1831, *Fort Tecumseh and Fort Pierre Letterbooks, Chouteau Collection*.
45. G.R. Brooks (ed.), 'The Private Journal of Robert Campbell', *Bulletin of Missouri Historical Society*, vol. 20 (1964), p. 109.
46. Maximilian, *Travels in the Interior*, vol. 22, p. 378.
47. Maximilian, *Travels in the Interior*, vol. 22, pp. 317–18, vol. 23, p. 92.
48. W. Gordon to W. Clark, 27 October 1831, *Fur Trade Envelope*.
49. The Western Department and Upper Missouri Outfit became relatively more important as the trade area of the Northern Department was eroded by encroaching settlement. In 1836, for example, Benjamin Clapp of the American Fur Company informed Curtis Lampson, the agent for that company in London, that 'the progress of civilization' was destroying the fur trade 'south of the Fox and Wisconsin rivers, worth annually $25,000'. B. Clapp to C.M. Lampson, 23 November 1836, *American Fur Company Letterbooks*. Yet even in 1840 the Upper Lakes region produced more furs than the western departments: see J.L. Clayton, 'The Growth and Economic Significance of the American Fur Trade, 1790–1890', in *Aspects of the Fur Trade* (St Paul: Minnesota Historical Society, 1967), p. 72.
50. Maximilian, *Travels in the Interior*, vol. 22, p. 379.
51. Ewers, *Five Indian Tribes*, p. 121.
52. Hewitt, *Indian Tribes*, p. 410–11.
53. W. Gordon to W. Clark, 27 October 1831, *Fur Trade Envelope*.
54. Hewitt, *Indian Tribes*, p. 462.
55. J.P. Cabanne to P. Chouteau Jr, 25 July 1825, *Chouteau Collection*.
56. P. Chouteau Jr to J.P. Cabanne, 31 May 1831, *Fort Tecumseh and Fort Pierre Letterbooks, Chouteau Collection*.
57. See, for example, J.P. Cabanne to P. Chouteau Jr, 27 March 1829. *Fort Tecumseh and Fort Pierre Letterbooks, Chouteau Collection*.
58. J. Dougherty to T.L. McKinney, 30 January 1830, *John Dougherty Papers, 1823–45* (St Louis: Missouri Historical Society).
59. Maximilian, *Travels in the Interior*, vol. 22, p. 277.
60. For the impact of this epidemic on the Canadian Indians and the Hudson's Bay Company system, see A.J. Ray, 'Diffusion of Diseases in the Western Interior of Canada, 1830–1850', *Geographical Review*, vol. 57 (1977), pp. 301–32.
61. Abel, *Chardon's Journal*, p. 127.
62. Devoto, *Across the Wide Missouri*, pp. 279–301.
63. An interesting alternative argument is presented in C.D. Dollar, 'The High Plains Smallpox Epidemic of 1837–38', *The Western Historical Quarterly*, vol. 8 (1977), pp. 15–38. Dollar suggests that three Arikara women who boarded the *St Peters* at Council Bluffs were probably the infectives. Dollar also shows that the environmental conditions at the Mandan villages were conducive to contagion.
64. J. Halsey to Pratte, Chouteau and Co., 2 November 1837, *Fort Union Letterbooks, Chouteau Collection*.

65. Ewers, *Five Indian Tribes*, p. 72.

66. Abel, *Chardon's Journal*, pp. 124–5. Dollar, in 'The High Plains Smallpox Epidemic' suggests that this speech was fabricated by Chardon (p. 31).

67. Holder, 'The Fur Trade as seen from the Indian's Point of View', p. 138.

68. The trapper Rufus Sage is representative of this body of opinion. See R. Sage, *Scenes in the Rocky Mountains* (Philadelphia: Carey and Hert, 1847), pp. 28–9, 41–2, 68–9.

69. Quoted in Chittenden, *The American Fur Trade of the Far West*, vol. 1, p. 23.

70. Hewitt, *Indian Tribes*, p. 465.

71. See F.P. Prucha, *American Indian Policy in the Formative Years* (Cambridge: Havard University Press, 1962).

72. When the Hudson's Bay Company was reorganised and reformed after 1821, following the merger with the Northwest Company, the quantity of liquor used in the trade was greatly reduced. Governor George Simpson was determined to eliminate alcohol from the fur trade except where competition with the Americans made it a necessity. Merk, *Fur Trade and Empire*, xx, pp. 110–11, 320–1.

73. Quoted in Chittenden, *The American Fur Trade of the Far West*, vol. 1, p. 27.

74. K. McKenzie to J.B. Cabanne, 10 December 1835, *Fort Union Letterbooks, Chouteau Collection*.

75. Ewers, *Five Indian Tribes*, p. 118.

76. Unless otherwise noted, the information on Sublette and Campbell is taken from J.E. Sunder, *Bill Sublette: Mountain Man* (Norman: University of Oklahoma Press, 1959), pp. 115–36.

77. Coues, *Forty Years a Fur Trader*, vol. 1, p. 62.

78. It was through this agreement that the Western Department acquired Fort William on the North Platte.

79. W. Laidlaw to P. Chouteau Jr, 10 January 1834, *Fort Tecumseh and Fort Pierre Letterbooks, Chouteau Collection*.

80. See D. Lavender, *Bent's Fort* (Garden City: Doubleday and Co., 1954).

81. The rather nebulous details of the chronology of these posts have been clarified in a series of articles written by LeRoy R. Hafen: 'The Early Fur Trade Posts on the South Platte', *Mississippi Historical Review*, vol. 7 (1925), pp. 334–41., 'Fort Jackson and the Early Fur Trade on the South Platte', *Colorado Magazine*, vol. 5 (1928), pp. 9–17, 'Old Fort Lupton and Its Founder', *Colorado Magazine*, vol. 6 (1929), pp. 220–6, 'Fort St Vrain', *Colorado Magazine*, vol. 29 (1957), pp. 241–55, and 'Fort Vasquez', *Colorado Magazine*, vol. 41 (1964), pp. 198–212.

82. Quoted in Sunder, *The Fur Trade on the Upper Missouri*, p. 49. See Sunder for details of the Union Fur Company and the Upper Missouri Fur Trade after 1840.

3 The Upper Missouri Fur Trade: Annual Cycle of Operations

The economic influence of the Upper Missouri Fur Trade reached from the Indian producers on the northern Great Plains to the factories and markets of the eastern United States and Europe. The lines of communication with this network were extended and often tenuous. The journey from St Louis to Fort Union by steamboat took more than forty days, the movement of furs and letters from St Louis to New York took about four weeks, and the round-trip passage between New York and Liverpool averaged 56.2 days in 1839.[1] During the long winter season the trading posts were virtually isolated. From early November, when the Missouri iced over, until the spring thaw, the sole communication link between the upper Missouri and St Louis was the winter express. In late December or early January two or three men, using a dog-sled, were sent from Fort Union to Fort Pierre, there to be met by a pack-horse express from St Louis. The two parties exchanged dispatches and retraced their journeys. Requisitions for trade goods, hunting equipment, seeds, provisions, and employees were returned to St Louis, together with detailed estimates of mid-season robe and fur production. In return, the traders on the upper Missouri were given preliminary market information that would be used to determine the exchange rates for furs in the spring trading.

Despite the problems of communication, the system was a tightly controlled unit, carefully supervised and organised, united by a continuous movement of furs, goods, and people, and regulated by information feedback which focused on St Louis, the main decision-making centre (Figure 8).

79

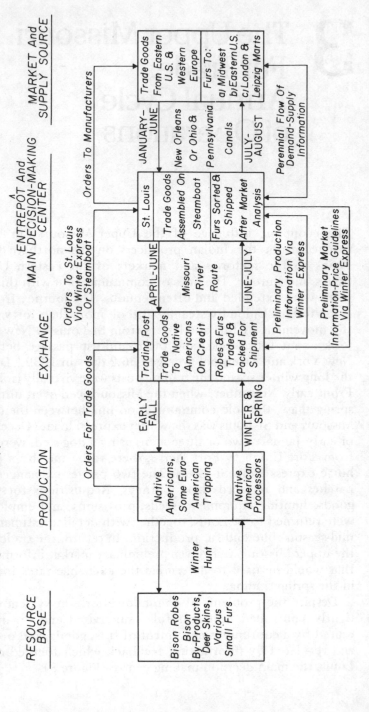

Figure 8: Spatial Organisation of the Upper Missouri Fur Trade

Supplying the Fur Trade

With the exception of ubiquitous items, the supplies and trade goods for the Upper Missouri Fur Trade originated in the factories of Europe and the eastern United States — the trading Indians of the northern Great Plains formed a small market for the products of the Industrial Revolution. Trade goods were requested by the Indians, the orders were relayed to St Louis via the express in winter and the steamboat in summer, and from St Louis the orders were placed with the manufacturers in Europe and the eastern United States.

The Indians were selective and specific in their demands for trade goods. They would not, for example, accept American vermillion, preferring instead the Chinese variety.[2] William Gordon listed the most demanded trade goods in 1831:

> Woollen goods of coarse fabric, such as blue and red strouds, Blankets etc. constitute the most costly items of trade — they are almost exclusively of English manufacture, and tho' coarse are good — the Indians are good judges of the articles in which they deal, and have always given a very decided preference for those of English manufacture — knives, guns, powder, lead, and tobacco are also among the primary articles, some of which are of American and some of English manufacture.[3]

By 1830 the trade goods were rather standardised.[4] Excavations at Kipp's Post and Fort Lookout II have revealed a large variety of glass beads, clay, catlinite and shale pipes, brass bracelets, arrowheads and pins, metal awls, nails and gun flints, and factory-made ear ornaments.[5] Not found in these excavations, but recognised as standard trade goods, are knives, kettles, firearms, necked hoes, gunpowder, tobacco, vermillion, bar lead, and a wide selection of brightly-coloured blankets, cloth and ribbons.

There were significant variations in the tribes' receptivity of trade goods — not all the Indians saw the advantages of antiquated guns, gaudy glass beads, and rather non-functional woollen clothing. Denig considered the Assiniboine, for example, to be 'far behind the other tribes' in their acceptance of European goods and, with uncharacteristic ethnocentrism, he attributed this to 'improvidence' rather than satisfaction with existing cultural baggage. The Assiniboine preferred their traditional weapons over guns and they refused to wear coats or pantaloons or to substitute metal utensils for wooden spoons and bowls. In contrast, wrote Denig, 'The Blackfoot and Crow nations perceive the convenience and utility of European articles, especially portions of clothing, horse gear and other things. . . They pride themselves on the cut of their coat.' The Crow, in particular, would accept only the 'very finest and highest priced goods' in exchange for their own high-quality leather products.[6]

The American Fur Company contracted with manufacturing companies in Europe for the importation of trade goods.[7] Blankets and cloth were provided by the Leeds textile companies, A. and S. Henry and Benjamin Gott and Sons, and by Crafts and Stell of Manchester, England. The Loubat Company of Le Havre, France supplied blue and scarlet blankets which, although of lower quality than the English products, were still highly demanded by the Indians of the northern Great Plains. By 1841 blankets from the textile mills of Lowell, Massachusetts had been introduced into the western fur trade, but their quality was poor and the Indians continued to prefer the European products. The American Fur Company also imported knives, traps, flints, and cutlery from Hiram Culter of Sheffield, beads from Alessandro Bertolla of Venice, and guns from Birmingham, England and from Belgium and Germany. The goods were bought on credit which was provided by George Wildes and Company of London and Wildes, Pickersgill and Company of Liverpool. They were dispatched to New York by the Liverpool shipping agents, Fielder Brothers and Company and Crary, Fletcher and Company. The New Orleans shipping company, Merle and Sons, then arranged the final transportation to St Louis.

During Manuel Lisa's time the fur companies were obliged to order their goods a year, even two years, in advance. Even then the deliveries were frequently delayed by transportation and logistical problems.[8] With the improvement of steamboat transportation in the 1820s, and with the standardisation of the types of trade goods (which allowed the American Fur Company to maintain standing orders with the suppliers), the system functioned more efficiently by 1830. Trade goods were generally sent from England in late winter and spring and, barring transportation delays, they were on hand at St Louis in early summer, ready for shipment to the upper Missouri. Nevertheless, there were inevitable delays inherent in such an extended transportation network. On 25 June 1836, for example, Ramsey Crooks apologised to Pratte, Chouteau and Company because the blankets that had been ordered from London in September 1835 had not been delivered.[9]

Transportation and Circulation on the Upper Missouri

The Upper Missouri Fur Trade spanned the 'Sail-Wagon' and 'Steamboat-Iron Horse' epochs in American transportation.[10] Before 1830 the fur trade relied on keelboats, mackinaws, and a variety of other cumbersome boats. Thereafter, the successful introduction of steamboat navigation in 1831 revolutionised Missouri River transportation. According to Sunder, 'Steam unsealed the upper river: unsealed its isolation, kept the seal broken, and strengthened, through improved communications, the Company's hand in the upper valley.'[11]

The Missouri River was extremely difficult to navigate. The channel meandered over a wide flood plain, its course changing frequently and sometimes rapidly. For much of the year the river was shallow, fed by an inadequate rainfall, and the boats frequently grounded on sand and gravel bars or caught on snags (Plate 4). The continuous navigation season was from mid March to late June. The early spring rise, beginning in mid March or early April, was caused by the snow melt and early spring rains on the northern Great Plains. The river abated by mid May, then was fed again in June by the snow melt in the high Rocky Mountains and by the early summer rains. This rise could last only days or for a period of months. Generally in late June the Missouri dropped quickly and navigation was closed by low water rather than by the ice which formed in the second half of November.[12]

Keelboats, which dominated the transportation system on the upper Missouri during the first three decades of the nineteenth century, needed the entire navigation season to

Plate 4: The Steamer *Yellowstone* on 19 April 1833 (Bodmer, 1840)

Northern Natural Gas Company Collection, Joslyn Art Museum, Omaha, Nebraska.

complete the upstream journey to the mouth of the Yellowstone.[13] They were powered by oars, sail, or cordelle — a long line that was attached to a central mast and pulled by twenty or thirty men who, at considerable risk from Indian attack, walked the shore. With these laborious methods of propulsion the keelboat averaged only fifteen miles a day upstream. They were expensive vessels, costing $2000—$3000 each in the Pittsburgh and Louisville shipyards. Moreover, the maximum load that a keelboat could carry was only twenty—thirty tons of cargo. Consequently, the advent of the steamboat signalled the end of the keelboat on the Missouri River, except above Fort Union which marked the limit of steamboat navigation before 1840.

The mackinaw was a clumsy but effective method of bulk carriage which continued to be used on the Missouri long after the introduction of the steamboat. These large, flat-bottomed vessels were built upriver at the boatyards (or chantier) that

were located near Fort Pierre, Fort Clark, and Fort Union.
Mackinaws were dispatched downstream on the June rise,
manned by a crew of five or six men. Driven by the current,
they often covered 100 miles a day. Audubon was on hand
when a fleet of four mackinaw boats were sent downstream
from Fort Pierre in 1843 carrying 10,000 bison robes, and he
left this description:

> These boats are strong and broad, the tops, or roofs are
> covered with the bent branches of trees, and these are
> covered by water-proof Buffalo hides, each has four oars-
> men and a steerman, who manages the boat standing on a
> broad board, the helm is about ten feet long and the
> rudder itself is five or six feet long.[14]

At St Joseph (where the furs were generally transferred to
barges or to the steamboat) or St Louis the mackinaw boats
were sold for firewood, fetching $4 or $5 each. In spite of
the difficulty of obtaining insurance for these boats (they
frequently sank) the mackinaw fleet carried more than
$100,000 worth of furs to St Louis in 1839. Mackinaw boats
remained an integral part of the Missouri River transportation
system until the 1870s.[15]

A wide variety of other, less important modes of transportation were used on the upper Missouri in the fur trade
era. Dugout canoes, hollowed out of long cottonwood trunks,
were used for short-distance haulage and communications
between the trading posts, but also for the shipment of high
value—low bulk products, such as honey and bear oil, to St
Louis. Piroques, which were made from two canoes fastened
together and decked over with planks, were used for downstream and upstream shipments, and they utilised the same
methods of propulsion as the keelboat. Bullboats were most
commonly used on the shallow tributaries of the Missouri
River, such as the Platte, the Bighorn, and the Niobrara. They
were used, for example, to move Pawnee robes down the
Loup and Platte rivers to the Council Bluffs. Their framework
was made of willowpoles bound together with rawhide
thongs.[16] Bison robes were sown together over this frame,
and the seams were waterproofed with a mixture of tallow
and ashes. Fully loaded these small, round boats carried 5,000

to 6,000 pounds of furs and drew only a few inches.

The first attempt to introduce the steamboat to the upper Missouri failed. The ill-fated Yellowstone Expedition, sponsored by the Federal Government in 1819, aborted when the *Western Engineer* reached only Council Bluffs. The expedition had been poorly organised and did not embark until 21 June, near the end of the summer rise. To the government and to many traders, this failure was proof that the Missouri River was unsuitable for steamboat navigation.

· It was left to the American Fur Company to establish a dependable steamboat service on the upper Missouri.[17] Kenneth McKenzie was the innovator, and by 1830 he had convinced Pierre Chouteau Jr that the steamboat would secure the American Fur Company's hold on the Upper Missouri Fur Trade. In the winter of 1830—1, the steamboat *Yellowstone* was built for the American Fur Company in the Louisville shipyard. The following summer, the *Yellowstone* reached Fort Tecumseh, but not without difficulty. This was only a qualified success, and the older more conservative traders continued to oppose the innovation: in 1832, for example, William Laidlaw noted in a letter to McKenzie that 'old Cabanne and Pratte are quite against steamboating'.[18]

The second journey of the *Yellowstone* dispelled any doubts. After leaving St Louis on 26 March 1832, the *Yellowstone* reached Fort Union on 17 June without encountering any significant problems. Time-distance was compressed. In November, Ramsey Crooks sent congratulations to Chouteau, writing 'you have brought the Falls of the Missouri as near comparatively as the River Platte was in my younger days'[19]

Even the first, comparatively crude steamboats were far more efficient than the keelboat. In subsequent years, as technology improved and as the pilots became familiar with the fickle character of the upper Missouri, the time for the journey to Fort Union was greatly reduced. By 1840, under favourable conditions, steamboats were ascending the Missouri at a rate of 50 to 100 miles a day. In 1843, the steamboat *Omega* made the trip to Fort Union in only fifty days and returned to St Louis in two weeks (Figure 7).

The advantages of the steamboat were speed and bulk carriage, which allowed the supply journey to Fort Union and the return journey to St Louis to be made in one season. The disadvantages were the initial cost, construction designs that were unsuited to the shallow Missouri River, the shortage of fuel, and the massive losses that were incurred when a vessel sank. In 1835, for example, the *Assiniboine* caught fire just below Fort Pierre and a cargo of furs valued between $60,000 and $80,000 was lost. The American Fur Company took this lesson to heart; thereafter Chouteau chartered vessels and insured the cargoes through New York firms.

The problem of fuel shortages was not so easily overcome. Steamboats consumed twenty-five to thirty cords of wood every twenty-four running hours. Cedar and cottonwood were the best fuels. Ash and oak also sufficed, but they were, according to Maximilian, 'poor wood for steam'.[21] The riparian woodlands along the Missouri River were rapidly depleted, and there were no professional woodcutters to supply fuel in the 1830s. Even Cedar Island, the traditional fuelling stop just below Fort Pierre, was deforested by 1840. Consequently, by that date, the steamboats were increasingly reliant upon driftwood and the decaying logs of old trading posts for fuel.

Despite these disadvantages, the steamboat greatly increased the efficiency of the Upper Missouri Fur Trade. Many of the upper Missouri Indians were greatly impressed by the spectacle of the steamboat and immediately proclaimed new allegiance to the American traders.[22] The Missouri River, more than ever before, became the aorta of this circulation system. Into this main arterial bullboats, mackinaws, skin and dugout canoes, Red River carts, and the Indians' travois carried furs from the hinterlands of the trading posts. These posts were the pivots of the Upper Missouri Fur Trade, outliers of the Euro-American settlement frontier and control points for the annual cycle of trading operations on the northern Great Plains.

The Morphology of the Trading Posts

The trading posts were the most apparent imprint of the fur trade on the cultural landscape of the Trans-Missouri West.

The fixed posts were built to serve a number of functions: they were trading centres, depots for the safe storage of goods and furs, defensible residential quarters for the traders, and small-scale agricultural and manufacturing sites. The posts were also social centres where news, ideas and customs were diffused among the various Indian tribes and between the Indians and the traders.[23]

As the patterns of commerce matured on the upper Missouri in the second half of the 1820s, the morphology of the trading posts began to take on a distinctive and definable form.[24] The larger posts were generally square or rectangular stockades built of wood, although adobe was used in the construction of the posts on the South and North Platte after 1835. There were dwellings for families and for single men, magazines for powder and arms, warehouses for the storage of furs and trade goods, and several types of workshops, all enclosed by picketed palisades.

The complexity of the internal structure of the trading post was a direct reflection of the post's external economic influence. The major depots were impressive landmarks. According to Maximilian (who was particularly meticulous in his post descriptions), Fort Pierre formed a quadrangle measuring 108 paces along each side and 114 paces along the front and back, and Fort Union was built as a square measuring 80 paces along each side.[25] Carl Bodmer, the young Swiss artist who accompanied Maximilian on his journey to the upper Missouri in 1833–4, painted Fort Pierre and its environs (Plate 1) and drew a detailed plan of the fort (Figure 9). The post was surrounded by squared cottonwood pickets, 20 to 30 feet high. At the northeast and southwest corners were the bastions, each with an upper storey fitted with small arms and a lower storey equipped with cannons. The bastions jutted out from the walls, allowing unobstructed surveillance of all the sides of the post. The internal arrangement of buildings reflected both the rigid social hierarchy and the economic functions of the trading post. The house of the bourgeois (who, in 1833, was William Laidlaw) occupied more than one half of the north side of the post. This was a one-storey building with large rooms, fireplaces and glass windows. Next to Laidlaw's house was a smaller building for the clerk. The engagés and their families, interpreters and

Figure 9: Plan of Fort Pierre

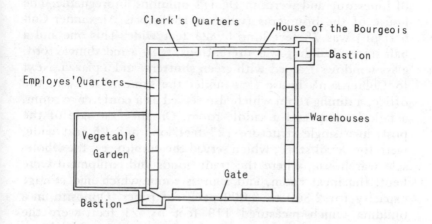

Adapted from Maximilian, *Travels in the Interior,* Vol. 22, pp. 317–18.

craftsmen (more than 100 people in all) lived in cramped quarters in a long building on the west side of the post. Opposite were the warehouses and stores, containing $80,000 worth of goods and furs, and the workshops. Attached to the post was a small vegetable garden. Fort Pierre was built on the first terrace of the Missouri River, near enough to afford easy access to water transportation, but secure from the floods and river erosion that had destroyed its predecessor, Fort Tecumseh. Surrounding the post on the native prairie sat the tipis of the various groups of Yankton and Teton Dakota.

Maximilian and Bodmer also left descriptions of Fort Union (Plate 2), but a more detailed account was given to Audubon by Edwin Denig in 1843.[26] Fort Union was built on an alluvial terrace on the north bank of the Missouri, 50 to 60 feet from the river, and far enough from the bluffs to be safe from surprise Indian attack. The river bottoms were wooded with elm, ash and cottonwood which supplied the fort with fuel and construction materials. The pickets, as at Fort Pierre, were made from hewn cottonwood trunks, but at Fort Union they were solidly set on a limestone foundation. The availability of local stone building material is also indicated by the structure of the bastions, which stood at the northeast and southwest corners of the fort — they were built of limestone and were, in Denig's opinion, impregnable. The house of the bourgeois (who, in 1843, was Alexander Culbertson) was 78 feet long by 24 feet wide. This one and a half-storey building was pretentious, with a red shingle roof, glass windows framed with green shutters, and a piazza. Next to Culbertson's house (and under the same roof) were the office, a dining room which also served as a conference room, a tailor's shop and a saddle room. On the east side of the post, in a single structure 127 feet long and 25 feet wide, were the retail store, which served the employees, the wholesale warehouse, where the trade goods and equipment were kept, the meat room, and a press room which had storage capacity for 2,800 to 3,000 packs of robes. Opposite, in a building which measured 119 feet by 21 feet, were the residential quarters, separated into sections for the clerks, hunters, and craftsmen. Smaller buildings included the ice-house, where meat was preserved during the summer, the kitchen, a cooper's shop, a blacksmith's shop, a coalhouse, a milkhouse and dairy, and ten stables with capacity for 50 horses. Facing the bourgeois' house, at the opposite end of the post, was the fortified entrance which, as at Fort Pierre, Fort Laramie, and many of the smaller fixed posts, consisted of a double gate. The outer gate was opened during trading operations, but the inner gate remained closed, excluding the Indians from the interior of the post. Trading was conducted through a window which opened into the corridor between the gates or into a reception room which was situated off the corridor. In times of tension, trading was done through a window which opened through the pickets to the outside. The outstanding construction at Fort Union was the powder magazine, a building which measured 25 feet by 18 feet, was made of limestone, and was, in Denig's opinion, absolutely fireproof.

Many of the regional posts on the upper Missouri were replicas of this model, but at a much smaller scale. Fort McKenzie measured 200 feet around the perimeter and housed 27 employees and their Indian wives. The morphology of Fort McKenzie was the same as at Fort Union but, in Maximilian's words, it was 'smaller and meaner' than the parent post: the buildings were small, the windows covered with parchment and the floors were dirt.[27]

The smaller posts were simple affairs. Kipp's Post, for example, measured only 96 feet around the pickets and had only one corner bastion.[28] The four small cabins at Kipp's Post were set against the north wall in an attempt to shield the employees from the prevailing northwesterly winds. But the wind swept through the gaps in the clay-chinked walls, and fuel was scarce — the life of a trader was much harder at a small post than at a large post on the upper Missouri.

On the lower reaches of the Missouri, at Council Bluffs, the posts were unenclosed because the threat, or perceived threat, of Indian attack had diminished with the progressive disintegration of the local Indian groups through war, famine and disease. Cabanne's Post, for example, consisted of only 'a row of buildings of various sizes, stores, and the house of the engagés married to Indian women'.[29]

On the South Platte, and later on the North Platte and the upper Missouri, adobe was used in trading post construction. The South Platte posts had close ties with Taos, and it is not surprising, therefore, that the traders experimented with adobe. According to the trapper Willard Smith, Fort Vasquez followed this 'Mexican plan of building'. Smith explained that because 'the atmosphere is very dry, and there is very little rain, the buildings are quite durable'.[30] Fort Laramie, which, as Alfred Jacob Miller's painting shows, was originally constructed on the Fort Union model (Plate 3),[31] was rebuilt using adobe in 1841. Its adjacent rival, Fort Platte, was also an adobe fort. 'Its walls are adobies,' observed Rufus Sage in 1841, 'four feet thick by twenty high — enclosing an area of two hundred and fifty feet in length by two hundred broad.'[32]

As early as 1831 William Laidlaw wrote to Chouteau asking for a man 'who understands making brick' to build the chimneys at Fort Pierre.[33] Only after 1842, however, did adobe construction come into widespread use on the upper Missouri. The Union Fur Company, Chouteau's main rival in the early 1840s was responsible for this architectural innovation.[34] Fort George, which the Union Fur Company built in August 1842 to oppose Fort Pierre, contained a number of masonry fireplaces made of sun-dried adobe-clay bricks, laid in adobe mortar and bonded with grass. Chouteau quickly recognised the advantages of adobe construction in an area where building timber was increasingly difficult to obtain. By the 1850s some of the buildings at Fort Pierre, and the walls, bastions, and buildings at Fort Benton were constructed of adobe.

The Annual Cycle of the Fur Trade on the Upper Missouri

The pattern of fur trading operations on the northern Great Plains was ingrained by 1830. This annual cycle represents a successful adjustment by Euro-Americans to a difficult environment for the purpose of acquiring furs. For much of the year the trading posts were virtually isolated. The traders were obliged, therefore, to strive for self-sufficiency and, to this end, most of the employees were involved not in fur production (a task which fell to the Indians), but in the up-keep of the trading posts. The round of activities at the fixed trading posts may be classified into three sections: production and trading, subsistence, and post maintenance and local industry (Figure 10).

Production and Trading

The production cycle commenced with the arrival of the steamboat at the trading posts bringing supplies and equipment. Denig described this inauguration of the trading year:

> The supplies for the trade are brought up each spring and summer from St Louis by steamboat and distributed at different forts along the Missouri River as far as Fort Union, mouth of the Yellowstone, from which point they are transported with keelboats to Fort Benton, near the mouth of the Maria River, in Blackfoot country. From these forts or depots the merchandise is carried into the interior in different ways, to wherever the Indians request trading houses to be established.[35]

In early September trade goods and hunting and trapping equipment were given to the Indians on credit. The debt was payable at the end of the season in furs valued against the robe standard, which was given a theoretical price of three dollars on the upper Missouri (Table 4). Denig's account

Figure 10: The Annual Cycle of Operations on the Upper Missouri, circa 1835

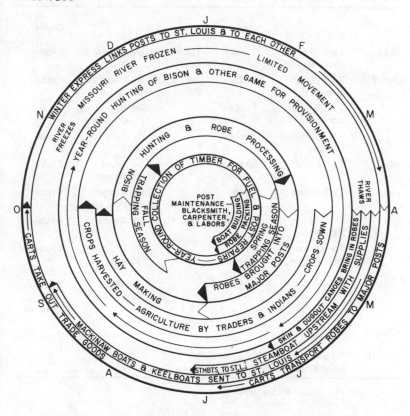

OUTER GROUP OF CIRCLES=<u>MOVEMENT</u>
SECOND GROUP OF CIRCLES=<u>PROVISIONMENT</u>
THIRD GROUP OF CIRCLES=<u>PRODUCTION</u>
INNER GROUP OF CIRCLES=<u>MAINTENANCE</u>

From D.J. Wishart, 'The Fur Trade of the West, 1807–40. A Geographic Synthesis', in Miller and Steffan (eds), *The Frontier: Comparative Studies*, p. 187. Copyright 1977, by the University of Oklahoma Press.

Table 4: The Operation of the Credit System: The Crazy Bear,
Assiniboine Chief

		Debit			Credit
1851	To 1—3 pt. white blanket	3 robes	1852	By 6 robes	6 robes
Dec. 3	To 2 yards blue cloth	2 robes	Jan. 8	By 2 dressed cow skins	1 robe
	To 3/4 year scarlet cloth	1 robe		By 30 pounds dried meat	1 robe
	To 2½ pounds tobacco	1 robe		By 2 red fox skins	1 robe
1852	To 1 horse	10 robes		By 2 raw cowhides	1 robe
Jan. 16	To 3 knives	1 robe		By 1 large elk skin, raw	1 robe
	To 1 kettle, 2 gallon	2 robes	Feb. 10	By 4 robes	4 robes
	To 100 loads ammunition	1 robe		By 12 wolf skins	4 robes
		21 robes		Balance forwarded	2 robes
					21 robes
1853					
Feb. 10	To balance on settlement	2 robes			

Source: Hewitt, *Indian Tribes,* p. 411.

books were replete with unpaid debts, and he complained
that 'a credit is considered lost as soon as given, or if after-
wards a trader receives half-pay he considers himself very
fortunate'. Yet Denig realised that this was often a consequence of inevitable misunderstandings in an economic
alliance which joined two disparate sets of cultures, and he
conceded that 'an Indian does not contract a debt actually
with the intent of deceiving, but before he has the means to
pay, new wants arise ...'[36] To many, less understanding
traders this was proof of the Indian's ingratitude and self-
interest (a prevailing sterotype held by the traders), and it
engendered bad relations.[37]

The traders arranged the production system to accommodate the producers, the plains Indians, and to fit the natural cycle of the fur-bearers. The Indians did not radically change their existing pattern of occupance to supply the traders, although they did intensify robe production to meet the new demands. Even small changes in lifestyle and attitude, however, had profound repercussions on societies that were already unbalanced from the stress of culture contact. As Fletcher and LaFlesche pointed out in their classic study of the Omaha, 'The quest for game for profit introduced new motives for hunting and also of cultivating the soil, motives not consonant with the old religious ideas and customs; consequently under their influence such customs slowly but inevitably fell into disuse.'[38] The fur trade brought the benefits of a new technology and the promise of higher standards of living, but inexorably it undermined the Indians' ways of life.

Horticultural groups like the Pawnee and the Omaha spent the spring and early summer seasons in their villages, cultivating beans, corn and squash. After the second hoeing of the corn, at the end of June, they set out on the communal summer bison hunt, leaving the village virtually depopulated.[39] During this hunt, which was generally made several hundred miles to the west, the main supply of meat was taken. The meat of both bulls and cows was prime in late summer and early fall. The meat was dried, or mixed with berries and tallow to make pemmican, and stored for winter consumption. The Pawnee returned to their villages on the Loup Fork of the Platte in early September, in time to reap the ripened corn. In early November, the entire village again migrated to the bison range of south-western Nebraska for the winter hunt. During this hunt the bulk of the robes for the fur trade was taken. Each part of the hunt — the preparation, the choosing of a leader, the migration, the surround, the kill, the butchering, and the allocation of meat and hides — was dignified with ritual and ceremony. The Pawnee returned to their villages at the beginning of March and initiated their continuing, age-old cycle with the spring renewal ceremonies.[40] The fur trade probably precipitated the abandonment of the horticulturalists' farming practices and it certainly expanded the bison hunts, particularly the winter hunt for robes.

The equestion nomads followed the bison at all seasons, occupying a loosely-defined hunting range in kinship bands which often merged and regrouped. The degree of nomadism, however, varied with the season and with the environmental conditions. In the Blackfoot yearly round there were four distinctive seasons: the period of the winter camp, from early November to early April; a brief, transitional hunting and collecting season in April and May; the communal summer hunting and Sun Dance season from June to September; and a brief fall hunting season which developed into the winter camp. The most 'nomadic' periods were spring, midsummer and fall; the longest 'sedentary' period was the five months of winter camp.[41]

The fur traders were interested only in the robes of cows and young bulls, taken from November to February when the fur was thick from the winter cold. The summer robes were too thin: 'teshna'ha', the Omaha called them, meaning 'hide without hair'. From the 'teshna'ha' the Omaha made moccasins, tent covers and other rawhide items that needed to be tanned on both sides. The Omaha called the winter robes 'meha', which were tanned on one side only, producing a pliable skin and thick robe. Denig estimated that only one quarter of the total bison kill went to the fur trade;[42] the remainder supplied the Indians with meat, leather products and a plethora of other uses.[43]

The nomadic Indians made their winter camp in broad, wooded river valleys which furnished grass for their horses and afforded shelter from the severe winds and blizzards of the northern Great Plains. They knew from experience that the bison also sought these valleys for shelter and for their winter forage of cottonwood bark, twigs and wild rosebuds. It was then a relatively simple task for the skilled hunter, equipped with snowshoes or mounted on a horse, to pursue and kill the bison. The Piegan, for example, generally wintered in the valley of the Marias, and the Crow habitually camped along the Bighorn or Wind rivers. The traders maintained temporary or fixed posts in proximity to the wintering grounds so that robes could be collected throughout the season.

The robes were produced, therefore, entirely within the framework of Indian culture and custom. As the trapper

Osborne Russell noted, the Crow 'laws for killing Buffalo are most rigidly enforced. No person is allowed to hunt Buffalo in the vicinity where the village is stationed without first obtaining leave of the council'.[44] Any breaches of the hunting ritual, either by Euro-Americans or Indians, resulted in the strictest punishment, meted out by the soldier division whose role was to regulate the hunt.

The production of robes was limited not by the number of bison that the men could kill (which, with the new hunting technology of the horse and gun, was large), but by the quantity of hides that the women could dress. According to Denig, 'Twenty-five to thirty-five robes is considered an excellent winter's work for one woman. The average is about 18 to 20 each.'[45] Whereas a Rocky Mountain trapper could easily perform the simple task of curing a beaver pelt, the few traders on the northern Great Plains could not handle the arduous task of processing the bison robes; hence the need for native labour. This increased demand for female labour resulted in an expansion of the practice of polygamy in the nomadic and horticultural societies and in a diversion of attention from the women's other traditional activities, such as farming.[46]

The processing of the hides was also performed within the context of the existing Indian milieu. Each step was dictated by custom and ritual. The hide was halved, scraped clean with the shinbone of an elk, dried in the sun in summer or over a small fire in winter, and rubbed with a mixture of liver and brains until it was soft and pliable and ready to trade.[47]

The robe was the most important, but not the only, item of trade. Deer and antelope were killed using the bow and arrow and the gun, or they were driven into parks or surrounds, in much the same way that the bison were taken. Wolves and foxes were killed using deadfall traps, but the traditional method of taking beaver by digging through the roof of the lodge was superseded in the early nineteenth century by the introduction of the steel trap. Of the northern plains Indians, however, only the Crow, Cree and, after 1831, the Blackfoot were accomplished commercial trappers. Again, only winter skins and furs were taken by the traders, although all of these animals were killed by the Indians year-round for food and clothing.

After the robes and skins had been dressed, they were exchanged for goods at the local trading hut or packed into small bundles, each weighing between thirty and thirty-five pounds, and transported on dog or horse travois to the nearest fixed post.[48] The ensuing trading process epitomises the merger of cultures that characterised the fur trade on the northern Great Plains. Each step was marked by ritual, and each culture honoured the customs of the other, although often without fully comprehending their meaning.

When the Indian trading party approached the gate of the post, the bourgeois would recognise the chief by raising the American flag and firing a cannon. In this way the chief's status was enhanced. The ceremony also affirmed the status of the bourgeois who at all times strived to maintain a dignified bearing in the eyes of the Indians. Adorned with splendid uniforms, men like Kenneth McKenzie were frontier diplomats as well as traders. The ceremony continued with the admittance of the Indians into the reception room, but at no time were they allowed into the heart of the trading post. The Indian leaders delivered eloquent speeches, generally directed at a softening of exchange rates. In deference to Indian custom, gifts were exchanged, particularly food, tobacco and alcohol. Gift-giving served a variety of functions, affirming friendship and representing a non-verbal form of communication.[49] The traders had no alternative but to adhere to this ritual, but they complained bitterly about the additional overhead cost and the Indian's apparent lack of appreciation for such 'generosity'. Even the American Fur Company, which generally defeated its opponents by taking the short-term losses that lavish gift-giving entailed in order to keep Indian allegiance in the long run, found the custom a heavy burden. Kenneth McKenzie attempted to curtail gift-giving in 1835, but he found that this was impossible, and he complained:

> I never was an advocate for large and indiscriminate distri-
> bution of presents: a good and industrious Indian may be
> encouraged to greater exertions by a well timed gratuity,
> but when all receive alike, every good effect is destroyed
> and the nation claims as a right what was intended as a
> boon.[50]

To the Indian, however, gift-giving was a right that could not be dispensed with. It was a prelude to the exchange of furs and trade goods (often done at night because liquor was an important but illegal item of trade), a day or two of celebration, and eventual departure from the trading post.

In general, both the trader and the Indian seemed satisfied with their economic rewards: 'The nature of the barter for robes and other skins,' wrote Denig, 'is such that the Indian receives what he considers an equivalent for his labor or he would not hunt.'[51] Under non-competitive conditions the traders were also satisfied with the exchange. The trapper, Zenas Leonard was amazed to discover that to 'get a beaver skin from these Indians [Wind River Shoshoni] worth eight or ten dollars never cost more than an awl, a fishhook, a knife, a string of beads, or something equally as trifling.'[52]

William Gordon estimated that the exchange of goods gave the trader 'a great ostensible profit upon primary cost, say from 200 to 2000 per cent'.[53] Denig agreed, but he noted that the profit margin was narrowed by the overhead costs of maintaining the trading post, by the gift-giving system and by the costs and risks of transportation:

> The cost of buffalo robes is about $1.35 in cash and we estimate the expenses in men, forts, and animals and other disbursements at $1.20 more each robe which would bring them to $2.25. Now the best sale of a large quantity is $3 each. Therefore, the loss of one or two boats loaded with furs must show a loss on the profits.[54]

Granted, Denig represented the fur trade in an idealised light and he glossed over the exploitative and damaging aspects of this culture contact. Nevertheless, he was probably correct in his assertion that there was 'no way in the nature of the business by which an Indian can be made to hunt, nor any means of getting his skins without paying a fair price.'[55] The Indians were not slaves to the fur trade. They were intelligent traders, selective in their cultural borrowings. As Denig pointed out, 'Should the merchandise be placed too high to be easily purchased by them they would and can dispense with nearly all the articles of trade'.[56]

The Indian was the main producer in the Upper Missouri

Fur Trade, but the trading posts did employ a few Euro-American trappers who led small parties of Indians and mixed-bloods on beaver hunts in fall and spring. At Fort Clark the trapping seasons were from the beginning of September until the beginning of November, when the streams iced over, and from the spring thaw, at the end of February, until the beginning of June, by which time the pelt had thinned. In 1836, for example, the main trapper, named Durant, was sent out six times on short trapping expeditions in September and October. Durant rarely caught more than three beaver on these hunts, which emphasises the scarcity of beaver on the Upper Missouri by the late 1830s. Fort Clark's annual return of beaver pelts was small: 1,100 lb (or about 12 packs) were produced between 18 June 1834 and 18 August 1835; four packs were produced in the year ending 30 June 1836; and five packs were sent downriver to St Louis at the end of the 1837 production year. In this same period Fort Clark returned 350 to 400 packs of robes each year, which underscores the fact that the bison robe was the basic product of the Upper Missouri Fur Trade.[57]

Subsistence

The most pragmatic activity at the trading posts on the upper Missouri was the procurement of food. Food supplies were obtained from a variety of sources, the importance of which varied with season and place. The problem of provisionment was most serious in winter, when famine was a constant threat, and at the northern and western trading posts where the possibilities for agriculture were limited.

Bison meat, either fresh or dried, was the most important food source on the upper Missouri. The trader and Indian agent John Dougherty estimated in 1831 that about one-half of the meat consumed at the trading posts was supplied by the Indians.[58] The remainder was procured by Euro-American hunters who were employed at each fixed post as provisioners. The meat was stocked in the fall when the flesh of the cows was prime. Fall was also the season for making pemmican which was prepared by the Indian women who mixed ripe berries with dried meat and melted bison fat in bags made from bison hides. The traders tried to accumulate enough meat and pemmican to last the long winter season, but the reserve was generally inadequate.

During most winters the trading posts teetered on the brink of starvation. As the supplies of stored meat and corn dwindled the traders were left at the mercy of the erratic bison migrations. Charles Larpenteur recalled that following a mild fall in 1833 the bison herds stayed far to the north of Fort William. With no fresh meat available, Larpenteur and his men were forced to subsist on pemmican, traded from the local Indians at a price-equivalent of fifty cents a bladder. This sufficed for breakfast, and corn soaked in lye was served for lunch and dinner.[59]

Chardon's journal at Fort Clark is filled with references to winter famines. On 16 January 1836, for example, Chardon wrote: 'Our prospect for the winter is now gloomy in the extreme. I have concluded to send off all my horses and hunters to make a living in the Prairies — or starve as fate may direct.'[60] Fortunately, later that month 'cattle' were found in the Knife River Valley, and the hunters and Mandan Indians brought in a saving supply of meat. Nevertheless, the constant threat of starvation, the intense cold, the isolation, and the merging grayness of the sky and land set a dismal tone for life at the trading posts in the winter.[61]

The provision of winter feed for the horses and other stock was also a difficult problem. At Fort Clark natural hay was gathered from July to August. This was a time-consuming task because 40 to 60 cartloads were needed for winter consumption. Around Fort Union, according to Edward Harris (who accompanied Audubon to the upper Missouri in 1843), there were 200 to 300 acres of big bluestem that were suitable for mowing.[62] The hay was cut in July and stored in a special enclosure, as Denig explained:

About two hundred feet east of Fort Union is an enclosure of about 150 ft. square, which is used for hay and other purposes. Two hundred and fifty good cartloads of hay are procured during the summer and stacked up in this place for winter use of horses and cattle, the winter being so severe and long, and snow so deep that little food is to be found for them on the prairies at that season.[63]

In spite of such precautions the hay supply was often exhausted before the end of the winter. The traders were then forced to turn the poorer horses out onto the prairie to fend for themselves.[64]

The horticultural Indians supplied the trading posts with substantial quantities of corn, beans and squash. In late September and early October the Mandan, Hidatsa and Arikara traded their surplus crops at Forts Union, Clark and Tecumseh: first beans and squash, then corn. The Arikara, for example, traded 500 to 800 bushels of corn at Fort Clark annually, and on one occasion in 1830 they supplied 1,000 bushels of corn to Fort Tecumseh.[65] The rate of exchange varied with supply and demand, but a bushel of corn could often be traded for a dollar's worth of goods.[66] At the trading posts the braided corn was hung on a scaffold to dry, packed in bags, then stored in a loft for winter consumption. Much of the corn reserve was eaten by Norway rats that had diffused up the Missouri River on the boats. At Fort Clark, for example, in 1833 and 1834, the rats consumed five bushels of corn each day.[67] Despite these losses during many winters corn was the only barrier between the traders and starvation.

In an effort to secure a firmer base of subsistence and to reduce operating costs many of the trading posts strived to become self-sufficient. This objective was particularly difficult to attain on the upper reaches of the Missouri River above the mouth of the Yellowstone. Drought and the short growing season were the major impediments. In 1823 Andrew Henry experimented with corn at the mouth of the Yellowstone, 'but the ground was so dry that it did not even swell or rot'.[68] In the same area, a decade later, Robert Campbell recorded in his diary of events at Fort William that 'there is not enough moisture here to raise vegetables, potatoes, grass etc.'[69] Even at Fort Union, where agriculture was practised, the yields were unreliable for a variety of environmental reasons, as Denig explained:

By experiments made at Fort Union it has been ascertained that oats, corn, potatoes and all garden vegetables grow well in favorable seasons. The soil being light and sandy requires frequent rains to produce good crops which happens 1 year in 3, the others fail from drought and destruction by grasshoppers, bugs and other insects.[70]

Nevertheless, farming was carried on at many of the Missouri River trading posts. The typical trading post agricultural system may be described as horticulture and small-scale stock raising. At Fort Union peas, turnips, radishes, beets, and onions were grown in the small garden attached to the post. The main garden was half a mile below the fort. There, on a one and a half acre plot, potatoes, corn and a variety of other vegetables were grown. The range of vegetables was wide: in 1835, for example, the trader Michael Hamilton submitted an order for seeds which included beets, carrots, four varieties of radishes, onions, lettuce, two kinds of beans, peas, sage, mustard, parsley, and thyme.[71] In addition thirty head of cattle, forty horses and a large number of hogs were kept at Fort Union.

In the description of Fort McKenzie that Alexander Culbertson gave to Audubon there is no mention of cultivation.[72] Culbertson did note, however, that 'the stock belonging to the fort consists of thirty to forty horses, ten or twelve cattle and a number of hogs' as well as a 'most splendid Durham bull'. It is probable that the constant fear of Blackfoot attack and the restrictions of a difficult physical environment vitiated any attempts to farm at Fort McKenzie.

Downriver from Fort Union, where the growing season is longer and precipitation higher, the possibilities for agriculture increased. At Fort Clark Audubon noted 'some small spots cultivated where corn, pumpkins and beans are grown', but according to Maximilian, 'Fort Clark possessed no oxen, nor any domestic animals, except some cows and hens, which latter began to lay in March'.[73] James Kipp, the bourgeois from 1831 to 1834, experimented with potatoes and manuring techniques, but the Mandan's agricultural surplus probably reduced the need for farming at Fort Clark.

At Fort Pierre, however, agriculture was well developed. In January 1834 (a winter of widespread famine on the upper Missouri), William Laidlaw informed Chouteau that Fort Pierre was self-sufficient, with a large reserve of dried meat and a garden that had yielded 170 bushels of corn and 200 bushels of turnips.[74] In addition, there were 150 cattle at Fort Pierre in 1833 which, in Maximilian's words 'afforded a sufficient supply of milk and fresh butter'.[75] Most of the crops consumed at Fort Pierre were grown on Farm Island, which was located three miles below the Fort. Audubon's party stopped at Farm Island in1843 to pick up potatoes, corn, and a pig, and Edward Harris noted that 'they raise the Mandan corn and it appears to do well'.[76]

The smaller posts further down the Missouri River also practised intensive small-scale agriculture. At Cabanne's Post corn was grown on fifteen acres of fertile bottom land. When this post was transferred to Joshua Pilcher in 1833, the inventory referred to a very large field of corn 'in flourishing condition'.[77] Nearby, at Bellevue, Fontenelle's Post kept five 'plantations' which yielded 100 bushels of corn per acre.[78] These lower-river trading posts, situated near cultivating Indians, with easy access to St Louis for supplies, and in a fertile area that would become part of the 'Corn Belt', did not face the severe problems of provisioning that were experienced farther upstream.

At many of the trading posts the nomadic and village Indians frequently stole or destroyed the traders' crops. In August 1830, for example, the *Fort Tecumseh Journal* recorded that 'The Indians have played great havoc in our garden, stolen corn, potatoes, pumpkins etc. etc.'.[79] Aside from this negative aspect, it is evident that the Indians' role in provisioning the fur trade was integral. Without the supply of fresh and dried meat which the nomads and village Indians provided and the crops which the horticulturalists produced, it is doubtful that the trading posts could have been maintained solely by their own hunting and farming activities.

The steamboat carried luxury items to the upriver posts each summer: Coffee, sugar, tobacco and various types of alcohol — high-priced products that could bear the costs of transportation. At certain times, such as Christmas, or on the occasion of a visit by an important traveller, the traders organised lavish feasts. When Nathaniel Wyeth returned from the Rocky Mountains by way of Fort Union in 1833 he was treated graciously by Kenneth McKenzie. A dinner was prepared which included fresh bison meat, beef, poultry and mutton, Mandan corn, fresh butter, milk and cheese, white bread and a variety of fruits, all accompanied by a fine selection of vintage wines and brandies. Such occasions, however, were rare, and they stood out conspicuously from a daily life that was austere, monotonous, and often dangerous.

Maintenance and Industry

Maintenance activities at the fixed posts were perennial. The most laborious task was the haulage of wood for structural repairs and for fuel. This drudgery became even more time-consuming and difficult when the accessible woodlands were depleted. The construction timber for Fort Pierre, for example, was brought from sixty miles upriver because the local supplies were exhausted. At Fort McKenzie in 1843 timber was so scarce that fuel was rationed and wood was stored behind locked doors.[80] Probably more man-hours were spent procuring wood at the trading posts than on any other single activity, including trading.

A variety of other maintenance and small-scale manufacturing activities were carried on throughout the year. In the fall the buildings were daubed and their roofs insulated and waterproofed with sod and hay in preparation for the winter. The trading posts were cleaned irregularly, generally by the Indian women. The blacksmith was responsible for shoeing the horses and maintaining the traps and other metal equipment, and tinners, coopers, tailors and other craftsmen and labourers performed mundane, but essential, duties.

At some of the larger trading posts there were boatyards, or 'Chantiers', where mackinaws were built in preparation for the June rise and their one and only journey downstream. Fort Pierre's 'Navy Yard' was located 20 miles above the post. As many as twenty carpenters and labourers were maintained there during the year, cutting wood with pit saws and structuring the two-inch cottonwood planks into large flat-bottomed boats. On 22 April 1830, for example, it was recorded in the *Fort Tecumseh Journal* that '2 men left for the Navy Yard with two Jack-asses loaded with Pitch, Cordage, etc. for the Batteaux'. Within a few weeks five mackinaws were dispatched from Fort Pierre with a large cargo of furs and robes.[81]

Winter was the slackest season at the trading posts. At that time of the year the main challenge was survival, and the predominant daily activities were the procurement of food and fuel. With the spring thaw came a flurry of activities. The warehouses were cleared in anticipation of the main trading season, raw-hide cords were cut for binding the packs of furs, and, starting in late March, the robes were pressed and packed in preparation for shipment to St Louis. By the middle of April the employees at Fort Clark were pressing about 50 packs of robes a day, using lever and screw presses. This activity continued until late June when the furs were loaded onto the steamboat and mackinaw boats. On 23 June 1832, for example, the *Yellowstone* left Fort Tecumseh with 1,300 packs of robes and furs on board. Three weeks later, 355 packs of robes and 10,230 pounds of beaver were loaded onto five mackinaw boats and shipped downstream.[82]

With a movement analogous to the flow of tributary water into the Missouri River, the furs were channelled from the hinterlands of the trading posts into the linear transportation route to St Louis. The volume of cargo increased as the steamboat collected the returns of each successive trading post and as more mackinaws and dug-out canoes joined the flotilla that headed for St Louis. In the late 1830s, between 8,000 and 10,000 packs of robes were conveyed each summer over the stretch of river between the Council Bluffs and St Louis.

Marketing the Furs

At St Louis the robes, pelts and skins from the northern Great Plains were gathered with the pelts and skins from the Rocky Mountains, sorted, then packed for transportation to the markets in the eastern United States and Europe. Furs of varying quality were included in each pack. This not only standardised the shipments but also ensured that the poorer furs were sold. Frequently the furs and skins were damaged by insects and moisture during the passage between St Louis and New York. On one occasion in 1823, for example, Ramsey Crooks complained that the batch of deerskins which he had received in New York had been riddled by worms and moths and looked 'as if they had been buried in the earth'.[83] By 1830 the American Fur Company had earned a bad reputation for delivering sub-quality furs. Subsequently, Pierre Chouteau instructed his main shippers, Merle and Company of New Orleans, to stow the furs between the decks of the steamboat.[84] This raised the freight costs but reduced the chances of spoilage. Nevertheless, Crooks continued to complain about the bad condition of the furs and skins that were sent from St Louis in the late 1830s.

By 1835 three routes were used to move the furs and skins to New York (Figure 11). The traditional method was by steamboat to New Orleans and thence by sea to New York. However, the heat and humidity of the southern summer often damaged the furs, and the 'endless, ruinous detention' of quarantine at New Orleans delayed the shipments.[85] Consequently, Crooks and Chouteau experimented with alternative routes. In the summer of 1835 the furs were shipped by steamboat on the Ohio River to Pittsburgh, then transferred to barges and sent on the Pennsylvania Canal to the east coast. The following summer the furs were moved from the Ohio River to Buffalo by way of the Ohio Canal, then shipped on the Erie Canal to New York.

None of these routes was totally satisfactory. The Ohio and Pennsylvania canals afforded direct passage to New York, but they were often in ill repair and impassable because of low water or ice. Moreover, the cost of shipment via Pennsylvania was three cents a robe more than on the New Orleans route.[86] A diversified transportation system emerged in the second half of the 1830s: the southern route was preferred in winter, particularly for the high-bulk robes, while the Pennsylvania and Ohio canals were used during the remainder of the year, especially for deerskins and small furs.

On the east coast the bison robes were distributed by rail to the markets in New York, Boston, and Montreal, where they were made into coats, wraps and blankets. In 1842 Crooks attempted to break into the European market with robes, but they cost 66 per cent more than domestic sheepskins, a complementary product, and the scheme failed.[87] Europe was, however, the primary destination for deerskins, beaver, muskrat and other small furs.

The furs were shipped from New York in July and January in order to reach London and Leipzig in time for the Michaelmas (29 September) and Easter trade fairs.[88] At the fur marts the American products came into competition with furs from a variety of sources. The Hudson's Bay Company sent beaver, otter, marten, lynx, and bearskins to Europe every year, and nutria were shipped from South America and goatskins from the Cape Colony. Curtis M. Lampson, an independent agent affiliated with the American Fur Company, kept Chouteau

Figure 11: Transportation Routes to Market, circa 1835

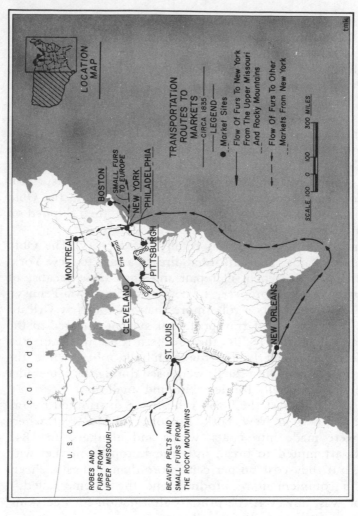

From D.J. Wishart, 'The Fur Trade of the West, 1807–40: A Geographic Synthesis', in Miller and Steffan (eds), *The Frontier: Comparative Studies*, pp. 190–1. Copyright 1977 by the University of Oklahoma Press.

and Crooks in constant contact with the market conditions in Europe. In 1838 and again in 1839, for example, Lampson reported that there would be no demand in Europe for American beaver, otter and muskrat, because the Hudson's Bay Company had inundated the market.[89] Each spring Lampson prepared lists of the furs and skins that were expected to do well at the fall auctions. This information was sent to Crooks and Chouteau who adjusted the trading exchange rates on the upper Missouri accordingly.[90] In April 1839, for example, Lampson informed Crooks that there would be a large demand for gray deerskins in Europe, and in 1837 Lampson reported that Russian duties on muskrat, raccoon and bearskins had been reduced and he expected large orders for these products from St Petersburg.[91]

The destination of the furs and skins from the Trans-Missouri West was decided only after a thorough comparative analysis had been made of the market conditions in the mid-west, on the east coast, and in Europe. In 1836, for example, Lampson announced that the prospects for the London spring fair were good but he advised Crooks to sell all the common skins in New York because the quality in London was high.[92] Or again, to choose a second example from many, in 1839 there was a large demand for beaver pelts in Missouri. Crooks advised Chouteau to sell only inferior furs locally, because beaver pelts were also in demand in New York, where higher prices could be obtained. A final decision was made to send the pelts to New York where they would be sold if a price of $4.50 a pound was forthcoming; otherwise the pelts would be sent to Europe for the Michaelmas fairs.[93]

The market for bison robes and bison by-products was good throughout the 1830s. Robes were worth $6 each in 1839 compared to the standard price of $3 in the early 1820s, and production rose from an average of 25,375 robes a year from 1828 to 1834[94] to 90,000 a year by 1840.[95] Despite the disequilibrium in the production system caused by the impact of the smallpox epidemic on the Indians, the Upper Missouri Fur Trade continued to prosper.

The Rocky Mountain trapping system, on the other hand, lacked this stability: its resource base was fragile, its production system overextended, and its market precarious. It is to this sub-system of the American fur trade of the Trans-Missouri West that attention is now turned.

Notes

1. Furs, trade goods, and mail were carried across the Atlantic on packet lines which had been introduced on a large scale after the 1812—15 war. The average sailing time for the eastward journey between New York and Liverpool in 1839 was 22.1 days and for the westward journey 34.1 days. Although Cunard introduced steamships on the trans-Atlantic route in 1838, reducing the time for the passage by half, sailing ships dominated ocean commerce until after 1840. D.B. Tyler, *Steam Conquers the Atlantic* (New York and London: D. Appleton-Century Co., 1939), p. 127; and E.R. Johnson, *Ocean and Inland Water Transportation* (New York and London: D. Appleton Co., 1911), p. 14.

2. Vermillion, a derivative of mercury, was brought from Kwa-Chow province of China and used by the Indians as body paint or dye. See C.E. Hanson Jr, 'A Paper of Vermillion', *The Museum of the Fur Trade Quarterly*, vol. 7 (Fall, 1971), pp. 1—3. Generally the Indians' preference for Chinese vermillion was observed. However, when the price rose to $.2.50 a pound in New York in 1839, the American Fur Company decided to substitute American vermillion, despite the Indians' preferences. G. Ehninger to Pratte, Chouteau and Co., 3 November 1839, *American Fur Company Letterbooks* (New York: New York State Historical Society).

3. W. Gordon to W. Clark, 17 October 1831, *Fur Trade Envelope*.

4. C.F. Miller, 'The Excavation and Investigation of Fort Lookout II (39LM57) in the Fort Randall Reservoir, South Dakota', in F.H.H. Roberts (ed.), *River Basins Surveys Papers* (Washington, DC: US Government Printing Office, 1960), p. 62.

5. Miller, 'Fort Lookout II', pp. 55—81, and A.R. Woolworth and W.R. Wood, 'The Archaeology of a Small Trading Post (Kipp's Post, 32MN1) in the Garrison Reservoir, South Dakota', in Roberts, *River Basins Survey Papers*, pp. 239—305.

6. Hewitt, *Indian Tribes*, pp. 459—60. Compared to the Crow and the Blackfoot the Assiniboine were a poor people and their purchasing power was low.

7. The information on the sources of trade goods is taken from the American Fur Company Letterbooks. For an introduction to, and a synopsis of, these papers see G.L. Nute (ed.), *Calender of the American Fur Company Papers*. Annual Report of the American Historical Association, vol. 2 (Washington, DC: US Government Printing Office, 1945).

8. Oglesby, 'The Fur Trade as Business', p. 116.

9. R. Crooks to Pratte, Chouteau and Co., 25 June 1836, *American Fur Company Letterbooks*.

10. This terminology is taken from J.R. Borchert, 'American Metropolitan Evolution', *Geographical Review*, vol. 57 (1967), pp. 301—32. Borchert argues that 1830 was the crucial census year that marked the build-up of steamboat tonnage on the Ohio-Mississippi-Missouri river system.

11. Sunder, *The Fur Trade on the Upper Missouri*, p. 19.

12. I have purposely written this description of the annual regime of the Missouri River in the past tense because the entire character of the river has since been changed by basin 'development' (notably the Pick-Sloan plan).

13. The best source on the keelboat era is L.D. Balwin, *The Keelboat Age on Western Waters* (Pittsburgh: University of Pittsburgh Press, 1941). Detailed descriptions of early methods of transportation on the Missouri River may be found in H.M. Chittenden, *History of Early Steamboat Navigation on the Missouri River* (New York: F.P. Harper, 1903), pp. 90–115; P.E. Chappell, 'A History of the Missouri River', *Transactions, Kansas State Historical Society*, vol. 9 (1905–6), pp. 237–316; and H.E. Briggs, 'Pioneer River Transportation in the Dacotahs', *North Dakota Historical Quarterly*, vol. 3 (1929), pp. 159–82.

14. Audubon and Coues, *Audubon and His Journals*, vol. 1, p. 499.

15. Sunder, *The Fur Trade on the Upper Missouri*, p. 23.

16. A useful source on the bullboat is G. Metcalf, 'The Bull Boat of the Plains Indians and the Fur Trade', *The Museum of the Fur Trade Quarterly*, vol. 8 (Summer, 1972), pp. 1–10.

17. See L.C. Hunter, *Steamboats on the Western Rivers* (Cambridge: Harvard University Press, 1949) and W.E. Lass, *A History of Steamboating on the Upper Missouri River* (Lincoln: University of Nebraska Press, 1962).

18. W. Laidlaw to K. McKenzie, 1831 (no exact date), *Chouteau Collection*.

19. R. Crooks to P. Chouteau Jr, 16 November 1832, *Fort Tecumseh and Fort Pierre Letterbooks*.

20. Steamboats cost about $8000 each in the 1830s. More than three-quarters of the steamboats used on western rivers from 1830 to 1880 were built on the Ohio River at Pittsburgh, Marietta, Cincinnati, and Louisville. Hunter, *Steamboats on the Western Rivers*, pp. 105–7.

21. Maximilian, *Travels in the Interior*, vol. 22, p. 292.

22. 'First Steamboat to Fort Union', *New York American*, 31 July 1832, reprinted in *The Museum of the Fur Trade Quarterly*, vol. 12, (Spring, 1976), pp. 1–2.

23. J.C. Ewers, 'Influence of the Fur Trade on Indians of the Northern Plains', in M. Bolus (ed.), *People and Pelts* (Winnipeg: Peguis Publishers, 1972), pp. 1–26.

24. G.H. Smith, 'The Buildings of the Fur Trade', Paper presented at the 1965 North American Fur Trade Conference (St Paul, Minnesota, 1–3 November 1965).

25. Maximilian, *Travels in the Interior*, vol. 22, pp. 317–18, vol. 23, pp. 77–8.

26. Audubon and Coues, *Audubon and His Journals*, vol. 2, pp. 180–2.

27. Maximilian, *Travels in the Interior*, vol. 23, p. 92.

28. Woolworth and Wood, 'The Archaeology of a Small Trading Post'.

29. Maximilian, *Travels in the Interior*, vol. 22, p. 271.

30. L.R. Hafen (ed.), 'With Fur Traders in Colorado, 1839—40: The Journal of E. Willard Smith', *Colorado Magazine*, vol. 27 (1950), pp. 161—88.

31. Alfred Jacob Miller was an American Romantic painter. In 1837 Miller accompanied Captain William Drummond Stewart of the British army to the Rocky Mountain rendezvous. Miller's paintings of the landscapes and inhabitants of the Trans-Missouri West are important historical records. See DeVoto, *Across the Wide Missouri*, chapter 12.

32. R. Sage, *Scenes in the Rocky Mountains*, p. 66.

33. W. Laidlaw to P. Chouteau Jr, 14 October 1831, *Fort Tecumseh and Fort Pierre Letterbooks*.

34. G.H. Smith, *Big Bend Historical Sites* (Lincoln, Nebraska: Smithsonian Institution River Basin Surveys, Publications in Salvage Archaeology, No. 9, 1968), p. 21.

35. Hewitt, *Indian Tribes*, p. 347.

36. Hewitt, *Indian Tribes*, pp. 459—60.

37. For an elaboration of this theme, see Saum, *The Fur Trader and the Indian*, pp. 141—5.

38. A.C. Fletcher and F. LaFlesche, *The Omaha Tribe* (Lincoln: University of Nebraska Press, 1972), vol. 2, p. 614.

39. This sequence does not apply to the Arikara, Mandan, and Hidatsa who had easy access to the bison range and did not, therefore, need to travel far afield to obtain their hides and meat.

40. G. Weltfish, *The Lost Universe* (New York and London: Basic Books, 1965). Weltfish gives an inspired account of one year in the life of the Pawnee.

41. J.C. Ewers, *The Horse in Blackfoot Culture* (Washington, DC: Smithsonian Institution Press, 1969), pp. 121—9.

42. Hewitt, *Indian Tribes*, p. 541.

43. For a comprehensive list of the complete use of the bison by the Blackfoot, see Ewers, *The Horse in Blackfoot Culture*, pp. 149—51.

44. Haines, *Journal of a Trapper*, p. 147.

45. Hewitt, *Indian Tribes*, p. 541.

46. This suggests that only wealthy Indians were able to participate in the fur trade on a large scale. Possibly this resulted in an accentuation of class differences within the Indian societies.

47. For detailed descriptions of the methods of bison hunting and robe processing see Hewitt, *Indian Tribes*, pp. 530—43; Fletcher and LaFlesche, *The Omaha Tribe*, vol. 1, pp. 270—312; and Weltfish, *The Lost Universe*, passim.

48. Only the Crow Indians, who carried on an extensive trade with the Shoshoni, Flathead, and Nez Perce, were rich in horses. The nomadic Assiniboine and Cree, on the other hand, had relatively few horses and continued to use the dog as a beast of burden.

49. W.R. Jacobs, *Wilderness Policy and Indian Gifts: The Northern Colonial Frontier, 1748—63* (Lincoln: University of Nebraska Press, 1963).

50. K. McKenzie to W.N. Fulkerson, 10 December 1835, *Fort Union Letterbooks*.

51. Hewitt, *Indian Tribes*, p. 457.
52. Ewers, *Zenas Leonard*, p. 57. The exchange rate was probably not as lucrative nearer the Missouri River where trade goods were more plentiful than in the Rocky Mountains.
53. W. Gordon to W. Clark, 17 October 1831, *Fur Trade Envelope*.
54. Hewitt, *Indian Tribes*, p. 460.
55. Hewitt, *Indian Tribes*, p. 457.
56. Hewitt, *Indian Tribes*, p. 457.
57. Abel, *Chardon's Journal*, pp. 43, 70, and 118.
58. J. Dougherty to L. Cass, 19 November 1831, *Dougherty Papers*.
59. Coues, *Forty Years a Fur Trader*, vol. 1, p. 55.
60. Abel, *Chardon's Journal*, p. 54. See also the entry for 31 January 1837 (p. 96). The winters of 1837−8 and 1838−9 were less difficult because the bison herds stayed close to Fort Clark.
61. Chardon was particularly subject to morbid depression during the winter season. His mood invariably lifted with the spring thaw.
62. J.F. McDermott (ed.), *Up the Missouri with Audubon: The Journal of Edward Harris* (Norman: University of Oklahoma Press, 1951), p. 143.
63. Audubon and Coues, *Audubon and His Journals*, vol. 2, pp. 187−8.
64. The cost of horses on the upper Missouri in 1836 ranged from $4.25 to $100 each, It was logical, therefore, to risk the loss of a few poor horses if it ensured the survival of the best stock. See Abel, *Chardon's Journal*, p. 311, footnote 438.
65. Ewers, *Five Indian Tribes*, p. 41; *Fort Tecumseh Journal*, 22 September 1830.
66. G.F. Will and G.E. Hyde, *Corn Among the Indians of the Upper Missouri* (Lincoln: University of Nebraska Press, 1964), p. 193.
67. Maximilian, *Travels in the Interior*, vol. 23, pp. 234−5. During his five years as head trader at Fort Clark, Chardon killed 3729 rats, but apparently this did not curb the infestation.
68. H. Leavenworth to A. McComb, 20 December 1823, *Indian Trade Papers*.
69. Brooks, 'Private Journal of Robert Campbell', p. 213.
70. Ewers, *Five Indian Tribes*, p. 68.
71. M. Hamilton to D. Lamont, 17 July 1835, *Fort Union Letterbooks*.
72. Audubon and Coues, *Audubon and His Journals*, vol. 2, pp. 188−95.
73. Maximilian, *Travels in the Interior*, vol. 24, p. 235.
74. W. Laidlaw to P. Chouteau, Jr, 10 January 1834, *Fort Pierre Letterbooks*.
75. Maximilian, Travels in the Interior, vol. 22, p. 320. Audubon and Coues, *Audubon and His Journals*, vol. 2, pp. 13−14.
76. McDermott, *Journal of Edward Harris*, p. 178.
77. Maximilian, *Travels in the Interior*, vol. 22, pp. 272−3.
78. A.L. Papin, 'Inventory of Establishment of Ottos on the occasion of delivery to Joshua Pilcher', 26 June 1833, *Fort Pierre Letterbooks*.

79. *Fort Tecumseh Journal,* 18 August 1830.
80. Audubon and Coues, *Audubon and His Journals,* vol. 2, p. 190.
81. *Fort Tecumseh Journal,* 22 April and 11 May 1830.
82. *Fort Tecumseh Journal,* 23 June and 11 July 1832.
83. R. Crooks to S. Abbot, 6 February 1823, *Chouteau Collection.*
84. P. Chouteau Jr, to Merle and Co., 23 March 1835, *American Fur Company Letterbooks.*
85. R. Crooks to Pratte, Chouteau and Co., 15 June 1835, *American Fur Company Letterbooks.*
86. R. Crooks to Pratte, Chouteau and Co., 15 June 1835, *American Fur Company Letterbooks.*
87. M.F. Klauche to R. Crooks, 3 May 1842, *American Fur Company Letterbooks.*
88. C.M. Lampson to R. Crooks, 28 August 1835, *American Fur Company Letterbooks.* In this letter, Lampson reminded Crooks that furs shipped from New York on or after 1 August always arrived too late for the autumn fairs.
89. R. Crooks to W. Brewster, 31 December 1839, *American Fur Company Letterbooks.*
90. R. Crooks to C.M. Lampson, 23 March 1835, *American Fur Company Letterbooks.* Crooks wrote to Lampson asking him to give estimates of prices to be paid for furs in the Trans-Missouri West, according to the market prospects.
91. C.M. Lampson to R. Crooks, 22 April 1839, and C.M. Lampson to B. Clapp, 28 January 1837, *American Fur Company Letterbooks.*
92. C.M. Lampson to R. Crooks, 6 February 1836, *American Fur Company Letterbooks.*
93. R. Crooks to P. Chouteau Jr, 22 April 1839, and P. Chouteau Jr, to R. Crooks, 5 July 1839, *American Fur Company Letterbooks.*
94. Pratte, Chouteau and Co., to R. Crooks, 28 March 1835, *American Fur Company Letterbooks.*
95. Sunder, *Fur Trade on the Upper Missouri,* p. 17.

4 The Rocky Mountain Trapping System: Strategy

The strongest magnet that drew Euro-Americans into the Trans-Missouri West after 1807 was the promise of a wealth of furs in the Rocky Mountains. (Both Lisa and Pilcher, it may be remembered, had set their sights on the Rockies, but they were repulsed by the Blackfoot and had to settle for the fur trade of the northern Great Plains.) This promise was based partly upon fact (the report of Lewis and Clark) and partly upon imagination and aspiration: the belief that the unknown recesses of Louisiana held riches in abundance. The 'terrae incognitae' beyond the western horizon had been the setting for Utopian visions ever since Europeans first set foot in North America. In the early nineteenth century, Oregon and the Shining Mountains became the mythical Kentucky once more removed.[1]

Associated with the lure of the Rocky Mountains was the search for the Passage to India, that Golden Fleece of Euro-American exploration. Lewis and Clark had attempted to forge a trans-continental passage that could be used to channel furs from the upper Missouri to the mouth of the Columbia and thence to Canton. This northern route would in time be proved impractical because of the contorted physiography of the northern Rocky Mountains, the extended lines of transportation, and the opposition of the Blackfoot and Arikara. Nevertheless, the Passage to India remained a persistent vision that lingered in the background of the American fur trade of the west.

The most notable attempt to enact the strategy of the Passage to India was John Jacob Astor's plan in 1810 to establish an international trade empire pivoted at the mouth of the Columbia River. Astor's 'magnificent enterprise'[2] almost made a reality of the Passage to India and was a prelude to the emergence of William Ashley's Rocky Mountain Trapping System.

The Pacific Fur Company, 1810–13

In the last two decades of the eighteenth century and first two decades of the nineteenth century there developed a tripartite competition for the furs of the Pacific Northwest. Under the monopoly of the Russian-American Company, Russian settlers and traders pushed southward from New Archangel (Sitka) after 1800, hunting the sea otter whose glossy pelt commanded a high price in China.[3] The Russians were opposed by the British who were drawn to the maritime fur trade of the Northwest after 1785, following the publication of the journal of Captain Cook's final voyage. The British came first by sea, then overland when Alexander Mackenzie and David Thompson discovered transcontinental routes for the Northwest Company traders. After 1788, enterprising American traders, mainly Bostonians, entered the competition. By 1800 they had virtually eliminated their British rivals from the Canton trade. Lewis and Clark substantiated the American claim to the Northwest in 1805–6 by establishing the Missouri–Clearwater–Snake–Columbia route. Despite its disadvantages Lewis was confident that he had discovered the most feasible passage to the Northwest.[4] It is against this background of political and economic rivalry that Astor's Pacific Fur Company is set.

Encouraged by Thomas Jefferson, Astor founded the Pacific Fur Company on 23 June 1810. Astor's plan was to establish a line of trading posts from the upper Missouri to the mouth of the Columbia, where the chief depot would be built. This depot would serve as a funnel for the distribution of trade goods and supplies into the interior, as a collection point for furs from the inland posts, and as a centre for the maritime fur trade. A ship would be sent annually from New York with merchandise and supplies. The same ship would be used to transport the maritime and Rocky Mountain furs to Canton and to carry Chinese goods (silk, tea, spices, vermillion) to New York (Figure 12).

Astor's goals, however, transcended economic gain. He hoped that the depot at the mouth of the Columbia would start 'a colony that would form the germ of a wide civilization' and 'carry the American population across the Rocky Mountains and spread it along the shores of the Pacific'.[5] Astor intended to undermine the British fur trade in the Northwest. To this end, in 1809, he made an agreement with the Russian Consul-General, Dashkov, to send two or three supply ships to Archangel each year and to market the Russian-American Company's furs in Canton.[6] Astor hoped that the expansion of Russian America southward and of the Pacific Fur Company northward would pinch the British presence in the Northwest. The agreement with the Russian-American Company was confirmed and expanded in a treaty negotiated in May 1812, whereby each party promised to respect the other's hunting grounds to the north and south of latitude 55°N.

Astor's plan was put into operation in 1810. On 8 September the *Tonquin* was dispatched from New York for the mouth of the Columbia, which was reached on 22 March 1811. On 18 May work commenced on the trading depot, which was aptly named Astoria. Astor's second party, headed by Wilson Price Hunt, was sent overland from St Louis on 21 October 1810. Hunt intended to follow the route of Lewis and Clark, contacting the Indians and selecting sites for potential trading posts. However, at the mouth of the Niobrara River Hunt was alerted to the Blackfoot threat by three trappers who had crossed the Rocky Mountains the previous year with Andrew Henry. Consequently, Hunt changed his plans. He acquired 82 horses from the Mandan and Arikara and veered overland from the Missouri River on a route that passed to the north of the Black Hills, up the Wind River, and through Union Pass to the upper Snake. After enduring terrible hardships while crossing the Snake River Plains, Hunt's party reached Astoria on 15 February 1812. A practicable route across the Rocky Mountains still had not been found.

Despite these problems of communication and the disas-

Figure 12: The Pacific Fur Company, 1810—13

LOCATION MAP

canada
u.s.a.

Kootenay Post
Flathead Post
Okanagan Post
Spokane House
Clearwater Post
Astoria (Ft. George)
Ft. Nez Percés
Willamette

Furs To Canton
Supplies From New York

Arikara Villages

Union Pass
South Pass

THE PACIFIC FUR COMPANY
1810-13
LEGEND
○ Pacific Fur Company Posts
● Northwest Company Posts
---- Hunt's Route Westward (1811)
→→→ Stuart's Route Eastward (1812-13)
Trapping And Trading Area Of The Pacific Fur Company

SCALE 100 50 0   100   200   300 MILES

tmk.

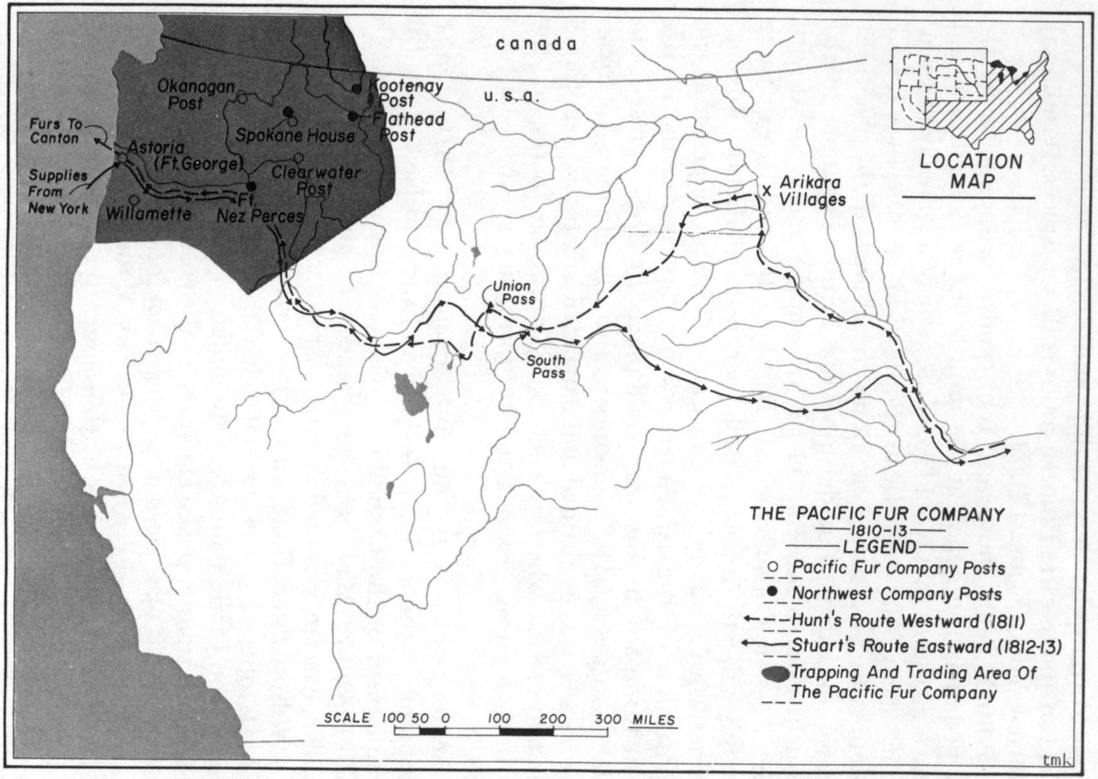

Adapted from Meinig, *The Great Columbia Plain*, p. 49.

trous sinking of the *Tonquin* off Vancouver Island in June 1811, the Astorians went into direct competition with the Northwest Company for the furs of the interior. In July 1811 a trading post was built at the mouth of the Okanagan, and in 1812 posts were established at the junction of the Spokane and Little Spokane rivers, on the South Thompson River (She-Whaps Post), and on the Clearwater and Williamette rivers (Figure 12). The locations of these trading posts were most rational. Okanagan, which proved to be an extremely profitable post, was situated on the border between the forrested mountains and the Columbia Plain. It was also the southern terminus of a trail that led north toward the She-Whaps Post, which drew furs from an extensive hinterland. Spokane Post was less profitable because of competition from the adjacent Northwest Company post, Spokane House, because the surrounding country was not rich in furs, and because the Indians were simply not interested in labouring for the traders. Nevertheless, Spokane Post gave access to the Cour d' Alene, Pend Oreille, and Flathead—Kootenay trapping grounds. The Williamette post was quite successful, and although the Clearwater Post was less productive, it was an ideal centre for procuring horses from the Nez Perce.[7]

The key to the entire system, particularly when the sea route proved to be unreliable, was the discovery of an effective overland routeway that would allow 'rapid' communication between Astoria and St Louis (and thence to New York). This was accomplished by Robert Stuart on an eastward journey from Astoria to St Louis, beginning on 29 June 1812 and ending on 30 April 1813. Stuart was probably the first Euro-American to use South Pass and the Platte overland trail, but it was not an effective discovery, and South Pass had to be rediscovered by Ashley's men in 1824.[8]

The promise of a lucrative Indian trade on the Columbia, the successful initiation of trading relations with the Russians, and the discovery of a direct route to St Louis indicate that Astor's strategy was quite feasible. In 1813, however, the entire enterprise was aborted when, faced with the prospect of armed encounter with the British (war had been declared on 18 June 1812), the Astorians sold their posts, equipment, and furs to the British for a fraction of their market value (Table 5).

Table 5: Fur Returns at Astoria, 1812—13

Furs	Price allowed by the Northwest Company	Market Value
	$ per skin	$ per skin
17,705 lb beaver	2.00	5.00
465 old coat beaver	1.66	3.50
907 land otter	0.50	5.00
68 sea otter	12.00	45—60
30 sea otter	5.00	25.00
179 mink,	—	0.40
22 raccoon	—	0.40
28 lynx	—	2.00
18 fox	—	1.00
106 fox	—	1.50
71 black bear	—	4.00
16 grizzly bear	—	10.00
Total	40,000	100,000+

Source: Irving, *Astoria,* p. 352. Meinig adds that roughly 50 per cent of these furs come from Okanagan and She-Whaps posts, 40 per cent from Spokane and tributary posts, and 10 per cent from the Williamette Post. See Meinig, *The Great Columbia Plain,* p. 52.

Astor toyed with the idea of reviving his scheme in 1816, and Nathaniel Wyeth attempted to put a similar plan into operation in 1832 and again in 1834—5. Despite the terms of the 1818 and 1828 treaties, however, whereby the United States and Britain agreed to share control of Oregon, the British were unassailable in the Northwest as long as the fur trade was the medium of competition. The British position was strengthened after 1821 when the Hudson's Bay Company absorbed the Northwest Company and Governor George Simpson reorganised the Columbia Department. The Hudson's Bay Company adopted an aggressive stance, and the main arena of competition between the British and American trappers moved eastward to the central and northern Rocky Mountains in the 1820s.

The Establishment of the Rocky Mountain
Trapping System, 1823—6

After a hiatus from 1814 to 1819, caused mainly by the economic and political repercussions of the war with Great Britain, the American fur trade of the west revived in the early 1820s. The economic situation improved, the constraint of the Indian Factory System was removed in 1822, the Santa Fe trade was opened to Americans in 1821, and in 1823 the publication of Edwin James' account of Stephen Long's expedition reactivated American interest in the Rocky Mountains.

By 1823, when William Ashley organised his second expedition to the upper Missouri, American trappers had been hunting and exploring in the Trans-Missouri West for almost two decades. They had worked throughout the northern Great Plains, crossed the continental divide with Andrew Henry in 1811, and probed to the mouth of the Columbia with the Pacific Fur Company. These men relayed a continuous flow of information on the geography of the West back to St Louis. There the knowledge was transmitted by 'street corner parley',[9] and in this informal way the map of the west clarified in the minds of the trappers and traders. Consequently, as information accumulated in the 1820s, the strategies for the exploitation of the furs of the Rocky Mountains were refined and rationalised.

William Ashley's drive to the Rocky Mountains, as we have seen, was temporarily halted at the Arikara villages in the summer of 1823. With his forces weakened, his capital diminished, and unable to continue by boat upriver, Ashley improvised. He dispatched one party, led by Andrew Henry, overland to the Yellowstone. A second party, under the charge of Jedediah Smith, headed westward from Fort Lookout toward the central Rocky Mountains. The plan was that a group of Henry's trappers under Captain John Weber would join with Smith's party on the Bighorn, and the united party would move across the continental divide for the spring hunt.[10]

In December 1823, Andrew Henry established a trading post at the mouth of the Bighorn River. He concentrated his trappers on the tributaries of the Bighorn and Yellowstone rivers, but constantly threatened by the Blackfoot, they obtained few furs. Henry's retirement from the field in 1824 symbolised Ashley's abandonment of the Upper Missouri Fur Trade.

Smith's party, which numbered at least eleven men (including William Sublette, Tom Fitzpatrick, and James Clyman), travelled westward along the north side of the White River, then veered northwestward to the Cheyenne where the river loops around the southern edge of the Black Hills.[11] They continued in a northwesterly direction across the fluted country between the Black Hills and Powder River and crossed the Owl Creek Mountains to the Bighorn River. The party moved up the Bighorn to the Wind River where they joined with Weber's trappers and shared winter quarters with the Crow Indians (Figure 13).

In February 1824 Smith attempted to cross the mountains via Union Pass, but the route was blocked by snow. When they returned to the Crow encampment the trappers were told of a wide depression in the mountains to the south of the Wind River Range. They set out again, crossed to the Sweetwater, and in March 1824 Smith's party made the effective discovery of South Pass.

Smith divided his trappers into small groups for the spring hunt and they scattered along the upper Green River and its tributaries. The hunt was successful. That summer, Fitzpatrick crossed the Great Plains to Fort Atkinson and relayed the good news to Ashley — not only was there rich beaver country in the central Rocky Mountains, but there was also a viable access route via South Pass and the Platte overland trail. In the course of two expeditions to the Rocky Mountains in the next two years William Ashley developed a successful production system based on beaver pelts, Euro-American trappers, the rendezvous, and the Platte supply route.

During the fall and spring trapping seasons of 1824 to 1825 Ashley's men separated into small parties and combed the tributaries of the upper Snake, upper Green, and Bear rivers for beaver. Only Jedediah Smith probed further afield. In the fall of 1824, Smith led his party of seven men northward from the Blackfoot tributary of the Snake to the Hudson's Bay Company post at Flathead Lake. This was an amiable confrontation, but it symbolised the mounting competition

Figure 13: The Rocky Mountain Trapping System, 1822–6

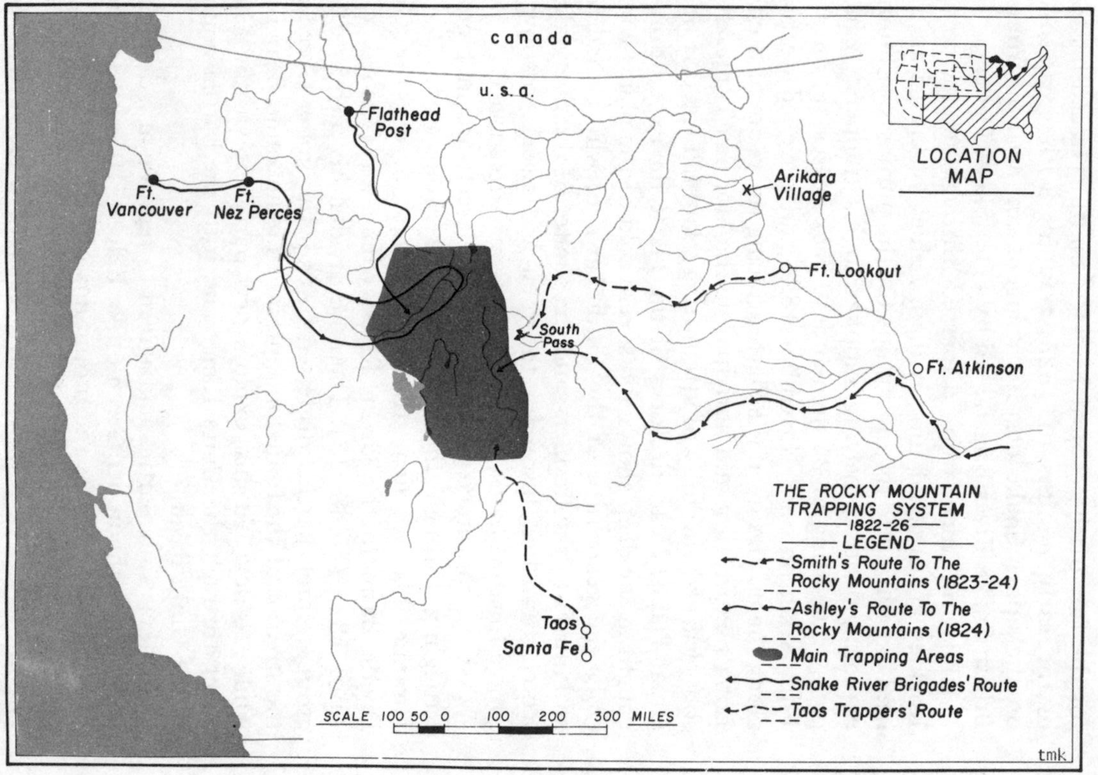

LOCATION
MAP

THE ROCKY MOUNTAIN
TRAPPING SYSTEM
1822–26
LEGEND

-·-·- Smith's Route To The
        Rocky Mountains (1823–24)
--- Ashley's Route To The
        Rocky Mountains (1824)
⬛ Main Trapping Areas
——→ Snake River Brigades' Route
---- Taos Trappers' Route

canada
u.s.a.

Ft. Atkinson
Ft. Lookout
Arikara Village
South Pass
Taos
Santa Fe
Flathead Post
Ft. Vancouver
Ft. Nez Perces

SCALE 100 50 0   100   200   300 MILES

tmk

for the furs of the central Rockies. Smith retraced his route in the early months of 1825, trapping with great success on the upper Snake despite stringent competition from the British Snake River Brigade led by Peter Skene Ogden.

While his men were dispersed throughout the central Rockies in search of furs, William Ashley organised an overland expedition to the mountains for the purposes of hunting, exploring, and conveying supplies to his trappers. Ashley's party, consisting of 25 men and 50 pack horses, set out from Fort Atkinson on 3 November 1824 and travelled westward along the north side of the Platte, tracing the route of Stephen Long's expedition and anticipating the Morman Trail. Ashley soon learned the folly of attempting a late fall traverse of the Great Plains. Near the forks of the Platte the expedition was caught in the deep snows and severe cold of the plains winter. Only the generosity of the Skidi Pawnee, who traded food and horses to the trappers, and the shelter of the river valleys, which furnished bison for the men and sweet cottonwood forage for the horses, enabled the trappers to survive.[12]

Ashley continued the arduous trek westward in January, struggling through the snows of the Front Range to the Laramie Plains, then striking westward across the Great Divide Basin to the Green River, which was reached on 19 April 1825 (Figure 13). There he divided his men into four groups: three parties dispersed to trap the upper Green and the streams of the folded mountains that surround Bear Lake, while Ashley led his exploratory party down the Green River through the Uinta Range and into the barren country of the Uinta Basin.

Ashley's four parties had agreed to regroup at a designated location on the upper Green on, or before, 10 July. The news of Ashley's arrival in the mountains diffused throughout the central Rockies, and by 1 July 1825 all of Ashley's employees — 120 men in all — had converged on Henry's Fork of the upper Green for the first official rendezvous of the Rocky Mountain Trapping System.

The fundamentals of the Rocky Mountain Trapping System emerged through improvisation in 1823—4 and by 1825 they were institutionalised. The production system functioned successfully only because the trappers were willing to remain in the mountains for extended periods of time.[13]

This reliance on the Euro-American trapper was an innovation in the American fur trade, where the Indian had normally assumed the role of producer. In the Rocky Mountain Trapping System the Native American played only a supplementary part, occasionally trading furs to the trappers or furnishing food and shelter for the trappers during the winter season.

There were three main categories of trappers. The 'engagés' were supplied and salaried by the company, and the furs which they collected were the sole property of that company. The 'skin trappers' were outfitted by the company on credit and, in a kind of sharecropping arrangement, they paid off their debt at the end of the season and retained any residue for themselves. The 'free trappers' owed allegiance to no single company. They worked alone, or in small groups, and they sold their furs to the highest bidder.[14] This system of labour, first introduced to the American fur trade by William Ashley in 1822,[15] cut the company's overhead costs by reducing the outlay of salaries. By 1830 there were several hundred free trappers in the Rocky Mountains, and their trade often determined the success or failure of the competing companies.

William Ashley left the Henry's Fork rendezvous on 2 July 1825 and headed for St Louis. Short of men and horses, and aware that there was an army security force on the upper Missouri that would provide an escort, Ashley decided to ship his furs down the Bighorn and Yellowstone rivers on bullboats instead of following the Platte overland route. At the mouth of the Yellowstone Ashley's party met with the military expedition and the trappers and their furs were carried on government boats down the Missouri. Ashley arrived in St Louis with 100 packs of beaver worth from $40,000 to $50,000.[16]

Encouraged by his success Ashley quickly outfitted a large expedition for the Rocky Mountains under the command of his new partner, Jedediah Smith. Smith's supply train, consisting of 70 men and 160 mules and horses, left St Louis at the beginning of November and travelled along the south side of the Platte, tracing the route that would soon become the Oregon Trail. The expedition crossed South Pass in midwinter and proceeded to Cache Valley where the trappers who had remained in the mountains were waiting for supplies and equipment.

After passing the winter season in two camps in the Bear and Weber valleys the trappers divided into three parties for the spring hunt: one group trapped northward into Flathead country, another group worked the Bear River and left-bank tributaries of the upper Snake, and Jedediah Smith led a trapping and exploratory party westward into the Great Basin. In the fur trade, exploration was generally motivated by the prospect of economic gain. Smith hoped to discover the virgin fur country that supposedly lay to the southwest of the Snake River and which was drained by rivers that flowed to the Gulf of California. Instead the trappers encountered the desolate Basin and Range country of northeastern Nevada. Faced by the prospect of starvation, they headed north to the Snake and made their spring hunts on the Boise, Payette, and Big Wood rivers before returning to Cache Valley for the summer rendezvous.

As many as 100 trappers converged on Cache Valley in July of 1826. There they were met by William Ashley's supply train, which had left St Louis on 8 March and followed the now conventional route through South Pass to Henry's Fork, then down the Snake to the Bear River. At the rendezvous Ashley sold his trapping interests to the new partnership of Jedediah Smith, William Sublette, and David Jackson for $16,000. The debt was to be paid in beaver delivered in the Rocky Mountains at a price of $3 a pound, or, alternatively, Ashley would transport the furs to St Louis and sell them on behalf of the new partners after deducting $1.12½ per pelt as his payment. Ashley further agreed to supply Smith, Jackson and Sublette with goods worth 'not less than seven thousand nor more than fifteen thousand' dollars at the Bear River rendezvous on 1 July 1827.[17] The arrangement would stand only if the trappers informed Ashley in Missouri by 1 March 1827 that they had taken sufficient furs to justify the contract.

Ashley returned to St Louis in the last week of September with 125 packs of furs worth about $60,000.[18] By his own estimation he had earned more than $200,000 from his four years in the Rocky Mountains, although he claimed that almost two-thirds of the profits had been consumed by the costs of transportation and supplies.[19] Nevertheless, the considerable fortune that Ashley had amassed from 1823 to 1826 was testimony to the efficacy of his production system. Why then, in 1826, did Ashley sell out and withdraw to a position of limited liability? Firstly, now that he had the capital he was able to pursue his political ambitions in Missouri, and this priority precluded full participation in trapping operations. Secondly, Ashley was a farsighted man, and even at this early date he may have anticipated the demise of the Rocky Mountain Trapping System. He had seen how quickly the accessible beaver streams were depleted by continuous trapping. Moreover, he probably realised that the central Rockies would soon be a vortex for competing American and British trappers, resulting in price inflation and resource destruction. Consequently, Ashley made the transition from production to supply, where the potential profits were greatest and the actual risks were less.

Competing Systems

There were competing forces in the field even during the first stage of the Rocky Mountain Trapping System. After 1824, for example, American trappers penetrated the southern and central Rockies in force from a convenient supply base at Taos. The most serious opposition, however, came from the Snake River brigades of the Hudson's Bay Company, which swept into the central Rockies each year, bent on creating a 'fur desert' that would prevent, or at least, delay, American expansion into the Pacific Northwest.

American traders and trappers were first drawn to Taos and Santa Fe in large numbers in 1821, following the independence of Mexico from Spain. During the next decade the fur trade and the Santa Fe trade developed hand in hand, and furs constituted a major portion of the overland commerce to Missouri.[20]

The Spanish fur traders had concentrated on the skins and hides of deer, antelope, elk and buffalo, which had immediate practical use as clothing, rather than on fine furs. Consequently, when the Americans converged on New Mexico in 1821, they found that the streams of the upper Rio Grande and Pecos rivers abounded with beaver. By 1824, this area, so convenient to the supply bases at Taos and Santa Fe, was depleted, and the trappers were obliged to expand their sphere of operations northward and westward into the Colorado Basin. There they contacted Ashley's trappers who were probing southward from the central Rocky Mountains (Figure 13).

By the close of the 1824—5 season at least six large trapping parties from Taos had trapped the streams of the Colorado Basin. One party of 20 to 30 men was led by Etienne Provost, who later was described by the St Louis trader Bartholomew Berthold as 'the very soul of the hunters in the Mountains'.[21] In the fall of 1824 Provost trapped westward from a supply base at the mouth of the White River into the Wasatch Range and, according to William Marshall Anderson, he was the first Euro-American to see the Great Salt Lake.[22] In May 1825 Provost's party fell in with Peter Skene Ogden's Snake River expedition in the Weber Canyon. Ogden was perturbed to learn of this new route of American ingress into the central Rockies, particularly when Provost told him that their supply base at Taos was only 15 days march from the Bear River.[23]

Ogden need not have worried on this account. The thrust of the Taos trappers into the Colorado Plateau petered out in 1825 because, in spite of the proximity of their supply base, they could not compete with Ashley's more efficient rendezvous system. The central Rockies were left to the British and to Ashley and his successors, who engaged in intense competition in an area that, ironically, was south of the forty-second parallel and, therefore, in Mexican territory.[24]

The two fur frontiers that collided along an arc from Flathead Post to the Snake River country were, as Merk explained, absolutely divergent in organisation and character:

One was British. Its home base was London — Fort Vancouver was its outpost. Its traditions were those of monopoly, of receiving government support and supporting government in turn. Its mode was long-range planning, synchronized with that of the Foreign Office, and corporation finance, with capital limited only by ability to pay dividends on it. The opposing frontier was American. It was based on St Louis. Its traditions were those of individualism and laissez faire. All it asked of government was to be let alone. Its makers of tactics were petty entrepreneurs, rival and secretive. Unthought of was long-range policy coordinated with that of government. Financing was of the individual mortgage variety, and the labor relied upon was youths bent on adventure.[25]

The British had shown in 1818, 1823–4, then again in 1826, that they were willing to yield to the United States that part of Oregon which lay to the south of a line extending along the forty-ninth parallel to the Columbia, then down that river to the sea. The policy of the London Committee of the Hudson's Bay Company was, therefore, to exploit relentlessly the furs of the southeastern part of Oregon while the opportunity was available and to 'leave it in as bad a state as possible' for the Americans.[26] The relinquished and devasted south side of the Columbia would then become a 'cordon sanitaire' protecting the northern side against American ingress.

The means of putting this strategy into operation was the Snake River Expedition, an institution that was inherited from the Northwest Company. From 1818 to 1821 Donald MacKenzie led these year-long trapping expeditions from the advance base at Fort Nez Perces to the upper Snake country. When the Hudson's Bay Company superseded the Northwest Company in 1821, the advance base was moved to Flathead Post. From 1822 to 1824 Michel Bourdon, Finian McDonald, and Alexander Ross successively led large brigades of 'engagés' and freemen into the central Rocky Mountains. The brigades left Flathead Post in mid-winter and followed the Missoula to the Bitteroot, then crossed through Gibbon Pass to the headwaters of the Missouri (a blatant invasion of American territory). The expeditions then re-crossed the continental divide through Lemhi Pass to the Salmon River and laboured through the snows of the Salmon River Mountains to the Big Lost River and, finally, to the Snake where the spring hunt commenced. The brigades trapped the rich beaver streams of the southeastern corner of Idaho or worked westward along the Snake River to the Boise, Payette, and Weiser tributaries.

They returned to Flathead Post in November, before the passes were blocked by the winter snows (Figure 13).

Although the returns from Snake River country were respectable ('upwards of 4000 Beaver' in 1823), Governor George Simpson was dissatisfied. In 1824 he criticised the organisation and management of the expedition, which he described as a 'forlorn hope'.[27] Consequently, in 1825, as part of his rigorous re-organisation of the Columbia Department, Governor Simpson overhauled the Snake River Expedition. Peter Skene Ogden was given command of the brigades, replacing Alexander Ross, whom Simpson considered a 'self sufficient empty headed man'.[29] From 1825 to 1832 Ogden and his successor, John Work, transformed the Snake River Expedition into a successful commercial enterprise and a powerful political weapon.

Every year from 1825 to 1832 the revitalised Snake River Expedition, generally consisting of more than 100 men and 200 to 300 horses, left Vancouver, Fort Nez Perces, or Flathead Post in late summer or early fall. The expeditions often ranged widely, as in 1827–8, for example, when Ogden led his men across the Great Basin to California. Every expedition, however, trapped around the curve of the Snake River Plains. The Snake River itself held no beaver, but the small tributary streams, bordered with birch, willow, and cottonwood, were richly stocked. The main brigade travelled parallel to the Snake River, and small trapping parties dispersed into the hinterlands. When all the streams in one area had been scoured, the main camp moved on. The process was repeated until a complete circuit had been made around the Snake River Plains[29] (Figure 13).

The Snake River Expeditions cut right into the core of the central Rockies where, on the upper Snake and Bear rivers, they came into headlong contact with William Ashley's trappers. The most serious clash occurred in May 1825 when British trappers from Flathead Post and American trappers from Taos and St Louis converged in Weber Canyon. A group of quarrelsome American free trappers led by Johnson Gardner accused Ogden of trespassing on American soil and, more damagingly, incited 23 British freemen to desert. As Ogden later explained to Governor Simpson, the Hudson's

Bay Company could not match the prices that the Americans offered to the British freemen for furs and supplies:

> In all the different expeditions to the Snake Country two thirds of the time is lost in travelling to and from head-quarters, far different is the mode the Americans conduct their trapping expedition, their trappers remain five and six years in their hunting grounds and their equippers meet them annually secure their furs and give them their supplies and although great the expence and danger they have to conduct their business in this way, and surely there is a wide difference in the prices they pay for their Furs and sell their Goods compared to us a difference of 200 PC.[30]

The reaction of the Hudson's Bay Company was prompt and decisive. The discrepancy between American and British prices was reduced in 1827 when the freemen trapping rate was substantially raised. The objectives of the Snake River Expedition remained as before: 'to hunt as bare as possible all the Country South of the Columbia and West of the Mountains,' but after 1825 the brigades were given express orders not to cross the continental divide south of 49° north and to avoid confrontations with American trappers. Where competition did occur, as around Flathead Post or in the maritime fur trade, the British traders were instructed to outprice their American opponents, even if it meant taking short-term losses.[31]

Simpson's plans were carried out efficiently and effectually. The fur returns from Snake country declined after 1831[32] (which was inevitable, given the British policy), but the geopolitical goal of the Snake River Expedition was achieved:

> It converted the Snake Country and much adjoining territory, with the support at a later date of several strategically located trade posts, into a fur desert. It helped to sterilize the southern and eastern sides of the Columbia Valley, to insulate the northern side against St Louis influence. It helped to convert the lower Columbia into a principality of the Hudson's Bay Company, governed until the time of the pioneers by Fort Vancouver and London.[33]

Expansion under Smith, Jackson, and Sublette, 1826–30

From 1826 to 1830 Jedediah Smith, David Jackson, and William Sublette expanded the scale of the production system that had been established by their predecessor and mentor, William Ashley. They employed from 80 to 180 men during these years, and their trapping parties radiated from the rendezvous northward into Flathead country, westward along the Snake River, and eastward across the continental divide into Crow and Blackfoot lands. In 1826, then again in 1827, Jedediah Smith led trapping and exploratory expeditions to California and the Pacific Northwest. Smith obtained few furs, but he clarified the geography of the Great Basin and spearheaded the American advance to the Pacific. [34]

These were, ultimately, profitable years for Smith, Jackson, and Sublette; but like widening cracks in the foundations of a building, the inherent weaknesses in the structure of the Rocky Mountain Trapping System became manifest in this period. The rapid depletion of a resource base that even under optimal conditions was only slowly renewable, the geographic expansion of an already extended production network, the inflation of prices at the rendezvous, and the mounting competition from American as well as British rivals all adumbrated the problems that would beset the Rocky Mountain Trapping System in the 1830s.

At the 1826 rendezvous Smith, Jackson, and Sublette arranged a division of labour that would characterise their strategy until the dissolution of the partnership in 1830. Jedediah Smith was primarily an explorer in search of new, untapped areas of furs. The main burden of organising trapping parties in the central and northern Rockies fell to David Jackson and William Sublette, and Sublette also assumed responsibility for supervising the transportation of furs and supplies between St Louis and the rendezvous.

On 16 August Jedediah Smith left Cache Valley with a party of 15 men and headed southwest into the barren, arid wastes of the Great Basin. Smith's primary objective was to determine the fur resources of an area that was 'terra incognita' to Euro-Americans. He was also searching for the mythical Buenaventura River, which supposedly headed with the Snake, Bighorn, Arkansas, and Rio Grande rivers and flowed into the Pacific south of Monterey.[35] Smith probably intended to trap north from California to the mouth of the Columbia[36] where, conceivably, he planned to revive the strategy of Astoria.

Smith's journey was epic, and the information that he furnished to William Clark, the Superintendent of Indian Affairs,[37] and which appeared in cartographic form in David Burr's map of 1839 (Figure 14),[38] elucidated the geography of the Great Basin. The trappers rode south to the Sevier River (which was probably the humble reality behind the magnificent myth of the Buenaventura) then followed the Virgin River to its junction with the Colorado. The exhausted trappers recuperated at the Mojave villages during October before striking out across the salt plains of the Mojave Desert to San Gabriel Mission. With considerable diplomacy and nerve Smith circumvented a serious confrontation with the Mexican authorities, and pushed northward along the San Joachin valley. He left his main party in camp on the Stanislaus River, promising to return within four months, and with two companions he crossed the Sierra Nevada and the Great Basin and reached the Bear River rendezvous on 3 July 1827 (Figure 15).

The first Southwest Expedition produced few furs, but, fortunately for the partnership, Jackson and Sublette had performed their roles well during the 1826–7 season, and the solvency of the company was assured. After the close of the 1826 rendezvous Jackson and Sublette led trapping parties to the upper Snake. There the parties separated: Sublette trapped north up Henry's Fork to the headwaters of the Yellowstone, while Jackson probably worked the lower tributaries of the Snake River. In late fall the trappers reassembled in Cache Valley to assess the results of the hunt. The catch was sufficient to justify the continuance of the company. While the main body of the trappers passed the winter in the sheltered haven of Cache Valley, Sublette and Moses Harris trekked across the snow-covered plains and confirmed the order with Ashley for a new outfit.

Ashley honoured the contract, and a supply train carrying $15,000 worth of merchandise was dispatched from St Louis on 15 March. The supply train followed the now well-established route which crossed the tall-grass prairies of eastern

Figure 14: David Burr's Map of the United States, 1839

Figure 15: The Rocky Mountain Trapping System, 1826—30

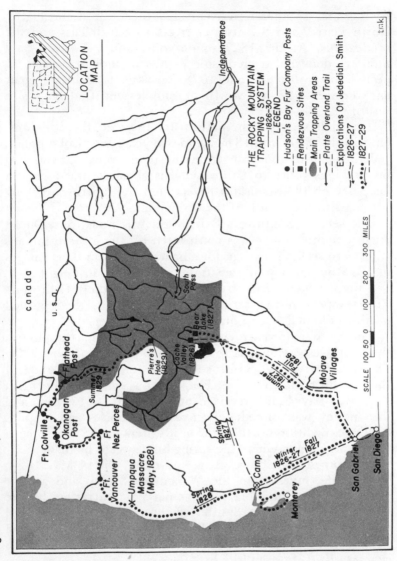

Kansas and southeastern Nebraska, then traced the Platte, North Platte, and Sweetwater rivers to South Pass and the rendezvous. At the 1827 rendezvous Smith, Jackson, and Sublette delivered a creditable 7400¼ pounds of beaver, 95 pounds of castoreum, and 102 otter skins to Ashley's agent and received $22,000 worth of supplies and trade goods in return.[39]

This first year set the pattern for the next three seasons. On 13 July 1827, with 18 men and two years' worth of supplies, Jedediah Smith rode out from the rendezvous and retraced his previous route to California. His objective was to rejoin his party on the Stanislaus River, then trap northward along the coast to the mouth of the Columbia.

The second Southwest Expedition was disastrous. On 18 August Smith's party was confronted by the Mojave Indians who were seeking revenge for a brutal attack on their villages in 1826 by a group of Taos trappers.[40] Smith lost eight men, and the disabled party struggled on into southern California. The trappers rested at San Gabriel Mission, then pushed north to the main camp on the Stanislaus River.

The total material rewards for three seasons trapping in the southwest amounted to only 1,568 pounds of beaver. On 18 November 1827, Smith sold these furs to the captain of the Boston trader, *The Franklin,* which was anchored off San Francisco Bay. Smith received only $3,920 for his furs, and this money was immediately invested in horses and supplies for the expedition north to the headwaters of the Sacramento River and Oregon where the spring hunt was to be made.

The expedition, however, was ill-fated. On 14 May 1828, only a few miles from the Willamette Valley and a clear passage to the Columbia, Smith's party was attacked by the Umpqua Indians. Only Smith and three others survived, and the furs and equipment were lost. The disabled party reached Fort Vancouver in August, where they were received with characteristic hospitality by the chief factor, Dr John McLoughlin. The British retrieved the pelts from the Umpqua and purchased them for $20,000. Smith passed the winter at Fort Vancouver and in the spring he travelled to Flathead Post where he was reunited with David Jackson. Finally, after an absence of two years, Smith joined William Sublette in August in Pierre's Hole, the site of the second rendezvous of 1829.

While Smith was exploring the Trans-Rocky Mountain West, his partners concentrated trapping operations in three main areas. American trappers continued to compete with the Hudson's Bay Company for the rapidly diminishing furs of the Snake River plains and Flathead country. As the traditional trapping areas of the central and northern Rockies were exhausted, the trappers moved across the continental divide to the headwaters of the Missouri, Yellowstone, and Bighorn rivers. In this cis-Rocky Mountain zone the expanding frontiers of the Upper Missouri Fur Trade and the Rocky Mountain Trapping System converged. This was, of course, the territory of the Blackfoot and Crow Indians, the area that had been the main objective of the St Louis fur trade since Manuel Lisa's time.

By 1827 the Snake River plains and the adjacent Bear River country had been trapped consistently for a decade, first by the British, then by the British and the Americans. The Hudson's Bay Company adhered steadfastly to their policy of trapping the Snake River country bare. Ogden, for example, carried more than 3,000 pelts out of the area in 1826, and again in 1827–8.[41] The Americans continued to send trapping parties to the Snake River (in the fall of 1827, for example), but the rewards hardly justified the effort and expense. In 1829, in return for the hospitality that he had received at Fort Vancouver, Jedediah Smith promised Dr McLoughlin that he and his partners would abandon the Snake River country. The promise was not kept, and David Jackson, the regional specialist, trapped the Snake River plains in the spring of 1830. By that year, however, the area was dominated by the British, and the American trappers were forced to look elsewhere for furs.

The rich beaver preserve around Flathead Lake was also controlled by the British by 1829, although the American trappers did not abandon this field. In the fall of 1827, the winter of 1827–8, and again in the fall of 1828, Sublette and Jackson dispatched trapping and trading parties to Flathead country. Their harvests were generally good, but the American freemen were tempted by the revised trade rates which the British had established in 1827. Moreover, the Americans were often forced to trade their furs at Flathead Post for essential supplies, and in this manner the British regained a large proportion of the catch. Nevertheless,

Governor Simpson was overly optimistic when he reported to the London Office in 1829 that 'the Flat Head Trade I do not think is likely to be disturbed in the future by the Americans'.[42]

In 1828 Jackson and Sublette turned their attention eastward to Crow country, an area from which the British were legally excluded. In the spring of that year, then again in the fall and spring of 1828–9, Robert Campbell led large trapping parties into the Bighorn and Powder basins, a barren area which, nevertheless, teemed with beaver and game. The location of the first rendezvous of 1829, which was held in the valley of the Popo Agie (near present-day Lander, Wyoming), symbolised this shift in trapping emphasis to the east of the Rocky Mountains.

On 1 July 1829 William Sublette rode into the Popo Agie rendezvous with a party of 54 men and a new outfit for the following season. After three years in the mountains, and despite some lucrative hunts, the company was barely solvent. The profit margin of the Rocky Mountain Trapping System was being eroded by the increased costs of trapping and trading, the inflated price of supplies, and the exhaustion of the most accessible trapping grounds. Heavy losses of men, horses, and equipment at the hands of the Indians increased the overhead costs of production (Table 6).[43] Moreover, the appearance of Joshua Pilcher's rival force on the Green River in 1827 had added a new element of competition to the Rocky Mountain Trapping System. Pilcher was a novice in the Rocky Mountains, and his venture disintegrated by the

Table 6: 'Amount of Property Lost by the firm of Smith, Jackson and Sublette, from depredations of different tribes of Indians from July 1826 to July 1830.'

480 head of horses at the lowest mountain price $60 per head	$28,000
Gross amount of Goods lost	10,000
Traps and Camp Equipage lost	1,000
Beaver furs taken from us by Indians	4,500
	$43,500

Source: Morgan, *Jedediah Smith*, p. 342.

summer of 1828. Nevertheless, Smith, Jackson, and Sublette probably viewed Pilcher as a harbinger of future American competition.[44]

With the future of their company precarious, the partners convened in Pierre's Hole in August 1829 and arranged their areal strategy for the upcoming season:

> Nothing Jedediah had seen in the country west and south-west of Great Salt Lake promised much. California was too far off, and they had had no luck there. The southern Rockies were overrun with trappers operating out of Taos. The Utah country was trapped out. The Flathead lands were not a likely prospect for this year. The Snake Country, trapped by British and Americans alike, seemed all but exhausted. Since they had left the Snake Country undisturbed for a year, Jackson might try his luck there. Milton Sublette had already been detailed to the Big Horn. That left just one likely possibility, the Blackfoot country.[45]

A precedent had been set for exploiting Blackfoot country in the fall of 1827 when, according to William Ashley, some of the Blackfoot bands 'invited a friendly intercourse and trade, and did actually dispose of a portion of their furs to Messers Smith, Jackson, and Sublette'.[46] This accommodation was short-lived, so it was probably with considerable trepedation that Sublette and Smith led their party to the headwaters of the Missouri and Yellowstone in November 1829.[47] Despite the constant threat of Blackfoot attack, the trappers made a successful fall hunt. In December they merged with Milton Sublette's Crow party on the Bighorn and proceeded to the pre-arranged winter camp in the Wind River. There they were joined by David Jackson who had trapped that fall on the upper Snake.

The fall hunt had been so successful that the partners decided to send an express to Missouri to arrange a new outfit for the following year. While William Sublette and Moses Harris made their second mid-winter crossing of the plains (this time in relative comfort, with snow-shoes and a pack of dogs), the trappers divided into large parties for the spring hunt. Jackson returned to his favourite trapping grounds on the Snake River where, according to Joe Meek, he caught 'plenty of beaver'.[48] Smith led his men north to the Musselshell River and the Judith Basin, the core area of Blackfoot territory. The Blackfoot again made trapping difficult, but Meek recalled that 'times were good on this hunt', and beaver were taken in abundance.[49]

In July the trappers reassembled in the Wind River Valley, where they were met by William Sublette with a supply train consisting of 81 men, ten wagons, and two deerborn carriages. 'This was the first time that wagons ever went to the Rocky Mountains', the partners later reported to the Secretary of War, 'and the ease and safety with which it was done prove the facility of communicating overland with the Pacific Ocean'.[50]

Nevertheless, despite the promise of this innovation and the success of the 1829—30 trapping season, Smith, Jackson, and Sublette decided to dissolve their partnership. They were motivated, perhaps, by Smith's desire to leave the mountains and by the exhaustion of the fur country, which forced the trappers to focus on Blackfoot country, where the costs and risks of operation were great. It is possible that they realised that the best years of the Rocky Mountain Trapping System were past, and that the next few years would be marked by increased competition for a diminishing resource. Already, in 1830, a powerful opposition loomed on the horizon. The American Fur Company, having secured its base on the upper Missouri and overcome its characteristic cautiousness, launched an expedition to the central Rockies under the leadership of Lucien Fontenelle, Andrew Drips, and Joseph Robidoux. Within four years the American Fur Company controlled the Rocky Mountain Trapping System.

Smith, Jackson, and Sublette sold out to Tom Fitzpatrick, Jim Bridger, Milton Sublette, Henry Fraeb, and John Baptiste Gervais — a group of experienced trappers who subsequently were known as the Rocky Mountain Fur Company. On 4 August Smith and his partners headed for St Louis with 190 packs of beaver, the largest single annual return to be taken from the Rocky Mountains to that date. The furs brought $84,500 in the Philadelphia and New York markets, which was enough to clear the company's debts and still leave a substantial profit.

In 1831 they invested their money in the Santa Fe trade.

On the first expedition, in late May of 1831, Jedediah Smith
was killed by the Comanches near the Cimarron River in
present-day southwestern Kansas. David Jackson entered the
Santa Fe and California trades, but his health rapidly deteriorated, and he died in Paris, Tennessee on 24 December 1837.
William Sublette followed Ashley's example and returned to
the fur trade as supplier and, therefore, controller of the
Rocky Mountain Fur Company.

The Rocky Mountain Fur Company and its Rivals, 1830 to 1834

After 1830 the Rocky Mountain Trapping System slipped
irreversibly into disequilibrium. The imbalance became
evident in both the resource and market sectors of the economic chain, and no adjustments in spatial strategy could
offset the decline in the efficacy of the production system.
The costs of production were greatly increased by the emphasis
on Blackfoot country, not only because of the attenuated
lines of transportation, but because of the additional overhead
costs that were incurred when the trapping parties were
expanded into brigades of 60 or 80 men for the purpose of
defence against Indian attack. Moreover, when the supply
train returned to St Louis after the close of the 1833 rendezvous the traders found that the market price for beaver had
fallen to $3.50 a pound. This was only the beginning of a
precipitous decline that would bring the price down to $2 a
pound by 1840.

Paradoxically, the scale of the Rocky Mountain Trapping
System continued to expand in the early 1830s, even though
the halcyon days of trapping were past. A diverse group of
aspirants converged on the Rocky Mountains, hoping to
emulate the success of William Ashley and Smith, Jackson,
and Sublette. The pitch of competition reached its greatest
intensity in 1832. In July of that year the principal contestants
gathered in Pierre's Hole for the eighth rendezvous. Nathaniel
Wyeth, a Massachusetts ice-merchant who intended to challenge the Hudson's Bay Company on the Columbia, was
present at the rendezvous with his party of ten or twelve
'sober and inexperienced New Englanders'. Wyeth noted

about 120 lodges of the Nez Perce and about 80 of the Flatheads, a company of trappers of about 90 under Mr Drips of the firm of Drips and Fontenelle, connected with the American Fur Company, many independent hunters and about 100 men of the Rocky Mountain Fur Company under Messrs Milton Sublette and Mr Fraeb.[51]

The 'many independent hunters' included 22 men who had formerly been associated with the St Louis-based Gantt and Blackwell party, which had disintegrated in 1832 after only one season in the Rocky Mountains.[52] Also present were 15 trappers from Arkansas led by Alexander Sinclair. These were the remnants of the Bean–Sinclair party, which had trapped (with little success) the headwaters of the South Platte, Arkansas, and Green rivers from 1830 to 1832.[53] In addition, an expedition of 110 men under the command of Captain Benjamin Bonneville was camped at the junction of Horse Creek and the Green River, about 150 miles southeast of Pierre's Hole.[54] Altogether there may have been 1,000 American trappers in the mountains that summer — probably the highest population that the Rocky Mountain Trapping System attained.[55] To this total should be added the 600 men that the Hudson's Bay Company employed in Oregon,[56] and the numerous, and largely anonymous, Mexican and American trappers who worked the southern and central Rocky Mountains from bases at Taos and Santa Fe.[57]

The Rocky Mountain Fur Company had a number of advantages over its rivals. Firstly, its leaders were experienced mountain men who had an intimate knowledge of the environments of the Trans-Missouri West. Secondly, their production system was based upon the successful model that had been established by William Ashley and continued by his successors, Smith, Jackson, and Sublette. Moreover, after 1832 the Rocky Mountain Fur Company was supplied by William Sublette and Robert Campbell, who invariably beat the rival supply trains to the rendezvous. This allowed the Rocky Mountain Fur Company to capture the trade of the free trappers.

During the early 1830s American trappers combed the streams in every corner of the Trans-Missouri West. The free trappers, who were the majority, dispersed 'to the Columbia, the Pacific Coast, the Virgin and perhaps the Gila, the South

Platte, the Arkansas, the Missouri, the Grand, the Canadian, the Rio Grande — and the thousand creeks that fed them'.[58] For the most part, however, neither their names nor their exploits are known, and the history of the Rocky Mountain Trapping System is largely an account of the activities of the major companies.[59]

After 1830 the Rocky Mountain Fur Company concentrated its trapping parties in a few main areas: the Snake River and Flathead lands, which still continued to yield furs despite continuous trapping by the British and Americans; the Blackfoot and Crow country circuit, which produced the greatest returns and held the greatest risks; and the Parks of the Colorado Rockies, a relatively new trapping ground.[60] (Figure 16).

For their fall hunts of 1830 and 1832 Fraeb and Gervais led trapping parties to the Snake River country. The trappers generally worked a circuit around the Snake River plains. Starting in September they trapped the tributaries of the Snake as far west as the Owyhee and Malheur, occasionally probing south across parched sagebrush plains and deserts to the Humbolt. In November the parties generally trapped up the Boise or the Payette, then repaired to winter quarters in the Salmon or Bear river valleys, which were sheltered and well-stocked with mountain bison and other game. The Snake River country could no longer be relied upon because in many areas the beaver had been trapped to extinction. Yet in the spring of 1831 Warren Ferris, a trapper associated with the American Fur Company, averaged 40 to 70 beaver a day on Henry's Fork of the upper Snake.[61] This suggests that some of the tributaries had been ignored by the British and American trappers for a few seasons and, as Ashley argued in 1827, beaver populations did rebound if given the opportunity.[62]

The Americans and the British also contested for the Flathead trade. In the fall of 1831, for example, Milton Sublette and Jim Bridger led a trapping and trading party north from the Snake to the Salmon River, then across to the Deer Lodge River and Flathead Lake. It is difficult to ascertain whether the British or the Americans held the upper land in Flathead country. William Gordon, for example, claimed in 1831 that the American trappers were 'only gleaning where

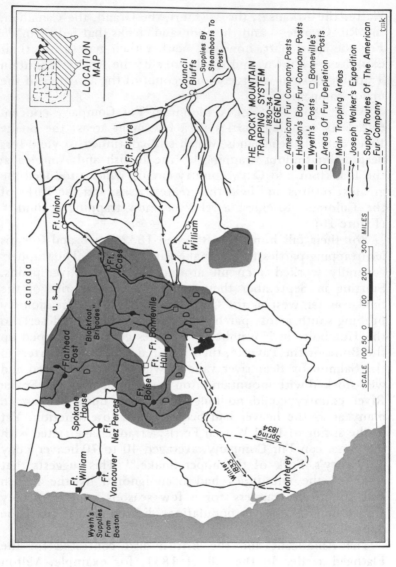

Figure 16: The Rocky Mountain Trapping System, 1830–4

the British have been reaping' in the northern Rockies.[63] On the other hand, and using the same analogy, Francis Ermatinger, the factor at Flathead Post, complained to his brother in the spring of 1833 that 'the Americans have reaped the harvest and all I can expect is part of the gleanings'.[64] The British, with their revised tariff rates and their superior trade goods, controlled the trade with the Flathead Indians and enticed the trade of the American freemen. The ubiquitous Americans, however, probably dominated trapping activities in Flathead country.[65]

There was one important new thrust of trapping operations in the early 1830s. In the spring of 1831 the Park country of the Colorado Rockies was worked for the first recorded time by trappers whose base was the rendezvous (as opposed to Taos or Santa Fe). Robert Newell recorded this event in his usual abridged style: 'Sublette went to the Park on the Platte I being one of Bridgers number went with him to the head of Laramas fork met Sublette in the Park'.[66] In subsequent years, as the focus of trapping operations shifted eastward, the Colorado Rockies became an important hunting ground, second only to the area that is now north central Wyoming and central Montana.

In 1830—1 and 1832—3 the Rocky Mountain Fur Company dispatched its main party of trappers to Blackfoot country. These parties were modelled on the Hudson's Bay Company Snake River brigades in that they were flexible, self-sufficient, and capable of defending themselves against Indian attack. They were generally led by the regional specialist Jim Bridger, and although their routes varied with the particular circumstances of each season, a number of basic geographic patterns may be discerned. One method was to use the Salmon River as a base camp. From the Salmon River the brigade moved across to the Bitteroot and Clark's Fork of the Columbia in September. The trappers then crossed the continental divide to the rich beaver streams of the Gallatin, Madison, and Beaverhead forks of the Missouri, deep in the heart of Blackfoot country. In late October, before the passes clogged with snow, the trappers withdrew to the west of Blackfoot territory and established their winter camp in the Salmon River or in the sheltered valleys of the upper Snake. In early spring, as soon as movement was feasible, the brigade would return to trap the headwaters of the Yellowstone and Missouri. Alternatively, the spring hunt would be conducted along the Bighorn, Powder, and Tongue rivers in the relatively safe country of the Crow Indians.

The potential rewards of trapping in Blackfoot and Crow lands were great because the streams were still well stocked with beaver. However, the problems and risks of operation in those areas were immense. Firstly, there was the very real threat of Blackfoot attack. The increased size of the brigades discouraged the Blackfoot from launching full-scale attacks on the trappers, but raiding and sniping were a constant danger. By 1834, according to Kit Carson (a member of Bridger's Blackfoot brigades), 'a trapper could hardly go a mile without being fired upon'.[67] Secondly, after 1830 the American Fur Company engaged the Rocky Mountain Fur Company in a bitter competition for the furs of the northern Rocky Mountains and adjacent Great Plains. Each year after 1830 the American Fur Company sent powerful trapping and trading expeditions to the mountains with express instructions 'écraser toute opposition'.[68] Moreover, the eastward shift of trapping operations brought the Rocky Mountain Fur Company into the hinterlands of Forts Union, Cass, and McKenzie. The competition reached a peak of intensity in the fall of 1833 when Tom Fitzpatrick's trapping party was robbed by the Crow, probably at the instigation of the American Fur Company. Fitzpatrick's furs, clearly branded with the Rocky Mountain Fur Company's mark, were subsequently traded at Fort Cass. His complaints were summarily dismissed by Kenneth McKenzie, who argued that the Indians were entitled to trade where, and with whom they wished.[69]

Despite these accumulating difficulties the Rocky Mountain Fur Company managed to collect 169 packs of furs from 1830 to 1832, 55 packs from 1832 to 1833, and 40 to 60 packs from 1833 to 1834.[70] These returns were satisfactory, but they were not sufficient to allow the Rocky Mountain Fur Company to escape the control of their suppliers, William Sublette and Robert Campbell.[71] As Ashley had realised in 1826, the suppliers always held the whip-hand, and the primary producers rarely had an opportunity to make substantial profits. This was particularly the case in the early 1830s. When the market price for beaver fell and the profit margin narrowed the suppliers were able to offset their losses by raising the price of goods at the rendezvous. The trappers did not have this flexibility. The Rocky Mountain Fur Company was stuck with the fixed costs of engagés' salaries and the standard rate of exchange for pelts. Indeed, the competition of the early 1830s produced a temporary inflation; at the 1833 rendezvous, the Rocky Mountain Fur Company was forced to pay $1500 a year for experienced mountain men and as much as $9 a pound for beaver. The American Fur Company could bear the short-term losses that

Table 7: Nathaniel Wyeth's Estimates of Beaver Production in the Rocky Mountains and Northern Great Plains, 1832 and 1833

Year		Packs (each containing 100 pounds)	Company
1832		90 packs	— from Sante Fe
	(seen)	30 packs	— American Fur Company party under Dripps and Fontenelle.
	(seen)	140 packs	— Rocky Mountain Fur Company, brought home by William Sublette.
		120 packs	— Traded by the American Fur Company at their posts on the Missouri.
Total		380 packs	
1833			
	(seen)	62 packs	— American Fur Company party under Dripps and Fontenelle.
	(seen)	61 packs	— Rocky Mountain Fur Company, brought home by William Sublette.
	(seen)	30 packs	— Bonneville and Co., brought home by Cerre.
		90 packs	— American Fur Company, traded at their posts on the Missouri.
		60 packs	— (probably) from Sante Fe
Total		303 packs	

Source: N. Wyeth to Mess. J. Baker and Son, 17 November 1833, in Young, *Correspondence and Journals of Nathaniel J. Wyeth,* p. 84.
Note: the form and spelling of the original table have been modified for the purpose of clarification.

resulted from this price fixing. The Rocky Mountain Fur Company, on the other hand, simply did not have the financial resources to compete.

The Challenge of the American Fur Company, 1830—4

If any one factor can be singled out to explain the demise of the Rocky Mountain Fur Company, it is the calculated campaign of opposition that the American Fur Company mounted after 1830. Viewed in the broadest sense, the expansion of the American Fur Company from the upper Missouri into the Rocky Mountains was part of John Jacob Astor's ambition to monopolise the fur trade of the United States. In the Rocky Mountains the American Fur Company succeeded in eliminating its rivals, but in the process the Rocky Mountain Trapping System was irredeemably damaged.

The Upper Missouri Outfit, headed by the dynamic Kenneth McKenzie, and the Western Department, controlled by the conservative traders Bernard Pratte and Company, eased into the Rocky Mountain Trapping System after 1827. McKenzie sent investigatory parties to the mountains in 1827, 1828, and 1829, and Pratte and Chouteau supplied Rocky Mountain expeditions led by Henry Vanderburgh in 1828 and 1829. The American Fur Company hesitated, however, before making a full commitment to the Rocky Mountains. Chouteau explained this hesitancy to McKenzie in 1828, noting that 'these enterprises have succeeded well with Gen. Ashley and with him alone', and that 'there is a great deal to gain if such an expedition succeeds, but there is also a great risk to run'.[72]

Caution prevailed until 1830. Thereafter, until 1832, both the Upper Missouri Outfit and the Western Department maintained large trapping brigades in the mountains and sent separate supply trains to the rendezvous.[73] This division of forces was wasteful, and in 1832 the ventures were combined under the able command of Lucien Fontenelle.

The American Fur Company's tactics were directed and logical. In an attempt to cut the costs of transportation and reduce the time of the supply journey, the American Fur Company sent its merchandise up the Missouri River by steamboat to the Council Bluffs, Fort Pierre, or Fort Union. The goods were then transferred to pack horses and dispatched to the mountains (Figure 16). In the Rocky Mountains the American Fur Company's operational strategy was straight-forward: Henry Vanderburgh and Andrew Drips (the field captains) intended to learn the best trapping grounds by following the Rocky Mountain Fur Company brigades and to capture the trade of the free trappers by offering inflated prices for their furs.

The American Fur Company's innovative supply system proved rather ineffectual. In 1832, for example, Fort Union was used as the supply base, but the steamboat was delayed on the journey upriver, and Fontenelle did not start for the mountains until 19 June. Consequently, he missed the Pierre's Hole rendezvous. Without merchandise, Vanderburgh and Drips were unable to compete with the Rocky Mountain Fur Company and William Sublette for the furs of the free trappers and the Flathead Indians.

In 1833, Fontenelle led the American Fur Company supply train overland from Fort Pierre, but he was outdistanced by the Rocky Mountain Fur Company's suppliers. Robert Campbell arrived at the Green River rendezvous eight days before Fontenelle, and the American Fur Company was once again deprived of the extra trade. Fontenelle simply could not compete successfully with his more experienced rivals who were masters of the supply system. From 1827 to 1832 Sublette crossed to and from the mountains ten times, and in 1827 he pioneered the trace that bore his name — from the Kansas River via the Little Blue to the Platte. After 1832, Sublette and Campbell successfully incorpor-ated wagons into the supply system, so increasing the amount of merchandise that could be carried, and in 1834 they built Fort William which served as a road ranch on the trail as well as a trading post. The alternative supply routes used by the American Fur Company did cut the costs of transportation but in every other way they proved inferior to the conventional central route. Consequently, in 1834 Etienne Provost delivered the American Fur Company's supplies to the Ham's Fork rendezvous via the Platte Overland Trail.

In the mountains, however, Fitzpatrick and his partners,

for all their experience, could not withstand the onslaught of the American Fur Company. Vanderburgh and Drips tailed the Rocky Mountain Fur Company's trapping parties, as Joe Meek explained:

> The rival company had a habit of turning up at the most unexpected places, and taking advantage of the hard-earned experience of the Rocky Mountain Company's leaders. They tampered with the trappers, and fereted out the secret of their next rendezvous; they followed on their trail, making them pilots to the trapping grounds; they sold goods to the Indians, and what was worse, to the hired trappers.[74]

This competition drove up prices, recklessly destroyed the resource base, and, in Meek's words, 'finally ruined the fur-trade for the American companies in the Rocky Mountains'.[75]

Viewed in purely economic terms, the American Fur Company's policy was rational. Astor's company had the financial resources to operate at a loss for extended periods of time in order to outprice and outlast its weaker opponents. Chouteau admitted to Astor in 1833 that 'these expeditions have been an annual loss', but he added:

> in spite of the unfavorable prospect I do not think it politic to abandon this trade for the present. Just at the time when Sublette and Company are opposing us on the Missouri it is not for us to leave the Mountains exclusively to them.[76]

In effect, after 1833 the two production systems of the St Louis fur trade converged. In 1833–4 William Sublette and Robert Campbell established a network of trading posts on the upper Missouri in direct opposition to the American Fur Company and probably with the objective of driving that company from the Rocky Mountains. The American Fur Company had never really been convinced that the Rocky Mountain Trapping System was worth the effort, but in 1833 their challenge in the mountains could be used as a bargaining force with Sublette and Campbell. In January of 1834 Sublette and Astor's representatives reached an accommodation in New York and agreed to partition the fur country of the West. Sublette and Campbell sold their properties on the upper Missouri to the American Fur Company. In turn the American Fur Company agreed to withdraw from the Rocky Mountains.[77]

The primary producer, the Rocky Mountain trapper, as usual had no say in these machinations: he was, in Nathaniel Wyeth's words, 'a mere slave to catch Beaver for others'.[78] Fitzpatrick and his partners were opposed by the American Fur Company on the one hand and controlled by Sublette and Campbell on the other. In 1832, in an effort to lessen the competition, Fitzpatrick tried to arrange a division of the trapping grounds with Vanderburgh and Drips, but the proposal was rejected.[79] A territorial division was organised after the 1833 rendezvous. Drips and Fontenelle would concentrate on Flathead country, the Snake River, and the environs of the Great Salt Lake, while the Rocky Mountain Fur Company would trap the Green River and the headwaters of the Missouri and Yellowstone.[80] The Rocky Mountain Fur Company had a poor year, whereas Drips and Fontenelle, no longer novices in the mountains, returned '5309 beaver, 90 of otter, 18 of bear, 130 of muskrats, and 150 pounds of castoreum'.[81]

In a sense, the results of the 1833 to 1834 trapping season were quite immaterial, because the future of the Rocky Mountain Fur Company (and of Fontenelle and Drips) had been decided in New York and St Louis. At the 1834 rendezvous, held on Ham's Fork of the Green River, the beleaguered Rocky Mountain Fur Company was dissolved. Fraeb and Gervais sold out for a pittance. The remaining partners, Fitzpatrick, Sublette, and Bridger, merged with Fontenelle and Drips to form a new company, Fontenelle, Fitzpatrick and Company. William Marshall Anderson witnessed this merger, and he recorded in his diary: 'The members of the two rival companies have associated themselves — they hunt and exist now una anima, uno corpore.'[82]

According to the terms of the 1834 partition, the American Fur Company could not compete with Sublette and Campbell for the furs of the Rocky Mountains. Sublette and Campbell, however, wanted to withdraw from 'Indian country' entirely and to concentrate on business in Missouri.[83] Consequently, in the winter of 1834—5, Fontenelle, Fitzpatrick and Company entered into an agreement with Pratte, Chouteau and Company, who had assumed control of the Western Department after Astor's retirement from the fur trade in 1834.[84] In this manner, the American Fur Company established control over the Rocky Mountain Trapping System and extended its monopoly over the entire American fur trade of the West.

Independent Competition: Bonneville and Wyeth

Nathaniel J. Wyeth and Captain Benjamin L.E. Bonneville merit attention not so much for the seriousness of their challenge to the Rocky Mountain Fur Company or the American Fur Company, but for the grandeur of their schemes. With strategies as ambitious as Astoria they vied with the Hudson's Bay Company for the fur trade of the Columbia. In theory their visionary plans were often magnificent; in practice their commercial successes were meagre.

On 1 May 1832, a party of 110 men led by Captain Benjamin Bonneville and with Joseph Reddeford Walker and Michael Sylvestre Cerre as field captains left Fort Osage, Missouri bound for the Rocky Mountains. Bonneville had obtained a two-year leave of absence from the army, and his purpose in the West, according to his chronicler Washington Irving, was 'to combine public utility with his private projects' by collecting information on the physical geography and native peoples of the Trans-Rocky Mountain West.[85] Subsequent events indicate that Bonneville's 'private projects' were given precedence over public service, although his reports to the Secretary of War and his journals and maps were major contributions to the opening of the West (Figure 17).[86]

Bonneville's party moved slowly across the central Great Plains to the Green River, hauling the first wagons across South Pass, thereby adding substance to the concept of a highway to the Columbia. At the junction of Horse Creek and the Green River Bonneville built a crude fortification which, rather pretentiously, was called Fort Bonneville. The trappers preferred to call it 'Fort Nonsense' or 'Bonneville's

Figure 17: Bonneville's Map of the Central Rockies

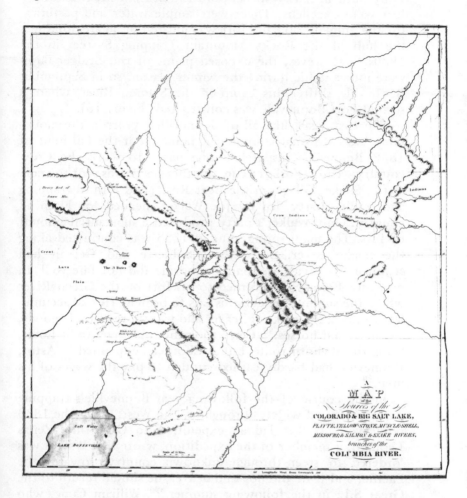

Library of Congress.

Folly', but in may respects both the site and situation of the fort were excellent. There were ample water and pasturage for the animals, and the fort was located in an area that was the hub of the Rocky Mountain Trapping System in the 1830s.[87] However, the exposed plains of the Bridger Basin were inhospitable during the winter season, so in September Bonneville shifted his camp to the Salmon River, where a second Fort Bonneville was constructed (Figure 16).

The first year, like all of Bonneville's years in the mountains, was a dismal commercial failure. For the fall hunt of 1832 Bonneville dispatched one party to work the Crow country—Three Forks circuit; another party was sent to trade at the Snake Village on the Bear River; and a third trapping and trading party, led by Joe Walker, headed for Flathead country. Only Walker's party produced a substantial amount of furs. The main spring hunt of 1833 was conducted along the Snake River, but Milton Sublette and Gervais had stripped the area bare, and Bonneville did not fare well. In mid-July Bonneville returned to his fort on the Green River where the summer rendezvous was to be held. He had accumulated only 22½ packs of beaver and was short of trade goods, supplies, and horses.[88] Cerre took the furs down to St Louis, using the Bighorn route, but as Chouteau explained to Astor, Bonneville had hardly earned enough to pay the wages of his men.[89]

In the course of the following year Bonneville's trapping parties diffused widely throughout the West. After the 1833 rendezvous Walker led an expedition to California. Zenas Leonard, a member of the expedition, wrote that Walker was 'ordered to steer through unknown country, towards the Pacific, and if he did not find beaver, he should return to the Great S.L. in the following summer.'[90] William Craig, who was also a member of Walker's party, later recollected that the purpose of the California expedition was to steal horses.[91] It is also possible that Bonneville was motivated by the persistent belief that the country to the southwest of the Great Salt Lake held undiscovered fur resources.[92] More likely, the expedition was one of those rambling commercial enterprises, so characteristic of the fur trade, whose objectives were diverse and rather indefinite.

From an exploratory point of view the expedition was

remarkable — Walker opened up the California Trail by fusing the routes that Jedediah Smith and Peter Skene Ogden had pioneered in 1826–7 and 1829–30 respectively (Figure 16). Commercially the expedition was an absolute failure, yielding no furs of any consequence and only a few horses. According to Irving, Bonneville was indignant and demoralised with Walker's failure to produce a wealth of furs, and the Captain never quite recovered from the failure of the California ventuer.[93]

While Walker's party crossed the Great Basin in the fall of 1833, Bonneville trapped the streams of Crow country. According to Tom Fitzpatrick, Bonneville's fall hunt produced only 112 skins.[94] After wintering on the Portneuf River Bonneville prepared a 'reconnoitering expedition' to test the feasibility of his grand design:

> This was, to penetrate the Hudson's Bay establishments on the banks of the Columbia, and to make himself acquainted with the country and the Indian tribes; it being one part of his scheme to establish a trading post somewhere on the lower part of the river, so as to participate in the trade lost to the United States by the capture of Astoria.[95]

Bonneville arrived at Fort Nez Perces on 4 March 1834. He was received with great hospitality, but, as Irving explained, he soon realised 'the difference between being treated as a guest, or as a rival trader'. Unable to obtain supplies, Bonneville retreated to the Bear River: 'he had seen enough to convince him that the American trade might be carried on with advantage in this quarter, and he determined soon to return with a stronger party, more completely fitted for the purpose.'[96]

In late June and early July of 1834 Bonneville's parties converged at a company rendezvous in the valley of the Bear River. Cerre brought up a small outfit from St Louis, then retraced his footsteps with the paltry returns from the previous year. A company of trappers under Antonio Montero was sent to trap in Crow country (Bonneville's most consistent hunting ground), and Bonneville assembled a party of 23 trappers for the Columbia.

In September Bonneville crossed the Blue Mountains and

reached the Columbia via the Umatilla. He moved to within 30 miles of Fort Nez Perces, but 'he could not subsist himself and company in a country where even every Indian refused to sell him either furs or provisions'.[97] Disheartened, and tired of eating horse-flesh, Bonneville travelled south along the John Day River in October, and by 15 November he was back in winter camp on the Portneuf.

Bonneville's courageous but naive challenge to the Hudson's Bay Company had ended ignominiously. His plans were in disarray and all his trapping ventures that year were unproductive. In the summer of 1835 Lucien Fontenelle informed Pierre Chouteau that Bonneville had 'sent down from twelve to fourteen packs of beaver', which was not even enough to pay the wages of his men.[98] Bonneville returned to Missouri in August 1835. He reappeared in the mountains in the summer of 1836 with a trading licence and an outfit for Montero's party, which had remained in Crow country. This venture was short-lived, and in the fall of 1836 Bonneville returned to the relative security of the army, where he rose through the ranks to become brigadier general in 1865.

Nathaniel Wyeth's ventures in the Rocky Mountains and Pacific Northwest from 1832 to 1836 were no more successful than Bonneville's, but like Astor's plan, upon which they were modelled, Wyeth's schemes were predicated on sound logic. They failed, perhaps, only because the historical circumstances were inauspicious.

Nathaniel Wyeth was a young, enterprising Yankee merchant who managed a Massachusetts ice-exporting company. In 1829 Wyeth met Hall J. Kelley, the foremost proselytiser for the settlement of Oregon country. Wyeth was inspired, but he soon withdrew from Kelley's visionary colonisation schemes and organised an expedition of his own to exploit the furs and fish of the Columbia River basin. Wyeth's strategy closely resembled Astor's plan for the Pacific Fur Company: a small party would be sent overland to the mouth of the Columbia, where a trading post would be built, and supplies would be shipped from Boston around Cape Horn (Figure 16).

Wyeth's party left Independence on 13 May 1832 and accompanied William Sublette's supply train to the rendezvous. The size of the party was whittled away by desertions, and at the close of the Pierre's Hole rendezvous Wyeth was left with only eleven men. Nevertheless, he persisted in his course, travelling down the Snake River in September and arriving at Fort Nez Perces on 14 October. Wyeth then descended the Columbia River on a Hudson's Bay Company barge and reached Fort Vancouver on 29 October. In the course of this journey Wyeth made the first westward crossing on the Oregon Trail from Missouri to the mouth of the Columbia.

At Fort Vancouver Wyeth learned that his supply ship had been wrecked in the Society Islands, which left him with no other option but to abandon his plan. Instead, as a guest of Dr John McLoughlin during the winter of 1832–3, then as an accompanier of Francis Ermatinger's inland brigade to Flathead Post, Wyeth 'took notice of everything . . . that could be of service to him in the further prosecution of his project; collected all the information within his reach, and then set off, accompanied by merely two men, on his return journey across the continent.'[99] Wyeth realised that he could not compete successfully with the Hudson's Bay Company for the fur trade of the Columbia. However, he was convinced that a multi-purpose plan which combined salmon packing, farming, trapping and trading, and supplying trade goods to the American freemen from interior posts was feasible.

Before he left the mountains Wyeth made an arrangement with Fitzpatrick and Milton Sublette to provide the Rocky Mountain Fur Company with an outfit worth 3000 dollars at the 1834 rendezvous, to be paid for in beaver priced at $4 a pound.[100] Wyeth regarded this agreement as a small detail in his major design: it would cover the costs of transporting his own expedition to the mountains. Since the Rocky Mountain Fur Company's financial situation was precarious, and since Wyeth was not positive that he could obtain backing for a second expedition, the contract provided for a 500 dollar forfeit if the terms were abrogated by either party.

By April 1834, Wyeth had secured financial support for his expedition and returned to Independence to prepare a supply train for the Rocky Mountains. The trapper Osborne Russell joined Wyeth's party, which he described in detail in his memoirs:

At the town of Independence Missouri on the 4th of

April 1834 I joined an expedition fitted out for the Rocky Mountains and Mouth of the Columbia River, by a Company formed in Boston under the name and style of the Columbia River Fishing and Trading Company. The same firm has fitted out a Brig of two hundred tons burthen, freighted with the necessary assortment of merchandise for the Salmon and Fur Trade, with orders to sail to the mouth of the Columbia River, whilst the land party, under the direction of Mr. Nathaniel J. Wyeth, should proceed across the Rocky Mountains and unite with the Brig's Company in establishing a Post on the Columbia near the Pacific. Our party consisted of forty men engaged in the service accompanied by Mess Nuttall and Townsend Botanists and Ornithologists with two attendants; likewise Rev's Jason and Daniel Lee Methodist Missionaries with four attendants on their way to establish a Mission in Oregon: which brot our numbers (including six independent Trappers) to fifty Eight men.[101]

At the Green River rendezvous, which Wyeth reached on 18 June 1834, the Rocky Mountain Fur Company 'refused to receive the goods, alledging that they were unable to continue business longer, and that they had dissolved'.[102] Sublette paid the forfeiture, and Wyeth was able to sell some of the goods at low prices, but, as Joe Meek observed, Wyeth's 'indignation was great and certainly was just'. Meek overheard Wyeth warn the partners of the Rocky Mountain Fur Company: 'Gentlemen, I will role a stone into your garden that you will never be able to get out.'[103] This threat was carried out in July of 1834 when Wyeth built Fort Hall at the mouth of the Portneuf River. There, strategically located in the buffer zone between the American and British spheres of influence, Wyeth contested for the trade of the Flathead, Nez Perce, Shoshoni, and Bannock Indians, and the American and British freemen (Figure 16).

In August Wyeth left Robert Evans in charge of eleven rather inexperienced trappers at Fort Hall and proceeded along the increasingly well-travelled route via Fort Nez Perces to Fort Vancouver, which he reached on 14 September 1834. The following day, Wyeth's brig reached the mouth of the Columbia. She had been struck by lightning at sea, forced to dock in Valparaiso for repairs and, consequently, she arrived in the Northwest too late for the salmon season. As Astor had discovered 23 years earlier the sea-route to the Northwest was not a dependable line of communication.

Despite this reversal Wyeth remained confident in the fall of 1834, believing that his fortunes must surely change: 'After so long an abstinence,' he wrote to his brother Leonard, 'I am hungry for a little success.'[104] Wyeth stayed on the lower Columbia for a year, energetically pursuing his multi-purpose scheme. He established a base, Fort William, on Savies Island at the mouth of the Willamette River and commenced farming further up the Willamette valley. He also negotiated a trapping and trading agreement with Dr McLoughlin, whereby Wyeth would obtain horses from the Nez Perce, trap the country to the south of the Columbia and lower Snake, and obtain supplies from, and sell his furs to the Hudson's Bay Company.[105]

By the fall of 1835, however, Wyeth had conceded defeat. The salmon business did not prosper — only 900 pounds of dried fish, worth $5,000 in Boston and the Hawaian Islands, were produced.[106] Wyeth's trapping ventures were plagued by accidents, deaths, and desertions, and yielded few furs.[107] The trappers at Fort Hall fared no better: the furs of the Snake River country were virtually extirpated, and Wyeth's men were directly opposed by the Hudson's Bay Company, which had built Fort Boise for that purpose in 1834. Only 600 beaver, worth approximately $4,500 in New York (if, indeed, they could be transported to that market) were produced at Fort Hall in 1834. Discouraged by these failures, Wyeth admitted to his backer, Francis Tudor, 'I have no means to prosecute this business further and, however mortifying, must give it up.'[108]

Wyeth returned briefly to Fort Hall in December 1835 with supplies and a new contingent of men to replace those whose contracts had expired. He visited Fort Vancouver again in February 1836, with a last, desperate proposal for Dr McLoughlin. Wyeth offered to place himself in the service of the Hudson's Bay Company and, as an American, to trap legally for the British in the country to the east of the continental divide. He also offered to abandon Fort Hall, if necessary, and to limit his trapping operators to 'the waters of the Salt Lake, the Colorado del Norte, and the Rivers of the Atlantic'.[109] This plan failed to materialise, and in the summer of 1836 Wyeth returned to Missouri via New Mexico. Captain Joseph Thing, who had replaced Robert Evans as factor of Fort Hall, sold Wyeth's equipment, supplies, and furs to Drips and Fontenelle at the 1837 rendezvous. Fort Hall passed into the hands of the Hudson's Bay Company, who maintained this 'stone in the American garden' until 1856. Nathaniel Wyeth returned to New England where he became a resounding success in the ice business.

According to Meinig, the Wyeth expeditions 'combined several frontiering instruments of America into a small but bold intrusion into British-held Oregon'.[110] The farms and missions that Wyeth and his companions established survived as embryonic forms of American settlement in the Pacific Northwest. The ventures in the fur and fish trades, however, were abysmal failures. The ambitious schemes of Bonneville and Wyeth failed for a variety of reasons: the powerful opposition of the firmly-established Hudson's Bay Company, the difficulties of operating trade and commerce in a remote area, and, as Joe Meek explained, the decadent condition of the American fur trade:

> The only conclusion which can be arrived at by an impartial observer of the events of 1832–35, is, that none but certain men of long experience and liberal means, could succeed in the business of the fur trade. There were too many chances of loss; too many wild elements to be mingled in amity; and too powerful opposition from the old established companies.
>
> Captain Bonneville's experience was no different from Mr Wyeth's. In both cases there was much effort, outlay, and loss. Nor was their failure owing to any action of the Hudson's Bay Company, different from, or more tyrannical, than the action of the American companies as has frequently been represented. It was the American companies that drove both Bonneville and Wyeth out of the field. Their inexperience could not cope with the thorough knowledge of the business and the country, which their older rivals possessed.[111]

Disequilibrium and Decline, 1834 to 1840

After 1834, when the maelstrom of the early 1830s subsided, the enervated Rocky Mountain Trapping System collapsed. The resource base had been virtually destroyed by the Euro-American incursion into the Rocky Mountains — only a change in fashion in the United States and Europe saved the beaver from extinction in extensive areas of the Trans-Missouri West. Faced with dwindling supplies of furs, the trappers were forced to expand their hunting territories, and this attenuation of trapping operations raised the costs of fur production. Moreover, many trappers worked year-round and found it impractical to return each summer to the rendezvous from distant trapping grounds. By 1840 the rendezvous, which had been the nub of Ashley's Rocky Mountain Trapping System, was an anachronism, and the fur boom, which in essence had lasted barely a decade, was over.

The falling productivity of the trapping system was parallelled after 1834 by a   protracted decline in the demand for beaver pelts. A major reason for this decline, as Astor explained to Chouteau, was that 'they now make hats of silk in place of beaver'.[112] The increasing availability of silk from China, new technologies for felting hats, and the whims of fashion combined to diminish the market for beaver, first in the United States, then in Europe.[113] The situation was aggravated by the financial panic of 1837, which, according to Chouteau, reduced confidence in American products abroad,[114] and by growing competition from other areas. For example, Ramsey Crooks complained to Chouteau in 1836 that South American 'nutria has diminished the consumption of beaver so much that we fear a decline in the price of that article must be submitted to'.[115] Lampson's market reports from Europe were consistently depressing, particularly after 1836. He described the Michaelmas fair of 1837 as 'one of the worst ever', and a similar phrase was used to characterise the situation in 1839, 1840, 1841, and 1842.[116] Even the manufacturers of army caps cut their orders by 1,000–1,500 pelts a year.[117] The price for beaver on the domestic and European markets plummeted: in the halcyon days of the early 1830s beaver was worth $5.99 a pound in Philadelphia; by 1843 the price had dropped to a nadir of $2.62 a pound.[118]

Unlike the fur trades of the northern Great Plains and the Midwest, the Rocky Mountain Trapping System was dependent upon one main product. When the supply of, and demand for, beaver declined, the traders on the upper Missouri and Ohio rivers simply shifted their attention to bison robes and raccoon pelts respectively.[119] The Rocky Mountain Trapping System, however, lacked this flexibility, and after 1840, in altered form, it became little more than an appendage to the lucrative robe trade of the central and northern Great Plains.

In the late 1830s, the status of the trappers, which had never been good, deteriorated rapidly. A disillusioned Zenas Leonard complained that when he 'first embarked in this business it was with the expectation that to ensure a fortune in the fur trade only required a little perseverence and industry'.[120] Instead, Leonard and his colleagues discovered that the only remaining substantial source of furs was in Blackfoot country, where the trapper risked his life in the pursuit of his livelihood. Moreover, the trappers were pawns to the St Louis merchants, particularly to Bernard Pratte and Pierre Chouteau who, as representatives of the American Fur Company, directed the Rocky Mountain Trapping System in its declining years. Pratte, Chouteau and Company monopolised the supply system and thereby controlled the fate of the Rocky Mountain trapper. When the beaver market collapsed the suppliers attempted to offset their losses by raising the prices of goods at the rendezvous until, in Osborne Russell's estimation, the trappers were paying 2,000 per cent above St Louis prices.[121] Many trappers abandoned the Rocky Mountain Trapping System. Others, bound by inertia and restricted by the lack of alternative opportunities, persisted until the withdrawal of the American Fur Company in 1840 forced them to relinquish, or else radically change, their way of life.

From 1834 to 1836 the firm of Fontenelle, Fitzpatrick and Company (the successors of the Rocky Mountain Fur Company) nominally controlled the Rocky Mountain Trapping System. They were backed, however, and deeply in debt to, the firm of Pratte, Chouteau and Company. At the 1836 rendezvous, held as usual in the Green River Valley, the

American Fur Company came to the fore when Joshua Pilcher, acting as an agent for Pratte, Chouteau and Company, assumed the debts of Fontenelle and his partners. 'By this new arrangement,' wrote Meek, 'Bridger and Fontenelle commanded' the field parties, and Andrew Drips 'was to be the travelling partner who was to go to St Louis for goods.'[122] As far as the ordinary trapper was concerned, nothing had changed: the trapping focus remained on Blackfoot country, and the Rocky Mountain Trapping System continued to sink into a state of morbundity.

Each year from 1834 to 1838 the Blackfoot brigades left the rendezvous and travelled to the headwaters of the Missouri and Yellowstone rivers. The brigades averaged 70 men and were usually commanded by Fontenelle and guided by Bridger.[123] Although the geographic details of the expeditions varied from year to year, the general pattern of operations was rather constant (Figure 18). The brigade generally moved from the Green River to Pierre's Hole, then across the continental divide to the headwaters of the upper Yellowstone. The fall hunt was conducted in September and October on the small tributaries of the upper Yellowstone (such as Cross Creek, 25-yard River, and Rocky Fork) and in the core of Blackfoot country at the Three Forks of the Missouri and in the Judith Basin.[124] During the first days of November the brigade generally established winter quarters near the junction of Clark's Fork and Yellowstone, or with the Crow Indians in the Bighorn or Powder river valleys. Beginning in late March, the spring hunt was made at the headwaters of the Yellowstone and Missouri. The trappers then worked back through Crow country, hunting along the Bighorn and Wind rivers, to reach the Green River in July, there to await the arrival of the supply train.

After 1836 the American Fur Company standardised the supply system. The goods were taken by steamboat to Bellevue, near the mouth of the Platte. From there they were transported in wagons to Fort William. At the fort, which served as a break-in-bulk point, the goods were transferred to small mule-driven carts which could manoeuvre the rough terrain from the North Platte to the Green River rendezvous (Figure 18).

In some seasons the harvests of furs from Blackfoot

Figure 18: The Rocky Mountain Trapping System, 1834—40

LOCATION MAP

THE ROCKY MOUNTAIN
TRAPPING SYSTEM
1834-40

LEGEND

○ — American Fur Company Posts
● — Hudson's Bay Fur Company Posts
— Main Trapping Areas
— Area Under Hudson's Bay
Company Control in 1840
- - - - Supply Routes

SCALE

100 50 0   100   200   300
MILES

Canada
U. S. a.

Council
Bluffs

Ft.
William

South Platte
Posts

North
Park

South
Park

Ft. Davy Crockett

Ft.
Uintah

Robideaux
Post

"Blackfoot
Brigades"

○ Ft.
Cass

Ft.
Bridger

Small-Scale
Trapping

Flathead
Post

Ft.
Hall

Ft.
Boise

Spokane House

Ft.
Nez Perces

Ft.
Vancouver

tmk

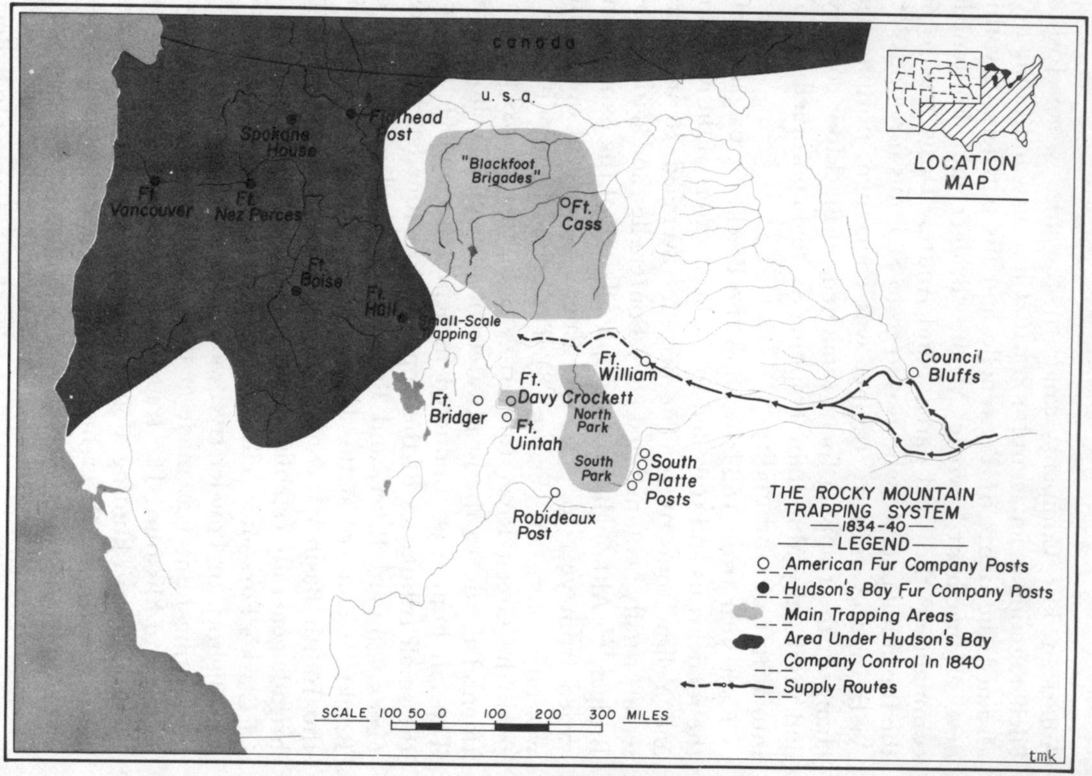

country were rich, but there was an air of desperation surrounding this final stage of the Rocky Mountain Trapping System. The death rate of the trappers was high as a result of the war of attrition waged by the Blackfoot. Yet stubbornly the trappers persisted in their quest for beaver: 'we determined to trap wherever we pleased,' Kit Carson recalled, 'even if we had to fight for the right.'[125] By 1837 the returns from Blackfoot country no longer justified the risks and costs. According to Joe Meek, 'The decline of the business of hunting furs began to be quite obvious about this time . . . The fact was becoming apparent that the beaver was being rapidly exterminated.'[126] The returns from the Rocky Mountains in 1837 were low, but, as Chouteau complained to Benjamin Clapp of the American Fur Company, this was of little consequence because the demand for beaver was also low.[127]

The Hudson's Bay Company enthusiastically monitored the decline of the Rocky Mountain Trapping System. They were represented at the 1836 and 1837 rendezvous by John McLeod, who informed Dr John McLoughlin that the American Fur Company had produced only 53 packs of beaver (each containing 90 pounds) in the 1836—7 season.[128] In 1838 James Douglas of the Hudson's Bay Company reported to his superiors that 'the collective hunts and trade of the American Fur Company . . . was little over 2000 Beaver and otter skins.' Douglas noted that the American Fur Company employed only 125 men in the Rocky Mountains and he added, perceptively, 'their trade cannot certainly support such expensive machinery.'[129]

The profitability of the Rocky Mountain Trapping System had always been unstable, but as long as the resource base was strong and the market steady the heavy costs of transportation and the frequent accidents and losses could be borne. Ashley's rendezvous system worked well under optimal conditions, but by 1838 the Rocky Mountain Trapping System was no longer profitable. Consequently, Pierre Chouteau, who had become the dominant power in the American Fur trade of the West after Bernard Pratte's retirement in 1838, began a systematic withdrawal from the Rocky Mountains.

At the 1838 rendezvous, held at the confluence of the Wind River and the Popo Agie, 'it was rumored among the men that the Company intended to bring no more supplies to the Rocky Mountains and discontinue all operations.'[130] The supply trains were sent to the Green River until 1840, but they were sadly diminished versions of the large convoys of the early 1830s. In 1839, for example, Andrew Drips brought only four carts of supplies to the rendezvous.[131] As with any men facing unemployment and dislocation, the trappers' morale deteriorated: 'times was certainly hard.' wrote Newell in 1840, 'no beaver and every thing dull.'[132]

The organised Rocky Mountain Trapping System disintegrated from 1838 to 1840. More trappers left the mountains in 1840 than in any other single year.[133] According to Joe Meek, 'some went to Sante Fe, some to California, others to the Lower Columbia.'[134] A few trappers, held as much by lifestyle as by livelihood, continued to work in the Rocky Mountains. They were outfitted from cis-montane trading posts on the South Platte, and from Fort William, Bent's Fort, and Sante Fe. The main emphasis of these posts was, however, the bison robe; the mountain trade was only a subsidiary interest. Fort Hall became a focal point for independent American trappers who worked the streams of the central Rockies and obtained their supplies from, and sold their furs to, the British.[135] Some short-lived trading posts (Fort Davy Crockett and Fort Uintah, for example) were established in the Colorado Rockies, which became the most important trapping ground in the 1840s. Symbolically, Jim Bridger's establishment in southwest Wyoming was primarily a road-ranch for the emigrants who signalled a new era in the settlement of the West.

Notes

1. John L. Allen, Henry N. Smith and Arthur K. Moore, amongst others, have stressed the importance of the myths that surrounded and stimulated American westward expansion. See Allen, *Passage through the Garden*, Smith, *Virgin Land*; and Arthur K. Moore, *The Frontier Mind* (New York: McGraw Hill, 1963).

2. The phrase is Washington Irving's. Irving wrote the official account of the Pacific Fur Company in *Astoria* (New York: The Century Co., 1909), first published in Philadelphia in 1836.

3. J. R. Gibson, *Imperial Russia in Frontier America* (New York: Oxford University Press, 1976). The sea otter was ruthlessly hunted and rapidly depleted, and production fell steadily after 1800.

4. Thwaites, *Original Journals*, vol. 3, pp. 334–7.

5. Irving, *Astoria*, p. 35. Also K. W. Porter, *John Jacob Astor* (Cambridge: Harvard University Press), vol. 1, p.243.
6. The Russians were barred from Canton, the best port of entry into China. They were forced instead to use the inland border town of Kyakhta which was far less accessible than the seaports. British traders were restricted by the monopoly of the East India Company which alone was allowed to import goods from China into Britain. The American traders had no such restrictions and they quickly came to dominate the carrying trade between the Northwest and Canton. Gibson, *Imperial Russia in Frontier America*, pp. 9, 155.
7. Meinig, *The Great Columbia Plain*, pp. 52–3, 60. Meinig explains that the Indians of the Pacific slope had a more secure subsistence base than those to the east of the Rocky Mountains. They were able, therefore, to adopt a rather independent stance toward the fur trade.
8. Robert Stuart's journal was not published in the United States until 1836, when Irving incorporated it into his study of the Astorians. However, the St Louis, and even the national, newspapers reported Stuart's discoveries in 1813, albeit rather vaguely. The concept of South Pass and the central route was known in 1813. It remained for William Ashley and his men to put the concept into operation. See R. A. Rollins, *The Discovery of the Oregon Trail* (New York and London: Charles Scribner's Sons, 1935), lxv–lxx.
9. W. H. Goetzman, *Army Exploration in the American West, 1803–1836* (New Haven: Yale University Press, 1959), p.23. Also DeVoto, *Across the Wide Missouri*, p.5.
10. The best source on Jedediah Smith and the early years of the Rocky Mountain Trapping System is D. L. Morgan, *Jedediah Smith and the Opening of the West* (Lincoln: University of Nebraska Press, 1967). This work supersedes, to a great extent, the earlier studies by Maurice S. Sullivan and Harrison C. Dale.
11. Morgan, *Jedediah Smith*, pp. 78–95, Also C. L. Camp, 'Jedediah Smith's First Far-Western Exploration', *The Western Historical Quarterly*, vol. 4 (1973), pp.151–70.
12. The primary souce material for this information is contained in the *Ashley Papers*, which include William Ashley's diary of his 1823-4 expedition. These materials have been reprinted and analyzed in Morgan, *The West of William H. Ashley*. See also Morgan, *Jedediah Smith*, pp.154–74; and H. C. Dale, *The Ashley–Smith Explorations and the Discovery of a Central Route to the Pacific, 1822-29* (Glendale: Arthur H. Clark Co., 1941).
13. For example, when Jim Bridger returned to St Louis for a brief visit in 1839, it was after an uninterrupted stay in the Rocky Mountains of seventeen years.
14. The price for furs at the rendezvous was standardised at three dollars a pound in the 1820s, but in the early 1830s, when competition was intense, the free trappers temporarily received as much as six dollars a pound for their furs.
15. See the letter written by Thomas Hempstead to Joshua Pilcher on 3 April 1822, in Morgan, *The West of William H. Ashley*, pp. 3–4.

16. *The Missouri Republican,* 3 October 1825.
17. W. H. Ashley to B. Pratte and Co., 14 October 1826, *Ashley Papers.*
18. *Missouri Intelligencer,* 28 September 1826.
19. *The Missouri Republican,* 21 September 1826.
20. D. J. Weber, *The Taos Trappers: The Fur Trade in the Far South-West, 1840–1846* (Norman: University of Oklahoma Press, 1971) p.64.
21. B. Berthold to P. Chouteau Jr, 9 December 1826, *Chouteau Collection.*
22. Morgan and Harris, *William Marshall Anderson,* pp.244–5.
23. P. S. Ogden to the Governor, Chief Factors and Chief Traders, 10 October, 1826, in Merk, *Fur Trade and Empire.,* p. 284.
24. Weber, *The Taos Trappers,* p. 80.
25. Merk, *Fur Trade and Empire,* xxv-xxvi. It should be noted that American trappers sought economic gain, as well as adventure, in the Rocky Mountains.
26. Governor G. Simpson to Dr J. McLoughlin, 10 July 1826, in Merk, *Fur Trade and Empire,* xxiii.
27. Merk, *Fur Trade and Empire,* p. 45.
28. Merk, *Fur Trade and Empire,* p.44.
29. The best source on the geography of the Snake River Expedition is Meinig, *The Great Columbia Plain,* pp. 82–4.
30. P. S. Ogden to Governor G. Simpson, 1 July 1826, in Merk, *Fur Trade and Empire,* pp. 276–7.
31. Governor and Committee to Governor G. Simpson, 12 March 1827; and Dr J. McLoughlin to Governor G. Simpson, 20 March 1827, in Merk, *Fur Trade and Empire,* pp. 286–90.
32. See table of returns in Meinig, *The Great Columbia Plain,* p. 88.
33. F. Merk, *The Oregon Question* (Cambridge, Massachusetts: Belknap Press, 1967), p.85.
34. Unless cited otherwise, the information for this section is drawn from Morgan, *Jedediah Smith;* Morgan, *The West of William H. Ashley;* Dale, *The Ashley–Smith Explorations;* and Sunder, *Bill Sublette.*
35. Morgan, *Jedediah Smith,* pp. 193–4. The myth of the Buenaventura is closely related to the concept of pyramidal height of land, which proposed that the major rivers of the western United States flowed symetrically from a central core of mountains. For the persistence of this belief in American geographical lore, see Allen, *Passage Through the Garden,* pp. 23, 243, 392.
36. This is suggested by a statement in a letter written by the trapper Daniel Potts to his brothers, dated 16 July 1826. The letter is reprinted in Morgan, *The West of William H. Ashley,* pp. 148–9.
37. J. Smith to W. Clark, 17 July 1827, in Dale, *The Ashley–Smith Explorations,* pp. 186–94.
38. David H. Burr's map of the United States of 1839 was largely derived from an original map of the West drawn by Jedediah Smith. The routes of the 1826–7 and 1827–9 expeditions are drawn on the map, which was the most complete portrayal of the West that had yet appeared. Smith's map was later incorporated more fully into George Gibb's 1845

map of the Fremont Expedition. Smith's original map has not been found.
See Wheat, *Mapping the Transmississippi West*, vol. 2, pp. 119–
39, 167–9.
 39. *Ashley Papers;* also cited in Morgan, *Jedediah Smith*, pp. 233–4.
 40. This was Ewing Young's party. See Weber, *The Taos Trappers*,
pp. 125–6. Dale, in *The Ashley–Smith Explorations* (p.230), suggests
that the Indians had been urged by the Mexican Government to prevent
Americans from crossing to California.
 41. The record of Peter Skene Ogden's 1826, 1827–8, and 1828–9
expeditions is presented in T. C. Elliott (ed.), 'The Peter Skene Ogden
Journals', *Oregon Historical Society Quarterly*, vol. 10 (1909), pp.330–
65; vol. 11 (1910), pp. 201–22, 355–97.
 42. E. E. Rich (ed.), *Part of Dispatch from George Simpson, Esqr,
Governor of Rupert's Land to the Governor and Committee of the
Hudson's Bay Company, London, March 1, 1829, Continued and Completed March 24 and June 25, 1829* (Toronto and London: Publications
of the Champlain Society, Hudson's Bay Company, 1947), p. 50.
 43. From 1826 to 1830, Smith, Jackson, and Sublette lost forty-one
men to the Indians, which amounted to one-third of the company's
average employment. More than three-quarters of the fatalities occurred
in the disastrous 1827–8 season. Smith, Jackson, and Sublette, and also
William Ashley, blamed the British for inciting the Indians against the
Americans. See 'A brief sketch of accidents, misfortunes, and depredations committed by Indians etc. onthe firm of Smith, Jackson & Sublette, Indian traders on the East and West side of the Rocky Mountains,
since July 1826 to the present [December ?] 24th, 1829', in Morgan,
Jedediah Smith, pp. 337–43.
 44. Pilcher's venture in the Rocky Mountains is detailed in Sunder,
Joshua Pilcher , pp.66–83.
 45. Morgan, *Jedediah Smith*, p. 307.
 46. W. H. Ashley to T. H. Benton, 20 January 1829, in Morgan, *The
West of William H. Ashley*, pp. 186–8. Possibly as many as thirty-nine
packs of beaver were traded from the Blackfoot.
 47. The details of this expedition were recalled by the trappers Robert
Newell and Joseph Meek. See D. O. Johansen (ed.), *Robert Newell's
Memoranda* (Portland: Champoeg Press, 1969), p.31, and F. F. Victor
(ed.), *The River of the West* (Newark: Bliss and Co., 1870), p. 64.
 48. Victor, *River of the West*, p. 89.
 49. Victor, *River of the West*, p. 85.
 50. Victor, *River of the West*, p. 110.
 51. Young, *The Correspondence and Journals of Captain Nathaniel
J. Wyeth*, pp. 158–9.
 52. The history of this company is told by the trapper Zenas Leonard
who joined Gantt and Blackwell in the spring of 1831 and worked for
them until 1832 when the company was dissolved. W. F. Wagner (ed.),
Leonard's Narrative (Cleveland: The Burrows Brothers Co. 1904),
pp. 59–92.
 53. L. R. Hafen, 'The Bean-Sinclair Party of Rocky Mountain Trappers, 1830–32', *Colorado Magazine*, vol. 21 (1954), pp. 161–71.

54. The story of Captain Bonneville's experiences in the Rocky Mountain is told in W. Irving, *The Adventures of Captain Bonneville* (New York: John B. Alden, 1886).

55. Meek recalled that there were 'not less than one thousand souls' at the Pierre's Hole rendezvous; Newell estimated 600 trappers and Indians; Leonard saw about 400 white people. See Victor, *River of the West,* p.110; Johansen, *Robert Newell's Memoranda,* p. 32; and Wagner, *Leonard's Narrative,* p. 109.

56. This figure was given by William Ashley in a letter to an unknown recipient, dated 11 January 1829. *Ashley Papers.*

57. A large proportion, perhaps one-third, of the total catch from the Rocky Mountains in the early 1830s was returned from Santa Fe. Weber, *The Taos Trappers,* pp. 206—7. (see Table 7.)

58. DeVoto, *Across the Wide Missouri,* p. 111.

59. LeRoy Hafen, in his monumental work, *The Mountain Men and the Fur Trade of the Far West* has assembled biographies for 292 trappers, which may represent about ten per cent of the total number of men who worked in the Rocky Mountains from 1807—40. The rest are anonymous.

60. The movements of the trappers in the Rocky Mountains during these years can be traced from the accounts of Meek, Newell, Leonard, and Bonneville.

61. P. C. Phillips (ed.), *Life in the Rocky Mountains* (Denver: The Old West Publishing Co., 1940), p. 85.

62. Morgan, *The West of William H. Ashley,* pp. 177—8.

63. W. Gordon to L. Cass, 3 October 1831, *Fur Trade Envelope.*

64. F. Ermatinger to E. Ermatinger, 11 March 1833. From *Selected Items Relating to the Fur Trade,* collected by D. L. Morgan (on microfilm at the Bancroft Library, University of California, Berkeley).

65. Meinig argues that the British success rested on 'solid advantages': superior trade goods and an ordered trading system. Josephy, however, maintains that the Flathead and Nez Perce Indians shifted their allegiance from the British to the Americans after 1830 because the Americans offered higher prices and an attitude of 'friendship and equality'. See Meinig, *The Great Columbia Plain,* p. 100, and A. M. Josephy Jr, *The Nez Perce Indians and the Opening of the Northwest* (New Haven and London: Yale University Press, 1965), pp. 71—6.

66. Johansen, *Robert Newell's Memoranda,* p. 32. Newell was referring to North Park, a synclinal basin in the Colorado Rockies which cradles the headwaters of the North Platte.

67. M. M. Estergreen, *Kit Carson: A Portrait in Courage* (Norman: University of Oklahoma Press, 1962), p. 63. The Blackfoot were particularly hostile toward the Rocky Mountain trappers (British and American alike) because they not only stripped Blackfoot country of its furs, so denying the Indians a source of wealth, but they also supplied the Crow, Flathead, and Nez Perce (all Blackfoot enemies) with guns.

68. DeVoto, *Across the Wide Missouri,* p. 95.

69. K. McKenzie to S. Tulloch, 8 January 1834, *Fort Union Letter-*

books, *Chouteau Collection.*
    70. Hafen, *The Mountain Men and the Fur Trade of the Far West,*
vol. 1, p. 126; Young, *Correspondence and Journals of Captain
Nathaniel J. Wyeth*, p. 69; and Sunder, *Bill Sublette*, p. 42. (See Table 7
for Wyeth's production estimates in 1832 and 1833.)
    71. Hafen, in *The Mountain Men and the Fur Trade of the Far West*
(vol. 1, p. 126) gives details of the contract between William Sublette
and the Rocky Mountain Fur Company. Hafen writes: 'The costs of
cleaning, shipping, commission fees, insurance, and interest charges
soon ate up the company's balance and left it indebted to Sublette.'
    72. P. Chouteau Jr, to K. McKenzie, 25 April 1828, *Fort Union
Letterbooks, Chouteau Collection.*
    73. Strictly speaking, the Upper Missouri Outfit was subordinate to
the Western Department, and both were under the control of Ramsey
Crooks and, ultimately, John Jacob Astor. However, both the Upper
Missouri Outfit and the Western Department had separate contracts
with the American Fur Company, and in practice the Upper Missouri
Outfit retained a great deal of autonomy. See Porter, *John Jacob Astor*,
pp. 746—71.
    74. Victor, *River of the West*, p. 103. In 1832, Fitzpatrick and Brid-
ger deliberately led Vanderburgh and Drips deep into Blackfoot country.
Vanderburgh was killed by the Blackfoot on the Madison River.
    75. Victor, *River of the West*, p. 104.
    76. Quoted in C. P. Russell, 'Wilderness Rendezvous Period of the
American Fur Trade', *Oregon Historical Quarterly*, vol. 42 (1941),
pp. 1—47.
    77. See above, pp. 72-8 .
    78. Young, *Correspondence and Journals of Captain Nathaniel J.
Wyeth*, p. 140. Wyeth expressed this opinion in a letter to Milton
Sublette, dated 1 July 1834.
    79. Victor, *River of the West*, p. 108. Meek believed that the pro-
position was rejected because Vanderburgh and Drips feared that they
would be allocated the poorest trapping grounds by their experienced
rivals.
    80. Victor, *River of the West*, p. 165.
    81. L. Fontenelle to P. Chouteau Jr, 17 September 1834, in Chit-
tenden, *American Fur Trade of the Far West*, vol. 1, pp. 304—5.
    82. Morgan and Harris, *William Marshall Anderson*, p. 173.
    83. Sunder, *Bill Sublette*, p. 144.
    84. The main reason for Astor's retirement was ill-health, although
he may also have been motivated by the unfavourable prospects of the
fur trade. Porter, *John Jacob Astor*, pp. 777—9.
    85. Irving, *The Adventures of Captain Bonneville*, pp. 3, 300.
    86. Bonneville's maps, one depicting the central Rockies and the
other covering the entire Trans-Rocky Mountain West, appeared in the
first edition of Irving's *The Adventures of Captain Bonneville*, which
was first published in Philadelphia in 1837, under the title *The Rocky
Mountains* . . . The map of the central Rockies (reproduced here as
Figure 17) was the best representation of that area that had appeared

by that date. Wheat, *Mapping the Transmississippi West,* vol. 2, pp.187–9.

87. DeVoto, who argued that Bonneville was primarily a military observer in the West, emphasised the strategic importance of Fort Bonneville, which commanded the main routway between Oregon and the United States. Morgan dismissed this argument, writing that Fort Bonneville had no military utility whatsoever. See DeVoto, *Across the Wide Missouri,* pp. 58–60; and Morgan and Harris, *William Marshall Anderson,* p. 254.

88. Young, *Correspondence and Journals of Captain Nathaniel J. Wyeth,* pp. 69–70. Elsewhere, Wyeth estimated that Bonneville accumulated thirty packs of beaver (see Table 7).

89. P. Chouteau Jr, to J. J. Astor, 25 September 1833, quoted in Chittenden, *American Fur Trade of the Far West,* vol. 1, p. 406.

90. Wagner, *Leonard's Narrative,* pp. 146–7.

91. T. J. Beall, 'Recollections of William Craig', *Lewiston Morning Tribune,* 3 March 1918. (On Microfilm at the Bancroft Library, University of California, Berkeley.)

92. Wagner, *Leonard's Narrative,* p. 145; and Irving, *The Adventures of Captain Bonneville,* p. 231. The details of the California venture are given in these two accounts.

93. Irving, *The Adventures of Captain Bonneville,* p. 241.

94. Cited in Morgan and Harris, *William Marshall Anderson,* p. 255.

95. Irving, *The Adventures of Captain Bonneville,* p. 179.

96. Irving, *The Adventures of Captain Bonneville,* p. 214.

97. Victor, *River of the West,* p. 164.

98. L. Fontenelle to P. Chouteau Jr, 17 September 1834, in Chittenden, *American Fur Trade of the West,* vol. 1, p. 425.

99. Irving, *The Adventures of Captain Bonneville,* p. 144.

100. Young, *Correspondence and Journals of Nathaniel J. Wyeth,* pp. 73–8. The details of this contract are given in a letter that Wyeth wrote to his backers, the Boston firm of Tucker and Williams. This letter, dated 8 November 1833, also contains an extremely perceptive analysis of the Rocky Mountain Trapping System.

101. Haines, *Journal of a Trapper,* p. 1. The diversity of the personnel on this expedition symbolises the growing American fascination with the western lands. Wyeth's journal of this second expedition is re-printed in Young, *Correspondence and Journals of Captain Nathaniel J. Wyeth,* pp. 221–51.

102. Young, *Correspondence and Journals of Nathaniel J. Wyeth,* p. 138.

103. Victor, *River of the West,* p. 164.

104. Young, *Correspondence and Journals of Nathaniel J. Wyeth,* p. 145.

105. Meinig, *The Great Columbia Plain,* p. 111. Meinig gives a brief, but incisive, analysis of the operations of Wyeth and Bonneville in the Northwest.

106. R. G. Beidleman, 'Nathaniel Wyeth's Fort Hall', *Oregon Historical Quarterly,* vol. 58 (1957), pp. 158–250.

107. By the summer of 1835, Wyeth had lost seventeen men to the
Indians and disease, and his letters indicate that he was concerned
about his own safety. See, for example, A. Wyeth to L. Wyeth,
22 September 1835, in Young, *Correspondence and Journals of
Nathaniel J. Wyeth*, p. 153.
108. Young, *Correspondence and Journals of Nathaniel J. Wyeth*,
pp. 149-51.
109. Dr J. McLoughlin to Governor, Deputy Governor, and Committee, Hon. Hudson's Bay Company, 5 May 1836, in *McLoughlin's Fort
Vancouver Letters*; E. E. Rich (ed.), *The Letters of John McLoughlin,
First Series, 1825–38* (Toronto: Champlain Society, 1943–4), pp.340-1.
110. Meinig, *The Great Columbia Plain*, p. 114.
111. Victor, *River of the West*, pp. 158–9.
112. Quoted in Chittenden, *American Fur Trade of the Far West*, vol.
1, p. 364.
113. R. Crooks to B. Clapp, 9 August 1836, *American Fur Company
Letterbooks*.
114. Pratte, Chouteau and Co. to J. B. Whetton, 6 April 1837,
American Fur Company Letterbooks. This contradicts James L. Clayton's conclusion that 'the depression of 1837–39 had little effect on
the American fur trade'. See J. L. Clayton, 'The Growth and Economic Significance of the American Fur Trade, 1790–1890', p. 67.
115. R. Crooks to Pratte, Chouteau and Co., 6 July 1836,*American
Fur Company Letterbooks*.
116. C. M. Lampson to R. Crooks, 19 October 1837; R. Crooks to
W. Brewster, 31 December 1839; C. M. Lampson to R. Crooks,
26 May 1841; and R. Crooks to S. Abbot, 24 May 1842, all from
American Fur Company Letterbooks.
117. C. M. Lampson to R. Crooks, 3 May 1842, *American Fur
Company Letterbooks*.
118. Clayton, 'Growth and Economic Significance of the American
Fur Trade', pp. 66–7.
119. Clayton, 'Growth and Economic Significance of the American
Fur Trade', pp. 67–8. Almost all of the raccoon skins gathered by the
American Fur Company came from the Ohio Valley.
120. Wagner, *Leonard's Narrative*, p. 142.
121. Haines, *Journal of a Trapper*, p. 60.
122. Victor, *River of the West*, pp. 198–9. After the amalgamation,
Fitzpatrick dropped out of the firm and became associated with the
company of Vasquez and Sublette on the South Platte.
123. According to Joe Meek, in the *River of the West* (pp. 189, 214),
the 1835 brigade numbered sixty men and the 1836 brigade 300
men. Osborne Russell recalled that the 1837 and 1838 brigades
consisted of sixty men and 110 men respectively. Haines, *Journal
of a Trapper*, pp. 41, 60.
124. Details of individual expeditions may be found in Victor, *River
of the West*, pp. 166–237; Haines, *Journal of a Trapper*, pp. 39–91;
and Johansen, *Robert Newell's Memoranda*, pp. 34–8.
125. H. L. Carter, *Dear Old Kit* (Norman: University of Oklahoma

Press, 1968), p. 67.

126. Victor, *River of the West*, p. 237.

127. Pratte, Chouteau and Co. to B. Clapp, 5 October 1837, *American Fur Company Letterbooks*.

128. J. McLoughlin to Governor, Deputy Governor, and Committee, Hon. Hudson's Bay Company, 31 October 1837, in Rich, *Letters of John McLoughlin*, First Series, p. 209.

129. J. Douglas to Governor, Deputy Governor, and Committee, Hon. Hudson's Bay Company, 18 October 1838, in Rich, *Letters of John McLoughlin*, First Series, p. 256.

130. Haines, *Journal of a Trapper*, p. 91.

131. Johansen, *Robert Newell's Memoranda*, p. 38.

132. Johansen, *Robert Newell's Memoranda*, p. 39.

133. Fehrman, 'The Mountain Man — A Statistical View', p. 12.

134. Victor, *River of the West*, p. 255.

135. After 1838 both Russell and Meek were based at Fort Hall, and Newell operated out of Fort Davy Crockett in 1839. In the early 1840s Russell, Meek, and Newell (and many less-renowned trappers) left the mountains for Oregon.

5 The Rocky Mountain Trapping System: Annual Cycle of Operations

Like the Upper Missouri Fur Trade, the Rocky Mountain Trapping System may be visualised as a production network, characterised by a distinctive infrastructure and linked through St Louis, the control point, to the fur markets and the sources of supplies and equipment in the eastern United States and Europe (Figure 19). The two main branches of the fur trade of the Trans-Missouri West were joined to a common national and international network, although the Rocky Mountain Trapping System depended less upon the European suppliers (the trappers had only occasional need for trade goods) and more on the European market than the Upper Missouri Fur Trade. The flow of furs, trade goods, and information between St Louis, New York, and Europe was discussed in connection with the upper Missouri Fur Trade (see above, pp. 79–83) and need not be reiterated. The focus of this chapter is placed upon the ecology of fur production in the Rocky Mountains and the movement of furs and goods between St Louis and the rendezvous as expressed through the annual cycle of operations.

The Trapping Seasons

The main trapping seasons were fall and spring (Figure 20). The fall hunt commenced immediately after the close of the rendezvous and ended when the streams iced over, generally

175

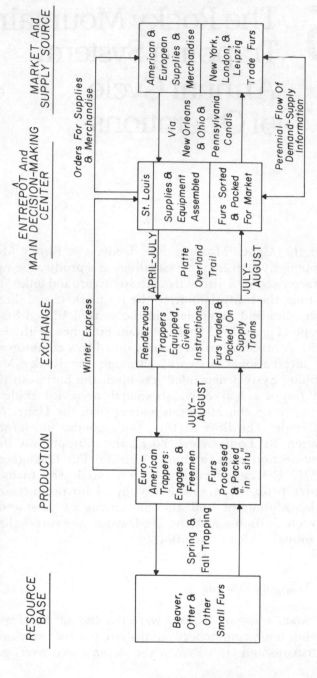

Figure 19: The Spatial Organisation of the Rocky Mountain Trapping System

Figure 20: The Annual Cycle of Operations in the Rocky Mountains, circa 1830

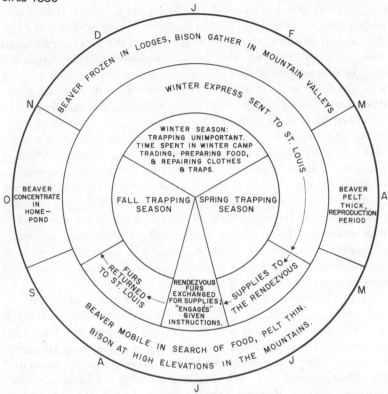

From D.J. Wishart, 'The Fur Trade of the West, 1807–40: A Geographic Synthesis', in Miller and Steffen (eds.), *The Frontier: Comparative Studies*, p. 180 (Copyright 1977 by the University of Oklahoma Press).

at the beginning of November, although this date varied from place to place and from year to year. In 1836, for example, Bridger's Blackfoot brigade was forced into winter quarters on the Yellowstone on 10 October, because the small streams were frozen and trapping was impracticable. On 25 October a brief warming trend allowed the trappers to resume their activities, but on 11 November the temperature dropped and the streams froze over for the duration of the winter.[1] In spring the hunt started in March or April when the ice melted and the flow of the swollen streams abated. In 1837 Bridger's brigade could not begin the spring hunt until 1 April, and even on 19 May, on the Wind River, they 'found the water overflowing the banks of all the branches so much that it was impossible to trap Beaver'.[2] The spring hunt continued until the advent of summer when the quality of the pelt deteriorated and the mobility of the beaver made trapping difficult. Spring was the most lucrative trapping season because the fur was thickest at that time of the year; but it was the most destructive hunt when the trappers indiscriminately killed newly-born cubs as well as adults.[3]

At the summer rendezvous the company trappers were divided into parties and delegated to the various hunting grounds. These trapping parties tried to maintain periodic contact during the year, 'to meet at certain times and places, to report progress, collect and cache the furs and "count noses" '.[4] The free trappers, of course, were not supervised in this manner. They chose their own routes and trapping grounds, although they often tagged the company parties, particularly in Blackfoot country where trapping alone, or in small groups, was hazardous.

With the exception of the Blackfoot brigades the trapping parties were small. In 1835, for example, Osborne Russell was a member of a party that was based at Wyeth's Fort Hall and consisted of 24 men, including 14 trappers and 10 camp-keepers.[5] The camp-keepers looked after the fires, prepared the food, cured the pelts, and performed a host of other mundane tasks. Warren Ferris estimated that about one-half of the 300 men attached to company parties in the Rocky Mountains in 1835 were camp-keepers.[6] They were, therefore, an integral, but largely unheralded, part of the Rocky Mountain Trapping System.

In his 'Guide to Camp Life', Joe Meek explained the procedure of a large trapping party on the march. The 'Booshway', or leader, rode at the head of the party, accompanied by a mule that carried the company's account books and employment contracts. He was followed by the camp-keepers (each in charge of three pack-animals), the trappers, Indian women and children, and the second-in-command, or 'little Booshway', who brought up the rear and supervised the order of the march and the formalities of the night-camp.[7]

Osborne Russell described in detail the accoutrements of

the Rocky Mountain trapper:

> A Trappers equipment in such cases is generally one Animal
> upon which is placed one or two Epishemores a riding
> Saddle and bridle a sack containing six Beaver traps a
> blanket with an extra pair of Mocasins his powder horn
> and bullet pouch with a belt to which is attached a butcher
> Knife a small wooden box containing bait for Beaver a
> Tobacco sack with a pipe and implements for making fire
> with sometimes a hatchet fastened to the Pommel of his
> saddle his personal dress is a flannel or cotton shirt (if
> he is fortunate enough to obtain one, if not Antelope skin
> answers the purpose of over and under shirt) a pair of
> leather breeches with Blanket or smoked Buffalo skin,
> leggings, a coat made of Blanket or Buffalo robe a hat or
> Cap of wool, Buffaloe or Otter skin his hose are pieces of
> Blanket lapped round his feet which are covered with a
> pair of Moccassins made of Dressed Deer Elk or Buffaloe
> skins with his long hair falling loosely over his shoulders
> complete the uniform.[8]

The parties travelled along the main river valleys, and small
groups of trappers dispersed to work the tributary streams. In
the fall of 1836, for example, Bridger's Blackfoot brigade
followed the Yellowstone down from its headwaters in
Yellowstone Park to the Missouri Plateau, near present-day
Billings. There, according to Russell, the trappers 'scattered
out in small parties of from 2 to 5 in number leaving Mr.
Bridger with 25 Camp Keepers to travel slowly down the
river'.[9] When all the surrounding streams had been exhausted,
and when the game had been killed or frightened away, the
main camp moved to another locale, and the pattern was
repeated. Typically, in the fall 'the trappers commenced
business on the headwaters of various rivers, following them
down as the early frosts of the mountains forced them to do,
until finally they wintered in the plains, at the most favored
spots they could find in which to subsist themselves and
animals.'[10] In spring this transhumant pattern was reversed —
the trappers followed the progress of the ice-melt upstream,
until in summer they were trapping in the 'beaver meadows'
at high altitudes in the mountains.

Plate 5: Setting Traps for Beaver (Miller, 1837)

Northern Natural Gas Company Collection, Joslyn Art Museum, Omaha, Nebraska.

They laid their traps at sunset, in preparation for the beaver's nocturnal activity (Plate 5). Joe Meek described the details of the rather brutal trapping procedure:

He has an ordinary trap weighing five pounds, attached to a chain five feet long, with a swivel and ring at the end, which plays round what is called the float, a dry stick of wood, about six feet long. The trapper wades out into the stream, which is shallow, and cuts with his knife a bed for the trap, five or six inches under water. He then takes the float out the whole length of the chain in the direction of the centre of the stream, and drives it into the mud, so fast that the beaver cannot draw it out; at the same time tying the other end by a thong to the bank. A small stick or twig, dipped in musk or castor, serves as bait, and is placed so as to hang directly above the trap, which is now set. The trapper then throws water plentifully over the adjacent bank to conceal any footprints or scent by which the beaver would be alarmed, and going to some distance wades out of the stream.[11]

The castor bait attracts the beaver, whose foot is caught in the smooth jaws of the trap.[12] The beaver struggles in an attempt to free himself and, unless he chews off his foot, he drowns, weighted down by the heavy trap.

The traps were generally raised at dawn. The beaver was skinned immediately and along with the perineal glands, which yield the castoreum, and the tail, which was considered a delicacy, the pelt was carried back to the main camp. There the camp-keepers performed the relatively simple task of processing the pelt. First the flesh side of the skin was scraped clean. Then the skin was stretched on willow hoops and dried in the sun for a day. Finally the pelts were folded, fur inward, marked with the company's insignia, and compacted into bundles of 60 to 80 skins in preparation for transportation.

The trappers dispensed with the burden of unnecessary transportation by caching furs, merchandise, and surplus equipment in the ground. The cache then became a base for trapping operations, a trading post without superstructure.[13] The cache was generally made on a rise where the soil was dry. The trappers dug a deep pit, lined it with sticks and leaves, and carefully deposited the materials. The pit was then filled with soil and the surface of the ground restored to a natural condition in an effort to conceal the cache from Indians. The furs and goods were generally raised when the trappers repaired to the summer rendezvous. The frequent occurrence of toponyms which include the word 'Cache' attests to the widespread nature of this practice. Cache Valley, for example, one of the most important sites in the fur trade of the West, was 'so called from its having been formerly a place of deposit for the Fur Traders'.[14]

In November, when the streams froze and trapping was curtailed, the American trappers went into hibernation in winter camp. They continued to hunt beaver during the winter months only if the fall trapping had been bad or if they were in urgent need of food. Warren Ferris, for example, trapped through much of the winter of 1832–3 on the

Blackfoot tributary of the upper Snake and on the Salmon River, and Zenas Leonard trapped in the Wind River country in December 1834.[15] Leonard's 'principal profits', however, came from trading with the Crow — the Indian trade was generally more important than trapping during the winter season.

In winter, when the beaver colony is frozen into the lodge, the conventional system of laying traps was impracticable. Trappers located the lodge by sounding the ice or by noting where the collective body heat of the colony had melted the ice. Then, using a traditional Indian method of hunting, the trappers broke through the roof of the lodge and killed the beaver. Alternatively, they traced the passages between the lodge and the bank of the stream and caught the beaver as he travelled in search of food.[16]

In the British system in the Pacific Northwest winter was the most important trapping season. To the west of the continental divide, in Flathead and Kootenay lands, on the Snake River, and along the Pacific slope, the streams are often free of ice, even during the coldest months of the year. The milder winter season in Oregon (compared to the country at similar latitudes to the east of the continental divide) allowed Governor Simpson to extend the Snake River Brigades' operations through December and January, when the beaver pelt was prime.[17] Nathaniel Wyeth also recognised that 'by approaching the seacoast where the climate is warmer the hunt might continue all winter and thus add a great amt. to the years hunt without adding anything to the expenses.'[18] Because of the opposition of the Hudson's Bay Company, however, neither Wyeth nor any other American trappers were able to take full advantage of this opportunity.

Of course, even to the west of the continental divide there were great variations in winter trapping conditions from year to year. In February 1839, for example, Osborne Russell set four traps in the Lewis Fork of the Snake and raised '4 large fat beaver' the following morning.[19] In contrast, during the harsh winter of 1827–8 Ogden's Snake River Brigade was immobilised by the deep snow on the upper Snake and trapping operations were suspended from December to April.[20]

Subsistence was generally not a problem in the central and

northern Rocky Mountains during the fall and spring trapping seasons. According to William Ashley, 'nothing . . . is actually necessary for the support of men in the wilderness than a plentiful supply of good fresh meat: it is all that our Mountaineers require or ever seem to wish.'[21] The most important sources of meat were bison, mountain sheep, mule deer, and elk, which were intercepted in fall and spring as they migrated between their high altitude summer ranges and their winter pastures in the mountain valleys.[22] In spring this fresh meat diet could be supplemented by camas roots, wild onions and carrots, and various types of berries.[23] If fresh meat was unobtainable, the trappers fell back upon pemmican which was prepared in winter camp.

By 1840 game had been depleted, or else had been pressured into more remote locations by the trappers. Osborne Russell, who was searching (in vain) for beaver on the Portneuf in 1840, recalled that 'in the year 1836 large bands of Buffalo could be seen in almost every little valley on the small branches of this stream.' In 1840, however, 'the only traces which could be seen of them were the scattered bones of those that had been killed.' 'It was time,' opined Russell, 'for the White man to leave the mountains as Beaver and game had nearly disappeared.'[24]

The trappers were blocked on the west by the desolate lands of the Great Basin. Nathaniel Wyeth explained that 'the reason why this country has been so much neglected is that in it there are no Buffaloe, and hunters cannot live in the luxury that they like.'[25] Expeditions to the Columbia and California stocked up with meat in the Portneuf and Bear Valleys before striking west beyond the bison range into 'Starvation Country.' Zenas Leonard, for example, tells that Joseph Walker's party laid in 60 pounds of meat for each man before leaving the Great Salt Lake on the South-West Expedition.[26] When the stores of fresh and dried meat were exhausted the trappers subsisted on roots, berries, and small game — the same fare that supported the Digger and Paiute Indians, the indigenous inhabitants of the Great Basin.[27] Mules were bled to quench the trappers' thirst. As a last resort the mules and horses were killed for food, the weakest first, and beaver skins and moccasins were eaten. Despite the pioneering efforts of Jedediah Smith and Joseph Walker, the

Great Basin and the Pacific Slope remained outside the main sphere of American trapping activities. There were rich reserves of beaver and otter in Northern California, but that area was remote from the core of the Rocky Mountain Trapping System, and the problems of provisionment on the trek across the Great Basin were insurmountable.

Winter Season

Winter was a period of rest for the trappers, a hiatus between two seasons of arduous and dangerous work. If the trappers chose their wintering sites carefully the harsh season could be passed in relative comfort. Meek recalled that winter was 'the occasion when the mountain man "lived fat" and enjoyed life: a season of plenty of relaxation, of amusement, of acquaintanceship with all the company, of gayety, and of "busy idleness".'[28] Russell also remembered the winter seasons fondly, as times of relaxation when the trappers lived 'on the fat of the land' and read (if they were able) and debated in the Rocky Mountain College.[29]

These idyllic accounts of winter camps were probably embellishments. Like most of the trappers, Meek and Russell wrote their memoirs with the benefit of hindsight, and, as Lowenthal has pointed out, 'memory transforms the past we have known into what we think it should have been'.[30] Certainly both the trappers and Indians of the central and northern Rocky Mountains experienced some winters of hardship and famine. Continental air masses frequently sweep down the eastern side of the Rocky Mountains from Canada and the Arctic, resulting in rapid drops in temperature and protracted cold spells. Occasionally these Arctic fronts break through the Rocky Mountains, and temperatures in western Montana and Idaho plummet to twenty or thirty degrees below zero.[31] This is probably what happened in the severe winter of 1827–8 when Ogden found the American trappers 'starving on the Bear River', immobilised by deep snow, and reduced to eating their horses and dogs.[32]

The trappers quickly learned the most suitable winter sites through experience and from the Indians. The sites were generally situated to the west of the continental divide where the inland penetration of Pacific air masses moderates the winter temperatures. The trappers chose sheltered, wooded river valleys that were well stocked with bison and other game. Valleys where temperature inversions frequently occurred, as in Jackson Hole, were avoided.[33] Often the trappers wintered with friendly bands of Bannock, Shoshoni, Ute, and Crow Indians who furnished trade, labour, and protection against the predatory Blackfoot.

A few select sites were particularly suitable for winter camps, and they were occupied habitually by the trappers during the late 1820s and the decade of the 1830s: the environs of Flathead Lake, where the trappers wintered with the Salish and obtained provisions from the Hudson's Bay Company post; the Lemhi and Salmon valleys, which were the traditional wintering grounds for the Nez Perce, Shoshoni and Bannock, and which Captain Bonneville favoured for his winter camps; the sheltered canyons that cut into the western wall of the Wasatch Range; and, particularly in the waning years of the Rocky Mountain trapping era, Brown's Hole (with its trading post, Fort Davy Crockett) and South Park in the Colorado Rockies (Figure 21). All these sites afforded shelter, food and forage, and security, and were havens for the trappers and the Indians during the hard winter months.

The most important wintering ground in the Rocky Mountains was the south-east corner of Idaho. The lush bottom lands of the Snake River above American Falls, the valleys of the Blackfoot and Portneuf rivers, and Cache Valley on the Bear were customary winter refuges for British and American trappers and for the Shoshoni and Northern Paiute-speaking Bannock. After 1834 Fort Hall became the focal point of this area, and the winter camps of the trappers and Indians were distributed in fingers along the valleys in the hinterland of the fort.[34]

These valleys were oases amidst the desolate sagebrush plains and plateaux of south-eastern Idaho. During the 1830s they swarmed with bison, mountain sheep, deer, and other game. Unless the trappers or the Indians carelessly ran the bison out of the valleys before the onset of winter (which happened in 1835–6),[35] subsistence was not a major problem. At the worst, the trappers were forced to subsist on pemmican. The animals thrived on the bunch grass which covered the

Figure 21: Rendezvous and Winter Sites

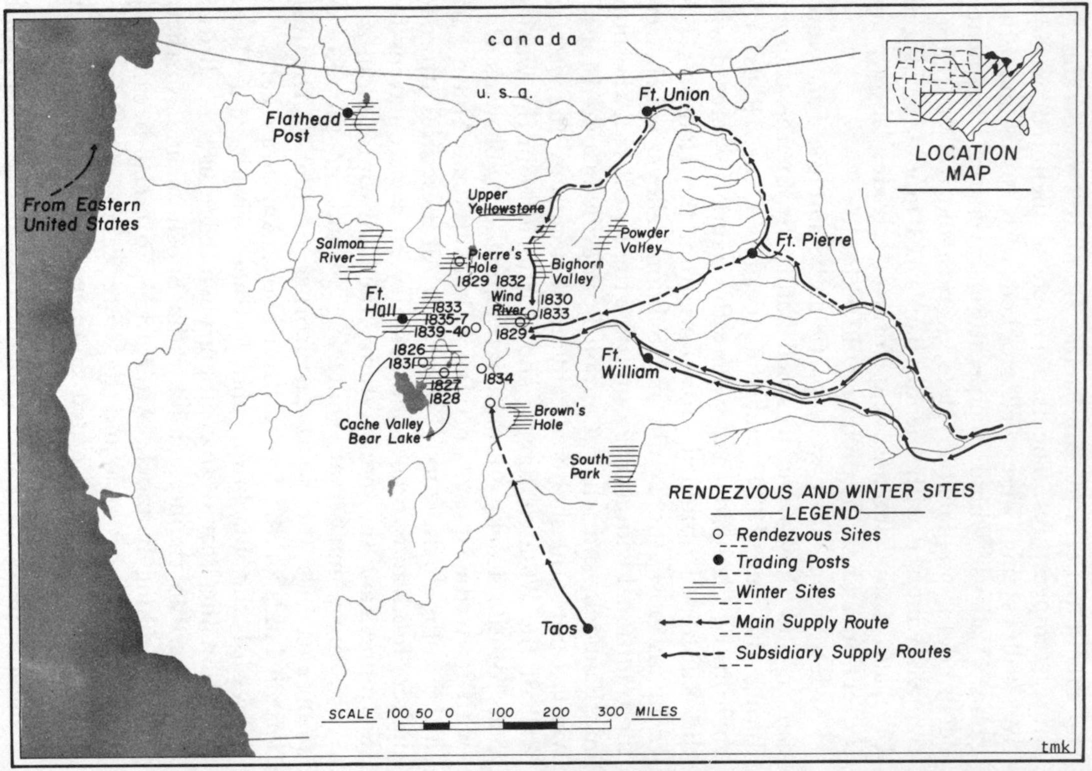

valley floors. Even during periods of heavy snow accumulation (annual snowfall averages more than sixty inches in this area), forage was generally available on the south-facing slopes. Winter temperatures are mild in the valleys — Pocatello, for example, has a January mean of 25.5°F. This combination of favourable environmental factors, plus the opportunities for a lucrative trade with the local Indians, made south-east Idaho the most densely populated area in the Rocky Mountains during the winter season.[36]

After 1830, when trapping operations shifted to the east of the continental divide, the trappers often wintered over on the northern Great Plains. This expediency allowed the trappers to work the streams of Blackfoot and Crow countries late in the fall and to recommence trapping at the earliest opportunity in the spring.

The winter season on the northern Great Plains is severe. The area around Fort Union, for example, experiences mean January temperatures of less than 10°F; and the cold is exacerbated by high winds. In the lee of the Rocky Mountains, however, the bitter cold is ameliorated by warm chinook winds and low humidity. Consequently, the trappers, Indians, and bison herds congregated in the winter in the cis-montane valleys of the upper Yellowstone, Bighorn, Powder, and Wind rivers. In these locations the trappers customarily built forti- fied camps (to ward off the persistent Blackfoot), or else they wintered under the protection of the Crow or the Wind River Shoshoni.

On 11 November 1836, for example, Bridger's Blackfoot brigade took up winter quarters near the junction of Clark's Fork and the Yellowstone. By late December the local supplies of food and forage had been consumed, and the camp was moved four miles over to the Yellowstone. The trappers lived in 'snug lodges of dressed Buffalo skins', six men to a lodge.[37] They passed the time comfortably, hunting bison, looking after the horses, and eating. On 22 February the camp was besieged by a large band of Blackfoot. Bridger's men hastily built a large breastwork of cottonwood logs and branches. Within a few days the Blackfoot moved on, and on 28 February the trappers left to commence their spring hunt on the Bighorn.

The Blackfoot danger aside, the upper Yellowstone was an

excellent location for a winter camp. The area teemed with game — elk, pronghorn antelope, white-tailed deer, mule deer, grizzly bear, and large herds of bison. With the onset of winter the bison herds assembled in the river valleys, seeking the shelter and forage of the cottonwood groves. Jedediah Smith was impressed by this phenomenon when he wintered at the junction of the Musselshell and the Missouri in 1822–3:

> When the weather had at length become extremely cold and the ice strong and firm across the River we were astonished to see the buffalo come pouring from all sides into the valley of the Missouri and particularly the vast Bands that came from the north and crossed over to the south side on the ice. We therefore had them in thousands around us and nothing more required of us than to select and kill the best for our use whenever we might chose.[38]

Often the bison herds were so large that the trappers were obliged to station a double guard to protect the camp.[39]

The trappers' animals thrived on the bark of the sweet cottonwood (Populus Sargentii), which was the dominant tree in the riparian woodlands of the northern Great Plains. Russell related that 'the horses and mules are very fond of the bark which we strip from the limbs and give them every night as the Buffalo have entirely destroyed the grass throughout this part of the country'.[40] William Ashley considered cottonwood bark to be 'quite as nutritious as Timothy Hay', and Meek noticed that 'the animals fatten upon it quite as well as upon oats'.[41]

Most frequently the Blackfoot brigades wintered in Absaroka, the land of the Crow, which was perceived as an arcadia by trappers and Indians alike. The Crow believed that the Great Spirit had put their country in 'exactly the right place'. 'When you are in it', the Crow Chief Arapooish told Robert Campbell, 'you fare well; whenever you go out of it, whichever way you travel you fare worse'. There were, claimed Arapooish, climates and resources for every season. In summer, when the Wyoming plains are parched, the Crow found game, fresh pastures and cool air in the mountains. In spring and autumn the plains swarmed with bison and the streams abounded with beaver. And in winter, Arapooish continued, you can take shelter in the woody bottoms along the rivers; there you will find buffalo meat for yourselves, and cotton-wood bark for your horses; or you may winter in the Wind River valley, where there is salt weed in abundance.[42]

The trappers concurred. The Powder River plains, where Bridger's trappers wintered in 1830–1 and 1837–8, were eulogised by Meek as a 'Land of Canaan' and a 'hunter's paradise'.[43] The Wind River Valley was, according to Leonard, 'one of the most beautiful formations of nature' and a common wintering ground 'on account of the abundance of buffalo and other game'.[44] Captain Bonneville, who placed great value on the Crow winter trade, established temporary posts in the Wind River and Powder River valleys in 1834–5. The Powder River post — a group of log cabins under the charge of Antonio Montero — was still operative in late 1837.[45]

The Crow, a proud and ethnocentric people, merely tolerated the trappers. Meek described the relationship between the two cultures as a 'state of semi-amity'.[46] The Crow welcomed the trade goods, particularly the guns and ammunition, and seemingly both sides were satisfied with the economic exchange.[47] Although the Crow, by custom, often stole the trappers' possessions, they did not pose a threat to the trappers' safety.[48] Indeed, in their own opposition to the Blackfoot, the Crow were a bulwark for the trappers against Blackfoot attack.

During the winter season only a thread-like connection was maintained between the Rocky Mountain trappers and their controllers in St Louis. As in the Upper Missouri Fur Trade, the winter express was a tenuous but vital means of co-ordinating the parts of the production system (Figure 19). In the winter of 1830–1, for example, Meek and a companion were sent from the Powder River camp to St Louis with dispatches.[49] These probably included orders for goods to be sent to the next rendezvous and mid-season information concerning the fur catch. If this information reached St Louis by May, Chouteau was able to forward the estimates to his agents in Europe, who could then arrange preliminary contracts for the Leipzig fair. The winter express was also used to confirm agreements between the trappers and their suppliers. In this sense, the express played a more fundamental role in the uncertain Rocky Mountain Trapping System than in the Upper Missouri Fur Trade where continuance was guaranteed by the monopoly of the American Fur Company.

For most of the year, however, and particularly in winter, the Rocky Mountain trappers were a detached fragment of Euro-American society, isolated by more than 500 miles from the western tier of settled states. Only in mid-summer, when the rendezvous was convened and the supply trains trekked across the Great Plains, was this isolation temporarily broken.

Summer Season

The rendezvous, as Ewers has suggested, may have drawn from an Indian precedent: the Shoshoni trade fair was traditionally held in the central Rockies during the summer season.[50] The general consensus, however, is that William Ashley should be credited with the innovation of the rendezvous system. Whatever the origins, the rendezvous was a successful fusion of Euro-American and Indian trading rituals, combining the pragmatism of a mart with the celebration of a social occasion. 'The resulting synthesis', writes Washburn, 'was revolutionary in its implications':

> The furs still got to St Louis. The trade goods still got to the Indians. But the emotional release for both white and Indian, the jubilant excesses, the liquor, the women, and the meeting in the context of equality redeemed a process which might otherwise have been merely a cold exchange of material goods.[51]

Like much of Ashley's system the rendezvous was an extemporaneous innovation, but by 1825 the institution was ingrained. Summer pelts were thin and of little value, and summer was the only season when supply trains could cross the Great Plains. Moreover, the rendezvous was flexible and allowed a year's trading to be accomplished in a few days without the expense of a trading post. From the first, informal gathering of Ashley's trapping parties on Henry's Fork of the Green River in 1825 until the last, diminished meeting in 1840, the rendezvous was the hub and distinguishing feature of the Rocky Mountain Trapping System.

The rendezvous was held in a location that was central to the main trapping grounds and accessible for the supply trains which crossed the continental divide through South Pass. In 1826, 1827, and 1828 the rendezvous were held in south-east Idaho and northern Utah, within easy reach of the rich beaver streams of the upper Snake, upper Green, and Bear rivers (Figure 21). After 1829 the rendezvous was shifted to the north and east, symbolising the increasing importance of the Crow and Blackfoot trapping grounds. From 1833 to 1840, with the exception of the 1838 meeting at the confluence of the Wind and Popo Agie rivers, the rendezvous were held in the valley of the upper Green. This was a convenient and traditional assembly point for the Nez Perce, Flathead, Shoshoni, Bannock, and Crow who traded at the rendezvous each summer. The Green River was also accessible from the main trapping grounds of the upper Missouri and Yellowstone and for the supply trains which after 1832 sacrificed mobility for bulk transportation by replacing pack animals with wagons drawn by oxen.

The specific sites for the rendezvous were chosen deliberately, generally a year in advance. The ideal site was a wide valley with ample grass and water for the animals, wood for fuel, and game for food and sport. However, no single site was capable of supporting the numerous men and animals for the entire duration of the rendezvous, which often lasted for most of the month of July.[52] The rendezvous, therefore, should be envisaged as a congeries of camps arranged widely around a central site. The camps were moved frequently as the local resources were exhausted, and each plied a separate trade with Indians and trappers, like booths in a market.

At the 1834 rendezvous, for example, the various groups of trappers assembled in mid-June in three or four camps on the Green River, all within 50 or 60 miles of each other.[53] By 20 June the parties had converged on Ham's Fork of the Green River, where the general rendezvous was to be held. The Rocky Mountain Fur Company's camp was established about eight miles upstream from the American Fur Company's camp. After a series of local moves, the two companies joined on 20 July and moved northward, establishing camps in the wooded valleys of the right bank tributaries of the Upper Green (LaBarge Creek, South Piney Fork, and Cottonwood Creek). At the end of July the rendezvous was concluded, trapping parties splintered off to their hunting grounds, the supply trains retraced their long journey through South Pass to Missouri, and the annual cycle began anew.

Cache Valley and Pierre's Hole, for example, both met all the prerequisites of a good rendezvous site. Cache Valley, which was the site of the 1826 rendezvous, is a broad, flat bottomland formed during a period of aggradation by the Bear River. Daniel Potts, one of Ashley's trappers, described Cache Valley in 1826 as the 'chief place of rendezvous and wintering grounds' because of the abundance of grass, timber, water, game and wild fruit.[54] Pierre's Hole, the site of the 1832 rendezvous, lies at the western foot of the Teton Range. The south fork of the Teton River flows out of Pierre's Hole to the north and other headwater streams of the Snake flow more directly southwestward from the basin to the main stream. Pierre's Hole was a crossroads, traversed by the main trail from the Green River to the upper Snake, and linked to Jackson Hole and the upper Yellowstone through Teton Pass.[55] According to Osborne Russell, who crossed this basin in the fall of 1834, Pierre's Hole was a 'Smooth plain intersected by small streams and thickly clothed with grass and herbage and abounds with Buffaloe Elk Deer etc.'[56] The main disadvantage of Pierre's Hole, however, was that it fell well within the range of the Blackfoot. The massacre of trappers and Indians in Pierre's Hole in July 1832 may have been the reason why this site was not used again for the rendezvous.[57]

The most suitable (and most frequented) rendezvous site was in the vicinity of the confluence of Horse Creek and the Green River, near present-day Daniel, Wyoming. Captain Bonneville built his log trading post in the angle between these two streams in 1832, and although Fort Bonneville quickly crumbled the site persisted as a convenient place of rendezvous.[58] In 1835, 1836, 1837, 1839, and 1840 the rendezvous was held on this grassy flood plain, which in summer stands out on the landscape as a ribbon of dark green amidst the pale green and silver sagebrush plains of the Bridger Basin. Western wheatgrass, buffalo grass, green needlegrass, sandberg bluegrass, and blue grama provided good summer grazing for the thousands of horses and mules, and the groves of cottonwood and willow furnished firewood to warm the cool summer nights.[59]

The trappers generally gathered at the pre-arranged rendezvous site in early June, anxiously awaiting the arrival of the supply train from Missouri bringing trade goods, luxuries such as sugar, coffee and alcohol, and news of the outside world. The scene is vividly portrayed by Russell, who joined the assembled trappers on 10 June 1837 on the Green River, about ten miles below the mouth of Horse Creek:

> Here presented what might be termed a mixed multitude the whites were chiefly Americans and Canadian French with some Dutch, Scotch, Irish, English, halfbreed, and full blood Indians, of nearly every tribe in the Rocky Mountains. Some were gambling at Cards some playing the Indians game of hand and others horse racing while here and there could be seen small groups collected under shady trees relating the events of the past year.[60]

The supply trains followed the central route from Missouri to the Rockies that had been established, if not initially discovered, by Ashley's trappers in 1824. Occasionally other routes were utilised. As we have seen, in the early 1830s the American Fur Company launched its drive to the Rocky Mountains from the Council Bluffs, Fort Pierre and Fort Union, in a vain attempt to cut transportation costs and time. In 1831 Tom Fitzpatrick supplied the Rocky Mountain Fur Company from Taos, after travelling to Santa Fe with the ill-fated caravan led by Smith, Jackson, and Sublette. On at least two occasions, in 1824 and 1833, furs were returned from the Rocky Mountains via the Bighorn-Yellowstone-Missouri river route. These were exceptions, however, because the Platte Overland Trail was by far the most effective connection between Missouri and the rendezvous.

In 1826 the Missouri newspapers heralded the discovery of the central route to the Rocky Mountains (and beyond to the Pacific). The reports were idealised. The route was described by the *St Louis Enquirer* as 'so broad and easy' a way that 'thousands may travel it in safety, without meeting with any obstruction deserving the name of a mountain'. Another newspaper announced that the 'whole route lay through a level and open country, better for carriages than any turnpike in the United States' and that the gradient to South Pass was 'so small as hardly to affect the rate of going of the caravan, and forming at the most, an angle of three degrees, being two degrees less than the steepest ascent on the Cumberland road'.[61]

In reality the route was far more difficult than the newspapers suggested. Wagons had to be hauled over the dissected terrain on the North Platte, the aridity of the western plains caused the wooden wheels to shrink and, unless a good supply of wood had been stocked in the early stages of the journey, it was impossible to replace broken spokes in an area which was largely devoid of trees. Despite the expertise of the suppliers, this basic factor of distance between the production area in the Rocky Mountains and the outlet in St Louis was the Achilles Heel of the system. Recognising this problem, William Ashley wrote in 1826 that he would willingly pay $1 a pound to have his furs delivered from the Rocky Mountains to St Louis, where the selling price in the 1820s was $4 to $6 a pound.[62] Nevertheless, the central route sufficed as long as beaver were plentiful and the market price remained high.

The supply trains left Lexington or Independence, Missouri in late April or early May.[63] This early start ensured that the mountains were reached before the summer heat parched the western plains and terminated the growth cycle of the short grasses which the pack-animals depended on for forage. The expeditions generally consisted of 50 to 70 men and more than 100 pack-horses and mules.[64] After 1832, wagons and 'charettes' (two-wheeled carts) drawn by oxen, mules or horses were incorporated into the transportation system. The pack-animals and wagons were loaded with trade goods (three-point blankets, coloured cloth, beads, vermillion, awls, etc.), equipment (traps, guns /and ammunition, knives, etc.), and enough provisions to last until the bison herds were encountered, generally near the forks of the Platte.[65] In 1833 Nathaniel Wyeth estimated that the cost of sending

Table 8: Estimated Costs of Sending a Supply Train to the
Central Rockies in 1833

	$
Ins. and Sundrys	160.00
Baling of the above and Sundrys bought at St Louis	100.00
50 pack saddles and 50 Riding Do	250.00
Hobbles and Halters for 100 animals	150.00
Shoeing for 100 animals	50.00
Corn and sundry for Horses	50.00
Saddle Blankets	100.00
50 men for 5 months at 15 per month	3,750.00
Provisions to Buffaloe	100.00
Pack Covers	50.00
Am(m)unition	100.00
100 animals	3,000.00
Guns	300.00
First cost of goods	3,000.00
Six months interest on all charges except wages	222.00
	$11,382.00

Source: Young, *The Correspondence and Journals of Captain Nathaniel J. Wyeth,*
p. 75.

a supply train from St Louis to the central Rockies was
$11,382, which included $3,000 worth of trade goods
(Table 8).[66]

From the western border of Missouri the expeditions
followed the course of the Kansas River to the Little Blue,
then angled across the verdant, rain-fed prairies of eastern
Kansas and Nebraska. The Platte was reached at the Grand
Island after a journey of about two weeks. John Ball, a
member of Wyeth's 1832 expedition, described the formalised
routine of the camp on the march:

We kept in strict military order, and marched double file.
Those first ready took their places next to the commander.
We always camped in the form of a hollow square, making
a river or stream the fourth side. The horses were hobbled

(fore feet tied) and turned out of camp to feed. When brought into camp at night they were left hobbled, and were tied to stakes driven close to the ground, giving each horse as much room as could be spared him within the square.[67]

The delays caused by loading and unloading the pack-animals at dawn, noon, and sunset were obviated by the introduction of wagons. The wagons also provided a potential wall of defence in case of Indian attack, but this threat was more perceived than real.

The supply trains proceeded along the south side of the river and forded the shallow waters of the South Platte about eight miles above the forks. West of the forks of the Platte the supply trains emerged suddenly into an unfamiliar semi-arid environment where grasslands looked more like a closely-grazed meadow than a flowing sea. To men born in the humid, forested environments of the eastern half of North America and Western Europe (as most of the trappers were) this area seemed desolate and not unreasonably called the 'Great American Desert'. 'It is one immense desert', wrote Anderson, 'a true American "Sahara" '.[68] The consensus of opinion was that the area would remain forever in 'a state of pristine wilderness' because it offered 'no inducements to civilised people sufficient to justify the expectation of permanent settlement'.[69]

On the North Platte travel became difficult and uncomfortable. The men were plagued by swarming gnats, and the land began to swell and heave, forcing the supply trains to make detours away from the incised river. After the uncompromising flatness of the Platte floodplain, Courthouse Rock, the Wildcat Ridge, and Chimney Rock were impressive landmarks. The travellers compared these erosional remnants to castles, pyramids, and ancient cities: 'it was scarcely possible,' wrote Irving (echoing Bonneville), 'to persuade oneself that the works of art were not mingled with these fantastic freaks of nature.'[70]

After about 30 days' travel, averaging 25 miles a day, the supply trains reached the Laramie River. There, on 1 June 1834, William Sublette founded Fort William, which would serve as a road ranch on the trail, as well as a trading post.

The Platte was crossed to the north side near the mouth of Labonte Creek, or at the Red Buttes where the trail left the North Platte and cut across the alkaline, sagebrush plains to reach the Sweetwater near Independence Rock.

The travellers were now crossing the Wyoming Basin, at an altitude of about 7,000 feet. The mountains surrounding the basin were capped with snow, and at night the temperatures fell well below freezing. Bonneville's men in 1832 'complained of cramps and colics, sore lips and mouths, and violent headaches'.[71] The horses were jaded, the wagons began to disintegrate. Unable to obtain wood for fuel, the men improvised and used dried buffalo dung. During the fifth week of the journey the supply trains crossed through the wide depression called South Pass and struck out across the untrammelled, gravelly plains of the Bridger Basin to the Big Sandy, and thence to the Green River where the expectant trappers were assembled.

The rendezvous, as noted above, served a dual function of celebration and business. Alfred Jacob Miller captured the feel of the 1837 rendezvous in his water colours and in the description which he entered in his notebook:

> At certain specified times during the year, the American Fur Company appoint a 'Rendezvous' at particular localities (selecting the most available spots) for the purpose of trading with Indians and Trappers, and here they congregate from all quarters. The first day is devoted to 'High Jinks', a species of Saturnalia, in which feasting, drinking, and gambling form prominent parts ... The following days exhibit the strongest contrast to this. The Fur Company's great tent is raised; — the Indians erect their picturesque white lodges; — the accumulated furs of the hunting season are brought forth and the Company's tent is a besieged and busy place.[72]

In return for their furs the company trappers were given an outfit for the following year, some luxuries such as alcohol and tobacco, and, if any credit remained, a note payable in St Louis. 'A good hunter,' wrote Wyeth, 'can take an average of 120 skins in a year ... worth in Boston about $1000.' Such hunters, Wyeth continued, 'can be hired for about $400 payable in goods at an average of 600 per ct profit'.[73] A few experienced trappers could command a higher salary. At the 1838 rendezvous, for example, Jim Bridger received a note from Pratte, Chouteau and Co., paying $3317.13 for two years' service.[74] This was exceptional. The trappers were generally paid poorly for their labour. There was little prospect for accumulating capital in the rank and file of the Rocky Mountain Trapping System. It is hardly surprising, therefore, that the trappers squandered their meagre profits on a brief release at the rendezvous. 'They care not what may come to pass tomorrow,' wrote Leonard, 'but think only of enjoying the present moment.' In Leonard's estimation, 'scarcely one man in ten' ever thought of saving 'a single dollar of their earnings'.[75]

The companies established two separate trading rates, one in cash or merchandise for the trappers, the other in specified trade goods for the Indians. The standard rates at Fort Hall in 1834 are probably representative, and they indicate that the companies made a much higher percentage profit from Indian trading than from trading with the trappers.[76] (Table 9). In the 1830s, the trappers, whether engagés or independent, were caught in an upward spiral of prices. At the 1836 rendezvous, Osborne Russell was obliged to pay $2 a pound for coffee, sugar and tobacco, $4 a pint for alcohol, $20 each for three-point blankets, and $5 each for common cotton shirts.[77] Horses could cost as much as $500 in the mountains.[78] Meanwhile, the price the trappers received for beaver was standardised at $3 or $4 a pound, $5 for a large skin.

This extortion continued until even these inflated prices could not offset the costs of operation. The fur companies then abandoned the effete Rocky Mountain Trapping System, leaving many trappers in limbo.

Compared to the durable Upper Missouri Fur Trade, the Rocky Mountain Trapping System was a brief, intense episode in the history of the West. Ashley's revelation of vast quantities of beaver in the central Rockies, his innovative production system, and high market prices inspired a 'fur rush' in the second half of the 1820s which was sustained into the first half of the 1830s. By 1834, however, the collapse of the beaver market and the blind destruction of the resource base had thrown the system into disequilibrium. By withdrawing the American Fur Company from the Rocky Mountains after

Table 9: Trading Rates at Fort Hall, 1834

Indian Tariff

For Robes and Beaver give the following articles for Elk skins and meat the same except the cloths, Blankets axes and large cut Beads

1	Bunch common beads cut
30	Loads Ammunition
20	Loads ammunition 1 Knife
20	Loads ammunition 10 Paper Vermillion
20	Loads ammunition Bunch small beads
20	Loads ammunition Small piece Tobacco
20	Loads ammunition ½ doz small Buttons
20	Loads ammunition 3 awls
20	Loads ammunition gun worm 1 flint
1	Fatham largest cut beads for Beaver or Robe
1	Common Blanket cost $4.25 for Beaver or Robe
1	Shirt for Beaver or Robe
½ yard	Blue cloth for Beaver or Robe
½ yard	Scarlet cloth for Beaver or Robe

Rifle 12 Beaver or Robes Fuzil 8 Beaver or Robe

For Rats or Mink give the following Articles

2	Flints	2	Loads Ammunition
1	Gun worm	1	Fire Steel for 3
1	Awl	4	Bells for one
1	Fish Hook		

For good Upishemays, Dressed Antelope and dear skins give ammunition only and trade only for good ones

10	Loads ammunition and trade only good ones
5	Loads ammunition for cords
12	Loads ammunition for saddles each

For all unnamed articles fix a price at your own discretion but purchase none only you are obliged.

Tariff for the Whites

The prices you will find in the Invoice and marked on the goods. Of the Whites you will trade only Beaver Rats and Mink. Paying as follows in goods

Viz.   Beaver $6 pr. large skin or $5 pr. lb.

Rats 25¢

Mink 25¢

Or cash $3.50 pr lb or $5 pr large skin

Male Beaver in proportion whether paid for in goods or cash.

Source: Beidleman, 'Nathaniel Wyeth's Fort Hall', pp. 217–18 (from the Fort Hall ledgers). Rats are, of course, muskrats, and Upishemays is one of the many names for skin saddle blankets or ground sheets (otherwise epishemores).

1838 and concentrating on the lucrative and stable robe trade of the northern Great Plains, Pierre Chouteau re-established equilibrium in the fur trade of the West. The retrenched production system continued to prosper until the 1860s when it was engulfed by the tide of permanent settlement.

Notes

1. Haines, *Journal of a Trapper*, pp. 49-51.
2. Haines, *Journal of a Trapper*, pp. 55—7.
3. In modern commercial trapping, beaver pelts are considered to be at their best about 1 February. The major trapping season is from the end of January until mid-April, and pelts taken during this period are worth twenty-five per cent more than fall pelts. H. McCracken and H. Van Cleeve, *Trapping* (New York: A. S. Barnes and Co., 1947), p.3.
4. Victor, *River of the West*, p. 57.
5. Haines, *Journal of a Trapper*, p. 14.
6. Phillips, *Life in the Rocky Mountains*, p. 228.
7. Victor, *River of the West*, pp. 52—4.
8. Haines, *Journal of a Trapper*, p. 82. Epishemores were made from pieces of bison skin that were sown together and used as a saddle blanket or a groundsheet.
9. Haines, *Journal of a Trapper*, p. 47.
10. Meek, *River of the West*, p. 214.
11. Meek, *River of the West*, pp. 64—5. For details on the characteristics and diffusion of the steel trap, see A. W. Schorger, 'A Brief History of the Steel Trap and its use in North America', *Transactions of the Wisconsin Academy of Sciences, Arts, and Letters*, vol. 40 (1951), pp.171—99. Also, C. P. Russell, *Firearms, Traps, and Tools of the Mountain Man* (New York: Alfred A. Knopf, 1967). Russell notes that the Chouteau family relied upon traps made by the New York blacksmith, Miles Standish (pp. 133—4).
12. Castoreum is a creamy, bitter, orange-brown substance from the perineal glands of the beaver. The perineal glands were taken from the base of the tail and dried in the sun or by smoking. They were then mixed in a bladder-like bag with nutmeg, cloves, cinnamon and alcohol, and the mixture was sealed in an air-tight wooden box. This pungent bait (which is still used in trapping) can entice beaver from as far as a mile away. Castoreum was an important item in the fur trade: a pound (about six pairs of castors) was worth three dollars in 1827. C. E. Hanson Jr., 'Castoreum', *Museum of the Fur Trade Quarterly*, vol. 8 (Spring 1972), pp. 1—4.
13. This analogy was made by Bonneville in Irving, *The Adventures of Captain Bonneville*, p. 67. A description of a cache is given in Wagner, *Leonard's Narrative*, p. 67.
14. Haines, *Journal of a Trapper*, p. 51.
15. Phillips, *Life in the Rocky Mountains*, p. 153; and Wagner,

Leonard's Narrative, p. 277.

16. Victor, *River of the West*, pp. 68–9.

17. Merk, *Fur Trade and Empire*, pp. 44–5. For example, the mean
January temperature at Boise, Idaho is 24°F., which is significantly
warmer than the Wind River Valley in Wyoming, where the January mean
is 14.8°F. Both stations are located between 43°and 44°N. US Department of Agriculture, *Yearbook of Agriculture 1941: Climate and Man*
(Washington, DC: Government Printing Office, 1941), pp. 829, 1201.

18. Young, *Correspondence and Journals of Captain Nathaniel
J. Wyeth*, p. 135.

19. Haines, *Journal of a Trapper*, pp.94–5.

20. Elliot, 'The Peter Skene Ogden Journals', pp. 370–2.

21. Ashley, *Diary*.

22. Information on migration habits of Rocky Mountain mammals
may be found in R. R. Lechleitner, *Wild Mammals of Colorado* (Boulder,
Colorado: Pruett Publishing Co., 1969), pp. 212–31; O. J. Murie, *The
Elk of North America* (Washington DC: Wildlife Management Institute
1951); and D. R. Smith, *The Bighorn Sheep in Idaho* (Boise, Idaho:
Idaho Department of Fish and Game, 1954). The bighorn sheep, for
example, lived in summer pastures in the subalpine zones above 8000
feet. In mid-October they migrated down the south facing slopes into
winter quarters in such areas as the Salmon, Lemhi, and Lost River
valleys. For a primary account of these migrations, see Haines, *Journal
of a Trapper*, p. 133.

23. No doubt the trappers learned from the Indians which plants
were edible and which were poisonous. Josephy, in his *Nez Perce Indians and the Opening of the Northwest* (pp.17–19) discusses the types
of plants which the Indians collected.

24. Haines, *Journal of a Trapper*, p. 123.

25. Young, *Correspondence and Journals of Captain Nathaniel J.
Wyeth*, p. 135.

26. Wagner, *Leonard's Narrative*, p. 149.

27. For food sources of the Great Basin see J. H. Steward, *Basin–
Plateau Aboriginal Sociopolitical Groups*, Bureau of American Ethnology Bulletin, No. 120 (Washington DC: Government Printing Office,
1938), pp. 21–44.

28. Victor, *River of the West*, p. 83.

29. Haines, *Journal of a Trapper*, pp. 51, 81, 109. Fort Hall served as
a 'lending library' during the late 1830s, and Dr John McLoughlin kept
the trappers well supplied with books.

30. D. Lowenthal, 'Past Time, Present Place: Landscape and Memory',
Geographical Review, vol. 65 (1975), pp. 27–8.

31. For example, the mean January temperature at Pocatello, Idaho
(near the Portneuf and Bear River wintering grounds) is a mild 25.5°F.
The minimum recorded temperature is 28°below zero. US Department
of Agriculture, *Climate and Man*, p. 829.

32. Elliot, 'The Peter Skene Ogden Journals', p. 371.

33. Osborne Russell noted that 'the cold descending the mountains
at nights' was a deterrent to wintering in Jackson Hole. Haines, *Journal*

of a Trapper, p. 18. Modern climatological data confirm Russell's observation: the mean January temperature at Jackson is 12.8° F; and the absolute recorded minimum is 52° below zero. US Department of Agriculture, *Climate and Man*, p. 1203.

34. See the map of Shoshoni and Bannock villages in Steward, *Basin Plateau Aboriginal Sociopolitical Groups*, facing p. ix.

35. Haines, *Journal of a Trapper*, p. 39. Russell reported that 'Mr. Bridger's men lived very poor and it was their own fault for the valley was crowded with fat cows when they arrived in Novr. But instead of approaching and killing their meat for the winter they began to kill by running on horse back which had driven the Buffaloe all over the Mountain to the head of the Missouri and the snow falling deep they could not return during the winter'.

36. In the winter of 1834–5, for example, Bridger's brigade, consisting of sixty men, camped at the forks of the Snake, sixty miles above Fort Hall. There were also sixty lodges of Fort Hall Shoshoni and 250 lodges of Bannock near Fort Hall. As Russell observed 'the Whites and Indians were very numerous in the valley all came to pass the winter on Snake River.' Haines, *Journal of a Trapper*, pp. 7–9.

37. Haines, *Journal of a Trapper*, pp. 50–1.

38. Quoted in Morgan, *Jedediah Smith*, pp. 45–6.

39. Victor, *River of the West*, p. 82.

40. Haines, *Journal of a Trapper*, p. 51.

41. Ashley, *Diary*; Victor, *River of the West*, p. 82.

42. Irving, *Adventures of Captain Bonneville*, pp. 135–6. Salt weed is an annual, silvery weed found in alkaline and arid areas of North America.

43. Victor, *River of the West*, pp. 83, 96.

44. Wagner, *Leonard's Narrative*, pp. 276–7.

45. Haines, *Journal of a Trapper*, p. 81.

46. Victor, *River of the West*, p. 225.

47. Wagner, *Leonard's Narrative*, p. 277.

48. In the 1850s Denig wrote that 'scarcely an incident has happened during the last 40 years when they (the Crow) have killed a (white) man.' See Ewers, *Five Indian Tribes*, p. 149.

49. Victor, *River of the West*, p. 96.

50. Ewers, 'Indian Trade on the Upper Missouri'. p. 431.

51. W. E. Washburn, 'Symbol, Utility, and Aesthetics in the Indian Fur Trade', *Aspects of the Fur Trade*, pp. 50–4.

52. At the 1834 rendezvous, for example, Osborne Russell estimated that there were 600 trappers in the Rocky Mountain Fur Company and American Fur Company camps, Haines, *Journal of a Trapper*, p. 3. It was not unusual for 2000 or 3000 Indians to gather at the summer rendezvous. See statistics in Russell, 'Rendezvous Period of American Fur Trade', pp. 21, 31, 38.

53. The details of this rendezvous are given in Morgan and Harris, *William Marshall Anderson*, pp. 128–74. Anderson's Diary and Journal are supplemented by the editors' copious and perceptive notes.

54. D. Potts to his brother, 1 July 1826, in Morgan, *West of William H. Ashley*, p. 148.

55.DeVoto, *Across the Wide Missouri*, pp. 49, 397. Basing his opinions on field work and contempary descriptions, DeVoto concluded that the rendezvous was probably held at the southern end of Pierre's Hole.

56. Haines, *Journal of a Trapper*, p. 15.

57. For a description of the Pierre's Hole massacre, see DeVoto, *Across the Wide Missouri*, pp. 80—91. Among the many contempary accounts of this incident are Victor, *River of the West*, pp. 112—18, and Irving, *Adventures of Captain Bonneville*, pp. 54—61.

58. In the summer of 1838, Osborne Russell came across 'an old log building which was formerly used as a storehouse', near the junction of Horse Creek and the Green River. This was not Bonneville's post, which apparently lay in ruins nearby. Haines, *Journal of a Trapper*, pp. 90, 169.

59. In the semi-arid areas of southwest Wyoming, where annual precipitation averages less than ten inches and fluctuates widely, only the floodplain grasses are suitable for summer grazing. Elsewhere, plant growth is terminated by drought before mid-summer. J. E. Weaver and F. W. Albertson, *Grasslands of the Great Plains* (Lincoln: Johnson Publishing Co., 1957), pp. 327—44.

60. Haines, *Journal of a Trapper*, p. 58.

61. *St. Louis Enquirer*, 11 March 1826, and *Missouri Herald and St. Louis Advertiser*, 8 November 1826.

62. Morgan, *West of William H. Ashley*, p. 308.

63. Unless noted otherwise, the information on the supply journal is taken from Morgan and Harris, *William Marshall Anderson*.

64. The size of the expeditions varied considerably. Sublette's supply train in 1834, for example, consisted of thirty-seven men and ninety-five horses. Compare this with Bonneville's expedition of 1832, which comprised 110 men and included twenty wagons. Sublette's party, of course, was purely a supply train, whereas Bonneville was launching an expedition and many of his men were trappers. Morgan and Harris, *William Marshall Anderson*, p. 72; and Irving, *The Adventures of Captain Bonneville*, p. 24.

65. Each horse carried a load of about 180 pounds.

66. Young, *Correspondence and Journals of Captain Nathaniel J. Wyeth*, p. 75. Wyeth was making the point that the cost of transporting the same goods from the head of navigation on the Columbia was less than half the cost of supplying from St Louis.

67. K.N.B. Powers, 'Across the Continent Seventy Years Ago', *Oregon Historical Quarterly*, vol. 3 (1902), p. 86.

68. Morgan and Harris, *William Marshall Anderson*, p. 127.

69. Irving, *The Adventures of Captain Bonneville*, p. 40; and William Ashley, in the *St. Louis Enquirer*, 11 March 1826.

70. Irving, *The Adventures of Captain Bonneville*, p. 34, For an analysis of these perceptual responses, see P. Shepard, *Man in the Landscape*, (New York: A. A. Knopf, 1967), pp. 238—46.'

71. Irving, *The Adventures of Captain Bonneville*, p. 42.

72. M. C. Ross (ed.), *The West of Alfred Jacob Miller* (Norman: University of Oklahoma Press, 1968), p. 110. Many other contemporary descriptions of the rendezvous are available, nearly all in the same vein

as Miller's account. William Marshall Anderson, however, was rather disappointed with the rendezvous: 'everything is novel and interesting', he wrote, 'but not as exciting as I had expected'. Morgan and Harris, *William Marshall Anderson*, p. 134.

73. Young, *Correspondence and Journals of Captain Nathaniel J. Wyeth*, pp. 60—1. Considering these potential profits it is not surprising that Wyeth wrote that there was 'a good chance to make money' in the Rocky Mountains.

74. *Chouteau Account Books, Chouteau Collection.* Joe Meek claimed in 1834 that the Rocky Mountain Fur Company paid him a salary of $1500 a year. This is quite feasible because experienced trappers were in great demand in the competitive years of the early 1830s. Victor, *River of the West*, p. 159.

75. Wagner, *Leonard's Narrative*, p. 248.

76. Beidleman, 'Nathaniel Wyeth's Fort Hall', pp. 217—18. Fire steels, for example, sold for three cents apiece wholesale in the eastern United States. The Indians, however, exchanged three muskrat skins (worth seventy-five cents total) for one fire steel at Fort Hall.

77. Haines, *Journal of a Trapper*, p. 60.

78. This figure is given by Daniel Potts in a letter written on 8 July 1827, which Morgan cites in *Jedediah Smith*, p. 232.

6 The Fur Trade of the West: Assessment

The sweep across the North American continent has traditionally been described in heroic terms, and the blemishes which stained each period of frontier settlement have tended to fade with time. Perhaps, as Bellow's protagonist Moses Herzog wrote (to himself), 'we have fashioned a new utopian history, an idyll, comparing the present to an imaginary past, because we hate the world as it is.'[1] Certainly the fur trade has generally been represented as a glorious episode in the opening of the West,[2] and the trapper, in Goetzman's words, is 'a figure of American mythology rather than history'.[3]

There is, as Sauer has argued, 'a dark obverse' to this romanticised view of American history.[4] The fur trade was an early stage in the progressive dissipation of the American environment. In any assessment of the fur trade as a frontier stage of occupance both the practical accomplishments and the destructive environmental impact should be weighed.

The assessment begins with the actors, who were a small, diverse group of men. The trappers and traders were complex characters, and their motivations for entering the fur trade were varied and probably ambigiuous. They were generally young men in their twenties and thirties. The majority of the trappers were married, although the American Fur Company preferred single men. They were mostly drawn from rural areas of Canada, the Midwest and the Upper South.[5] There is reason to believe that the Rocky Mountain Trapping System attracted a rougher type of individual than the Upper Missouri

Fur Trade which, by comparison, was a steady, mundane occupation. To Edwin Denig the trappers were a 'desperate set of men', more outlandish and brutal than the traders, and more than half-Indian in appearance and habits.[6]

At least three stereotypes have been used to categorise the Rocky Mountain trappers.[7] Each one, like most reasonable stereotypes, is partly valid. The trapper has been portrayed as an epic hero who confronted and partially tamed the wilderness. Conversely, he has been cast as an outsider, a daring but degraded character who was escaping the strictures of a civilised society. To these standard stereotypes Goetzman has added a third which seems to be most tenable: the trapper was a Jacksonian man, an 'expectant capitalist' like most other Americans of that time. Goetzman substantiates his thesis with statistical evidence which indicates that a primary motivation for participating in the fur trade was to accumulate capital quickly. This capital could subsequently be invested in more permanent and less demanding occupations.[8]

Each of these stereotypes draws support from the contemporary literature of the fur trade. Zenas Leonard, as noted above, was an expectant capitalist who entered the Rocky Mountain Trapping System with the hope of making a fortune from what he termed a 'toilsome occupation'.[9] In this endeavour, unlike most of his peers,[10] Leonard was partially successful. Following the disintegration of Bonneville's schemes in 1835, Leonard returned to Clearfield Country, Pennsylvania with $1,100 accumulated capital from five years' labour. Some of his colleagues, however, were unwilling or unable to leave the Rocky Mountains:

> Many were anxious to return to the States, but feared to do so, lest the offended law might hold them responsible for misdemeanors committed previous to their embarking in the trapping business, and others could not be persuaded to do so for any price — declaring that civilized life had no charms for them.[11]

Some trappers, therefore, were escapists who, in Russells's words, had been 'banished to the wilderness' by 'some mishap in life'.[12] Others, like Russell, were romantics who developed an attachment to the remote, solitary life in the

Rocky Mountains.[13] Most, perhaps, were simply men trying to earn a living. The categories overlap and in any one trapper motivations surely varied with time, experience, even with mood.

Like most frontiersmen, the trappers and traders predominantly viewed the environment with antipathy. Romanticism was not allowed to interfere with the pragmatic aspects of making the wilderness productive.[14] The trappers and traders were determined to draw from the environment any resource that was easily exploitable and valuable. When the resources of one area were depleted they moved on to exploit other areas of frontier opportunity. This was characteristic of the settlement process in North America which, in Zelinsky's words, 'can be viewed as a series of environmental traumas or conflicts, in each of which the modern American has won the immediate decision through a technical knockout'.[15]

The fur trade was never an important part of the American economy: only in one year (1833) during the 1820s and 1830s did fur exports from the United States exceed $800,000.[16] However, contrary to Clayton, the fur trade was extremely important in the regional economy of the Trans-Missouri West, particularly with reference to the growth of St Louis.

St Louis was the major collecting and dispersing depot for furs and trade goods. It is estimated that from 1807 to 1840 an average of $200,000–$300,000 worth of furs were channelled annually through St Louis to the east coast and Western Europe. The value of the return flow of trade goods was about the same.[17] This represents an early stage in Vance's mercantile model of settlement, and it supports Harold Innis' thesis that the trade in staples was of basic importance to the economic development of North America.[18] The fur trade stimulated the early growth of St Louis, established a spirit of enterprise, and resulted in an accumulation of knowledge and capital that was a prerequisite to the diversification of the wholesaling base of the city.

Thomas Jefferson, it may be recalled, envisaged the fur trade as the overture to the American settlement of the West. In this geopolitical context the fur trade accomplished a great deal. The leading trappers were well aware of the catalytic role they were playing in the settlement process. In their 1830 letter to John Eaton, the Secretary of War, Smith, Jackson and Sublette warned of the danger of British activities in Oregon, and they emphasised that the American government should counteract this presence by utilising the transcontinental routeway which the trappers had established. Having thus stated 'the facts', Smith, Jackson and Sublette felt that they had 'complied with their duty, and rendered an acceptable service to the administration'.[19]

The trappers completed the initial work of American exploration in the West. It was an unsophisticated process compared to the scientific, government-sponsored surveys which followed after 1840. Generally the trappers' explorations were a by-product of the search for furs. Nevertheless, this conversion of second-degree and third-degree geographical knowledge into first-degree knowledge expressed on maps was a major achievement of the fur trade.[20] By 1840 the transcontinental trails were established, the main tenets of western geography were known, and the West had become, in Goetzmann's words, 'a place to move into — to occupy and settle and develop'.[21] Jefferson's vision of the fur trade as a preliminary stage in the settlement of the West had been realised.

The fur trade was instrumental in the establishment of two of the most important routeways in the early development of the West — The Missouri River and the Oregon Trail. The Missouri River never fulfilled its promise as a transcontinental channel of commerce and migration: The Passage to India proved to be no more than a 'macrogeographical dream'.[22] The Missouri River did, however, afford access to the northern Great Plains and Rocky Mountains. In the three decades following 1840 the river was used as a transportation line by fur traders, miners, the military and, eventually, by settlers. Dependable steamboat service, first introduced on the upper Missouri by the American Fur Company in 1831, continued to expand and reached a peak in the decade 1860 to 1870. Thereafter the railroads cut across the plains from Iowa, Minnesota and the eastern Dakotas, and the river route was truncated.

William Ashley and Jedediah Smith established the concept of a central route to the Pacific in the 1820s. In the following

decade Nathaniel Wyeth, Captain Bonneville and Joe Walker
added substance to this concept and proved the practicality
of the Oregon and California trails. Walker, Tom Fitzpatrick
and Caleb Greenwood, amongst other trappers, continued to
apply their accumulated geographical knowledge in the 1840s
by guiding emigrant trains to the Pacific. Justifiably this forg-
ing of the emigrant trails has been described as 'the climax of
the "mountain man" era of western exploration'.[23]

After the collapse of the Rocky Mountain Trapping System
the trappers formed the vanguard of American settlement in
Oregon, California, and New Mexico. Fehrman in his statistical analysis of the biographical sketches that were included
in Hafen's 'Mountain Man' series, concluded that 90.5 per
cent of the trappers (218 men) eventually died to the west of
the Mississippi. The four areas of Missouri (41), California
(39), New Mexico (31), and Oregon (28) accounted for 64 per
cent of these men.[24]

This migration of what Merk derisively called 'broken-
down trappers' is epitomised by Robert Newell's exhortation
to his colleague and brother-in-law Joe Meek in 1840:

'Come,' said Newell to Meek, 'We are done with this life in
the mountains — done with wading in beaver-dams and
freezing or starving alternatively — done with Indian trading
and Indian fighting . . . Let us go down to the Wallamet
and take farms.'[25]

There the trappers formed 'a nucleus of a steadily growing
pioneer force'.[26] With typical frontier versatility they engaged
in a wide variety of occupations, both in farming and in
trade. They were often successful because men were in short
supply on the frontier, particularly men with accumulated
capital (no matter how small) and experience. Many trappers
became prominent members of these embryonic communities.
Joe Meek, for example, was Oregon's first sheriff, elected in
1843, and first US Marshall, appointed in 1848. Robert
Newell was elected to membership in Oregon's first territorial
legislature in 1849 and in the same year he was named one
of the three United States sub-Indian agents for Oregon
Territory. As Zelinsky has pointed out in his Doctrine of
First Effective Settlement, 'the activities of a few hundred,

or even a few score, initial colonizers can mean much more for the cultural geography of a place than the contributions of tens of thousands of new immigrants a few generations later'.[27]

This trickle of American settlers to Oregon swelled into a flood after 1843. To the British Oregon remained primarily a 'company frontier'; to the Americans it was part of their 'natural frontier' and their national destiny. In 1841 Governor Simpson responded with a 'counter-immigration' policy, but his efforts were in vain. Four years later the Hudson's Bay Company moved the headquarters of the Columbia District north to Fort Victoria on Vancouver Island, and the 'Oregon Question' was virtually settled.[28]

In a spatial sense, however, the influence of the fur trade on the northern Great Plains and Rocky Mountains was generally rather transitory. Derwent Whittlesey, writing in 1929, argued that the human occupance in an area could be divided into discrete stages, each stage being linked genetically 'to its forbear and to its offspring'.[29] Perhaps the structure of an oil painting is analogous to this process of sequent occupance. Each successive layer of paint builds on the foundation of previous layers and largely obliterates them. Eventually only remnants of the earlier layers show through on the landscape. The fur trade influenced the stages of occupance which followed close after, but its imprint was soon erased from the land by new forms of use.

The geography of the missionary frontier on the northern Great Plains and in Oregon was greatly influenced by the existent network of the fur trade. This is hardly surprising, because the missionaries, like the traders, arranged their system primarily to afford access to the Indians.

The missionaries who worked among the Indians on the Upper Missouri in the 1840s and 1850s used the trading posts as bases and the company steamboats for transportation. The American Fur Company welcomed the missionaries, believing that peaceful, christianised Indians would make more dependable producers. The trading posts became the nuclei of later Catholic parishes in the Dakotas and Montana.[30]

In Oregon the mission frontier on the Columbia Plain and to the west of the Cascades was closely fitted to the patterns of the fur trade. In the second half of the 1830s missionaries (such as Marcus Whitman and Henry Spaulding) travelled with the fur parties to Oregon, and in subsequent years the Platte Overland Route served as the main line of communication between the missions and their headquarters in New England. The missions were located near the Hudson's Bay Company posts for the purposes of protection, companionship, and access to the Indians and the main routes of travel. The influence of the fur trade was fundamental. Indeed, in Meinig's opinion, 'without that established framework, the Oregon missions could have been neither inaugurated nor maintained'.[31]

Until 1870 the military frontier closely traced the general pattern of transportation and locations established during the fur trade. The forts, like the trading posts, were generally built on the terraces of the Missouri, within easy reach of the river for the bulk transportation of men and goods, but above the level of the flood waters. Ideally the sites provided fresh water, grass for forage, and flat land for the same type of small-scale agriculture that had been practised around the trading posts.

There was, however, very little continuance of site, as opposed to situation, even before 1870. Of 68 military forts established on the northern Great Plains from 1846 to 1891 only six were built around the nucleus of a former trading post.[32] In 1855, for example, the army purchased Fort Pierre from the American Fur Company to serve as a base for operations against the Dakota. They soon found that Fort Pierre was quite unsuitable for its new role. The buildings were in poor repair, there was insufficient pasture for the animals, and there was no fuel within twenty miles. A quarter of a century of continued occupance by traders had exhausted the resources of the surrounding country. Consequently in 1857 Fort Pierre was abandoned. By 1859 the post lay in ruins.[33]

After 1870 military forts were dispersed throughout the northern Great Plains to protect the emigrant routes, the Bozman Trail, and the workers on the Union Pacific and Northern Pacific Railroads, and to support the relentless campaign that was waged against the Indians after the Battle of the Little Big Horn. By the 1880s the military had virtually crushed the resistance on the northern Great Plains and the surviving Indians were incarcerated on reservations. The fur trade, mission, and military frontiers — geographic systems which were predicated in one form or another on the Indians — gave way to new patterns on the land. Thereafter towns developed as central places on an agricultural frontier not as entrepots in a mercantilist system.

Symbolically the northern loop of the Oregon Trail, which traced the North Platte and Sweetwater to the Big Sandy and Green, was abandoned after 1870 when the Union Pacific was built on a direct route across the Great Divide Basin. The Oregon Trail, Vance explains, 'was located where nature came closest to maintaining the traveler rather than where the effort was least'. The Union Pacific on the other hand (and subsequently Interstate 80) were established along lines of 'least wasted effort' in an attempt to reduce overall costs.[34] South Pass, the most important gateway in the early settlement of the West, is now crossed by Highway 28, a rather remote state road. Contrary to Turner, a neat continuity of routes did not exist on this frontier.[35] Instead routes were altered as the purposes of transportation changed.

In comparison with later stages of frontier settlement the fur trade barely scratched the surface of the West. The trappers and traders were too few in number, too limited in technology, and too focused in their objectives of exploitation for it to be otherwise. The fur trade did, however, set the pace for subsequent Euro-American activity in the West. The attitude of rapacious, short-term exploitation which was imprinted during the fur trade persisted after 1840 as the focus shifted from furs to minerals, timber, land, and water.

The fur trade did, of course, result in a serious depletion of beaver reserves throughout the northern Great Plains and Rocky Mountains. Yet, as Denig noted in 1854, beaver populations quickly rebounded after 1840 once the pressure of continuous overtrapping was removed:

> This animal has been trapped and killed to such an extent as to threaten his entire extinction, though for the last 10 or 12 years, since beaver trapping by large bodies of men has been abandoned, they have greatly increased.[36]

Even in the Rocky Mountains total depletion was averted

by the decline in the demand for beaver pelts in the late 1830s (aided, perhaps, by favourable trends in the natural cycle). The beaver was given a 'breathing-time', wrote Ruxton in 1849, 'and this valuable fur-bearing animal, which otherwise would, in the course of a few years, have become extinct, has now a chance of multiplying, and will in a short time again become abundant'.[37] By the late 1840s beaver were again numerous on the Arkansas and Platte rivers and in the Parks of Colorado.

Nevertheless, unregulated trapping continued throughout the second half of the nineteenth century, often as a secondary activity by miners and farmers. By 1900 in Colorado, for example, beaver populations were again dangerously low.[38] Thereafter, largely as a result of the pioneering work of Aldo Leopold who sparked the wilderness movement, beaver were protected by state legislation. Public trapping was restricted to designated periods of the year and in the twentieth century the streams of the western United States once again teem with beaver.

Protection, of course, came almost too late for the bison herds. By 1890, when many Americans first became aware of the dimensions of the slaughter, less than 1,000 bison remained as remnants of the once massive herds. As early as 1840, as a result of hunting by the trappers and the Indians, bison were no longer found to the west of the Rocky Mountains. On the northern Great Plains, however, the great destruction came not before 1840 but in the 1870s when the railroads afforded easy access for hide hunters and so-called sportsmen who systematically destroyed the herds. Even as late as 1854, Denig opined that 'Buffalo are very numerous and we do not, after 20 years experience, find that they decrease in this quarter, although upward of 150,000 are killed annually throughout the extent of our trade'.[39]

Nevertheless, the attitude of unconstrained exploitation was inculcated during the initial stages of the Upper Missouri Fur Trade. The traders began the process of depletion by furnishing the producing Indians with guns and a commercial incentive to produce hides and tongues above the needs of their own subsistence and inter-tribal trade. The herds were saved from greater destruction before 1840 only because the market and the scale of production were limited.[40]

The fur trade was also directly responsible for extensive deforestation of the riparian woodlands along the upper Missouri. Large supplies of wood were needed to stoke the steamboats, to construct the batteaux, and to build, maintain, and heat the trading posts. By 1854, for example, Fort Pierre consumed 1,000 cords of wood each year. Wood for construction was carried on rafts from 80 miles above the post and wood for fuel was hauled more than ten miles.[41]

The repercussions of this deforestation were also felt by the village Indians on the upper Missouri. In the second half of the 1840s the Mandan—Hidatsa were forced to move their villages 40 miles upstream from the traditional Knife River sites because of a serious shortage of wood. The traders, being dependent on the Indians for production, followed suit and built a trading post, Fort Berthold, at the new site.

According to Chittenden, 'The relation of the trader to the Indian was the most natural and congenial of any which the two races have ever sustained toward each other'.[42] The traders and the Indians interlocked in what Spicer has called a non-directed form of culture contact.[43] Neither culture was locally dominant but each accepted innovations from the other according to its needs. The traders adopted Indian foods and clothes, assimilated Indian geographic knowledge, were subject to Indian laws, and were encouraged by the companies to unite with Indian women. The Indians in turn welcomed the trade goods that the traders brought and willingly expanded their production of robes to meet the new demands.

Yet in the process of this contact the relationship between the Indian and the trader soured. The Indians became increasingly reliant on European trade goods, and the deleterious effects of alcohol and disease strained the existing social systems. The introduction of new commercial motivations weakened the traditional religious aspects of hunting which had given meaning and cohesion to Indian societies. The Indian was co-opted as a partner in the destruction of his most fundamental resource, the bison herds. Unintentionally, unthinkingly, the fur trader undermined the Indian societies and paved the way for a settlement process that would eventually result in the dispossession of the Indians' lands and in the shattering of Indian culture.

Viewed in the broadest sense the fur trade was the vanguard of a massive wave of Euro-American colonisation which brought into contact two sets of cultures with disparate and irreconcilable ways of life. The native Americans were, to use Dasmann's terminology, ecosystem people.[44] They were dependent on a single ecosystem, or at the most a few adjacent ecosystems, for their survival. If they violated the ecosystem — by persistent bison overkill, for example — then their very existence was jeopardised. Intimately connected with the land by livelihood and religion, ecosystem people were basically conservationist.

The fur trappers and traders were biosphere people. They were not dependent on a single ecosystem, but drew support (equipment, trade goods, supplies, markets) from many areas. As biosphere people the trappers and traders possessed a licence for unconstrained exploitation that was untenable for a people who were totally dependent on the ecosystem. They were able to exert great pressure on the environments of the northern Great Plains and Rocky Mountains with relative impunity. When these environments had been stripped of their furs the trappers and traders simply turned to other resources and to other areas. The impact of this exploitation was destructive to the physical environment and to the native inhabitants alike. Perhaps it is through this dark lens, rather than through the rosy lens of frontier romanticism, that the fur trade of the West should be viewed.

Notes

1. S. Bellow, *Herzog* (Greenwich, Conn: Fawcett Publications Inc., 1965), pp. 202–3.

2. See, for example, the treatment in J. A. Hawgood, *America's Western Frontiers* (New York: Alfred A. Knopf, 1967), pp. 93–128. On the other hand, R. A. Bartlett in *The New Country* (New York: Oxford University Press, 1974) devotes considerable attention to the fur trade as a destructive form of occupance.

3. W. H. Goetzman, 'The Mountain Man as Jacksonian Man', *American Quarterly*, vol. 15 (1963), p. 402.

4. Sauer, 'Theme of Plant and Animal Destruction', p. 49.

5. R. J. Fehrman, 'The Mountain Men — A Statistical View', in Hafen, *The Mountain Men and The Fur Trade of the Far West*, vol. 10, pp. 9–15. Also, R. Crooks to P. B. Barbeau, 28 March 1842, *American Fur Company Letterbooks*. Crooks explicitly stated in this letter that

he preferred to employ young single men, aged 21—5 who were 'country men rather than from cities'.

6. Ewers, *Five Indian Tribes*, p. 149.

7. H. L. Carter and M. C. Spencer, 'Stereotypes of the Mountain Man', *The Western Historical Quarterly*, vol. 6 (1975), pp. 17—32. See also, Smith, *Virgin Land*, pp. 88—98.

8. Goetzman, 'The Mountain Man as Jacksonian Man', pp.402—15.

9. Wagner, *Zenas Leonard*, pp. 280—2.

10. Carter and Spencer, 'Stereotypes of the Mountain Man', p.26.

11. Wagner, *Zenas Leonard*, p. 281.

12. Haines, *Journal of a Trapper*, p. 84.

13. Russell strove to express his feelings for the Rocky Mountains. See, for example, his description of the Lamar Valley of northwestern Wyoming and the poem which he wrote as a eulogy to his life as a trapper. Haines, *Journal of a Trapper*, pp. 46, 153—4.

14. Nash, *Wilderness and the American Mind*, p. 65.

15. W. Zelinsky, *The Cultural Geography of the United States* (Englewood Cliffs, New Jersey: Prentice Hall, 1973), p. 61.

16. Clayton, 'The Growth and Economic Significance of the American Fur Trade', pp. 71—2.

17. Chittenden, *The American Fur Trade of the Far West*, vol. 1, p.8.

18. J. E. Vance, Jr *The Merchant's World* (Englewood Cliffs, New Jersey: Prentice Hall, 1970), pp. 148—59. H. A. Innis, *The Fur Trade in Canada* (New Haven: Yale University Press, 1962), pp. 383—402.

19. Quoted in Morgan, *Jedediah Smith*, pp. 343—8.

20. The concept of graduations of geographic knowledge is presented in J. L. Allen, 'An Analysis of the Exploratory Process: The Lewis and Clarke Expedition of 1804—1806', *Geographical Review*, vol. 62 (1972), pp. 13—39.

21. W. H. Goetzmann, *Exploration and Empire* (New York: Alfred A. Knopf, 1906), p. 179.

22. Allen, 'An Analysis of the Exploratory Process', p. 39.

23. Goetzmann, *Exploration and Empire*, p. 169.

24. Fehrman, 'The Mountain Men — A Statistical View', in Hafen, *The Mountain Men and the Fur Trade of the Far West*, vol. 10, p.14.

25. Victor, *River of the West*, p. 204.

26. Merk, *Fur Trade and Empire*, xxvii.

27. Zelinsky, *Cultural Geography of the United States*, p. 14.

28. Meinig, *The Great Columbia Plain*, pp. 115, 146—7.

29. D. Whittlesey, 'Sequent Occupance', *Annals*, Association of American Geographers, vol. 19 (1929), pp. 162—5.

30. Sunder, *Fur Trade on the Upper Missouri*, p. 100.

31. Meinig, *The Great Columbia Plain*, p. 130.

32. R. H. Mattison, 'The Military Frontier on the Upper Missouri', *Nebraska History*, vol. 37 (1956), pp. 159—82; and 'The Army Post on the Northern Plains, 1865—1885', *Nebraska History*, vol. 35 (1954), pp. 17—44.

33. F. T. Wilson, 'Old Fort Pierre and Its Neighbours', *South Dakota Historical Collections*, vol. 1 (1902), pp. 259—440.

34. J. E. Vance, Jr, 'The Oregon Trail and the Union Pacific Railroad: A Contrast in Purpose', *Annals*, Association of American Geographers, vol. 60 (1961), pp. 357—79.

35. F. J. Turner, *The Significance of the Frontier in American History*. (Madison: State Historical Society of Wisconsin, 1894). Turner wrote (p.13) that 'the buffalo trail became the Indian trail, and this became the trader's "trace"; the trails widened into roads, and the roads into turnpikes, and these in turn were transformed into railroads.'

36. Hewitt, *Indian Tribes*, p. 411. The artist Rudolph Kurz made the same point in 1851 when he wrote: 'The low price placed on their skins is to the advantage of the beavers. There are said to be a great many of them not far from here [Fort Union]. . . J.N.B. Hewitt, *The Journal of Rudolph Friederich Kurz* (Fairfield, Washington: Viking Press, n.d.), p. 81.

37. G. F. Ruxton, *Adventures in Mexico and the Rocky Mountains* (London: John Murray, 1849), pp. 239—40.

38. Lechleitner, *Wild Mammals of Colorado*, pp. 125—6.

39. Hewitt, *Indian Tribes*, p. 410.

40. The traders did occasionally try to limit robe production, but the motives were economic, not conservationist. In 1838, for example, Ramsey Crooks advised Chouteau to 'restrain the Indians from over-exploiting'. There was a poor demand for robes that year and Crooks feared that the market would be swamped and the price would fall. R. Crooks to Pratte, Chouteau and Co., 28 July 1838, *American Fur Company Letterbooks*.

41. 'Fort Pierre in 1854', *New York Daily Tribune*, 6 April 1854, reprinted in *The Museum of the Fur Trade Quarterly*, vol. 2 (1975), pp. 8—9.

42. Chittenden, *American Fur Trade of the Far West*, vol. 1, p.8.

43. E. H. Spicer, 'Types of Contact and Processes of Change', in E. H. Spicer (ed.), *Perspectives in American Indian Culture Change* (Chicago: University of Chicago Press, 1961), pp. 517—44.

44. R. Dasmann, 'Future Primitive', *The CoEvolution Quarterly* No. 11 (1976), pp. 26—31.

Bibliography

Manuscripts

American Fur Company Letterbooks. New York Historical
 Society, New York City
Ashley (William H.) Papers. Missouri Historical Society, St
 Louis
Chouteau Collection, including the Fort Union and Fort
 Tecumseh-Pierre Letterbooks. Missouri Historical Society,
 St Louis
Dougherty (John) Papers. Missouri Historical Society, St
 Louis
Drips (Andrew) Papers. Missouri Historical Society, St Louis
Fur Trade Envelope. Missouri Historical Society, St Louis
Indian Trade Papers. Missouri Historical Society, St Louis
Selected Items Relating to the Fur Trade. Bancroft Library,
 University of California-Berkeley
Sublette (William L.) Papers. Missouri Historical Society, St
 Louis

Newspapers

Beall, T.J. 'Recollections of William Craig', *Lewiston Morning
 Tribune,* 3 March 1918
'First Steamboat to Fort Union', *New York American* (31
 July 1832), reprinted in *The Museum of the Fur Trade
 Quarterly,* vol. 12 (1976), pp. 1–12

'Fort Pierre in 1854', *New York Daily Tribune* (6 April 1854), reprinted in *The Museum of the Fur Trade Quarterly*, vol. 12 (1976), pp. 1—12
Missouri Advocate and *St Louis Enquirer*, 8 October 1825
Missouri Herald and *St Louis Advertiser*, 8 November 1826
Missouri Intelligencer, 11 March 1826; 28 September 1826
Missouri Republican, 3 October 1825; 21 September 1826
St Louis Enquirer, 11 March 1826

Books, Reports, and Articles

Abel, A.H. (ed.). *Chardon's Journal at Fort Clark, 1834—9* (Pierre, South Dakota: State Historical Society, 1932)
Alford, T.L. 'The West as a Desert in American Thought prior to Long's 1819—20 Expedition', *Journal of the West*, vol. 8 (1969), pp. 515—25
Allen, J.L. 'An Analysis of the Exploratory Process: The Lewis and Clark Expedition of 1804—1806', *Geographical Review*, vol. 62 (1972), pp. 13—39
—— *Passage Through the Garden: Lewis and Clark and the Image of the American Northwest* (Urbana: University of Illinois Press, 1975)
—— 'Geographical Knowledge and American Images of Louisiana', *The Western Historical Quarterly*, vol. 2 (1971), pp. 151—70
Annals of the Congress of the United States. Eighth Congress, Second Session, 1803 (Washington, DC: Gales and Seaton, 1852)
Audubon, M.R. and Coues, E. (eds.). *Audubon and His Journals* (New York: Charles Scribner's Sons, 1897)
Balwin, L.D. *The Keelboat Age on Western Waters* (Pittsburgh: University of Pittsburgh Press, 1941)
Bartlett, R.A. *The New Country* (New York: Oxford University Press, 1974)
Beidleman, R.G. 'Nathaniel Wyeth's Fort Hall', *Oregon Historical Quarterly*, vol. 58 (1957), pp. 157—250
Bellow, S. *Herzog* (Greenwich, Connecticut: Fawcett Publications, 1965)
Berkhofer, R.J. Jr. *A Behavioural Approach to Historical Analysis* (New York: The Free Press, 1969)

Borchert, J.R. 'American Metropolitan Evolution', *Geographical Review*, vol. 57 (1967), pp. 301—32

Bowden, M.J. 'The Perception of the Western Interior of the United States, 1800—1870: A Problem in Historical Geosophy' *Proceedings*, Association of American Geographers, vol. 1 (1969), pp. 16—21

Brackenridge, H. *Journal of a Voyage up the Missouri in 1811*, vol. 5 of Thwaites, R.G. (ed.) *Early Western Travels* (Cleveland: Arthur H. Clark Co., 1904)

Briggs, H.E. 'Pioneer River Transportation in the Dacotahs', *North Dakota Historical Quarterly*, vol. 3 (1929), pp. 159—82

Brookfield, H.C. 'On the Environment as Perceived', in Board, C., Chorley, R.J., Haggett, P., and Stoddart, D.R. (eds.), *Progress in Geography*, vol. 1 (London: Edward Arnold, 1969), pp. 51—80

Brooks, G.R. (ed.). 'The Private Journal of Robert Campbell', *Bulletin of Missouri Historical Society*, vol. 20 (1963—4), pp. 3—24, 107—18

Camp, C.L. 'Jedediah Smith's First Far-Western Exploration', *The Western Historical Quarterly*, vol. 4 (1973), pp. 151—70

Carter, H.L. *Dear Old Kit* (Norman: University of Oklahoma Press, 1968)

—— and Spencer, M.C. 'Stereotypes of the Mountain Man', *The Western Historical Quarterly*, vol. 6 (1975), pp. 402—15

Chappell, P.E. 'A History of the Missouri River', *Transactions, Kansas State Historical Society*, vol. 9 (1905—6), pp. 237—316

Chittenden, H.M. *History of Early Steamboat Navigation on the Missouri River* (New York: F.P. Harper, 1903)

—— *The American Fur Trade of the Far West* (New York: F.R. Harper, 1902)

Christman, G.M. 'The Mountain Bison', *American West*, vol. 8 (1971), pp. 44—7

Clayton, J.L. 'The Growth and Economic Significance of the American Fur Trade, 1790—1890', in *Aspects of the Fur Trade* (St Paul: Minnesota Historical Society, 1967), pp. 62—72

Colorado Game, Fish, and Parks Department. *The Beaver in Colorado. Its Biology, Ecology, Management and Economics*. Technical Bulletin No. 17 (1964)

Coues, E. (ed.). *Forty Years a Fur Trader on the Upper Missouri: The Personal Narrative of Charles Larpenteur, 1833—72* (New York: Francis P. Harper, 1898)

Cowan, J.M. 'The Fur Trade and the Fur Cycle: 1825—1857', *British Columbia Historical Quarterly*, vol. 2 (1938), pp. 19—30

Dale, H.C. *The Ashley-Smith Explorations and the Discovery of a Central Route to the Pacific, 1822—29* (Glendale: Arthur H. Clark Co., 1941)

Dasmann, R. 'Future Primitive', *The CoEvolution Quarterly*, No. 11 (1976), pp. 26—31

Davis, W.B. *The Recent Mammals of Idaho* (Caldwell, Idaho: Caxton Printers, 1939)

'Deposition and Interrogation of Michael E. Immel, June 25, 1821', *Bulletin of Missouri Historical Society*, vol. 4 (1948), pp. 78—81

DeVoto, B. *Across the Wide Missouri* (Boston: Houghton Mifflin Co., 1947)

Dollar, C.D. 'The High Plains Smallpox Epidemic of 1837—38', *The Western Historical Quarterly*, vol. 8 (1977), pp. 15—38

Douglas, W.B. 'Manuel Lisa', *Missouri Historical Society Collections*, vol. 3 (1911), pp. 233—68, 367—406

Elliott, T.G. (ed.). 'The Peter Skene Ogden Journals', *Oregon Historical Society Quarterly*, vol. 10 (1909), pp. 330—65

Estergreen, M.M. *Kit Carson: A Portrait in Courage* (Norman: University of Oklahoma Press, 1962)

Ewers, J.C. (ed.). *Zenas Leonard: Fur Trapper* (Norman: University of Oklahoma Press, 1959)

—— 'Influence of the Fur Trade on Indians of the Northern Plains', in Bolus, M. (ed.), *People and Pelts* (Winnipeg: Peguis Publishers, 1972), pp. 1—26

—— *The Horse in Blackfoot Culture* (Washington, DC: Smithsonian Institution Press, 1969)

—— 'The Indian Trade of the Upper Missouri before Lewis and Clark: An Interpretation', *Bulletin, Missouri Historical Society*, vol. 10 (1954), pp. 429—46

—— (ed.). *Five Indian Tribes of the Upper Missouri* (Norman: University of Oklahoma Press, 1961)

Fenneman, N.J. *Physiography of Western United States* (New York: McGraw Hill, 1931)

Fletcher, A.C. and LaFlesche, F. *The Omaha Tribe* (Lincoln: University of Nebraska Press, 1972)

Gibson, J.R. *Imperial Russia in Frontier America* (New York: Oxford University Press, 1976)

Goetzman, W.H. 'The Mountain Man as Jacksonian Man', *American Quarterly*, vol. 15 (1963), pp. 402–15

—— *Exploration and Empire* (New York: Alfred A. Knopf, 1906)

Hafen, L.R. 'The Early Fur Trade Posts on the South Platte', *Mississippi Historical Review*, vol. 7 (1925), pp. 334–41

—— 'Fort Jackson and the Early Fur Trade on the South Platte', *Colorado Magazine*, vol. 5 (1928), pp. 9–17

—— 'Old Fort Lupton and Its Founder', *Colorado Magazine*, vol. 6 (1929), pp. 220–6

—— 'Fort St. Vrain', *Colorado Magazine*, vol. 29 (1957), pp. 241–55

—— 'Fort Vasquez', *Colorado Magazine*, vol. 41 (1964), pp. 198–212

—— 'With Fur Traders in Colorado, 1839–40: The Journal of E. Willard Smith', *Colorado Magazine*, vol. 27 (1950), pp. 161–88

—— 'The Bean-Sinclair Party of Rocky Mountain Trappers, 1830–32', *Colorado Magazine*, vol. 21 (1954), pp. 161–71

—— *The Mountain Men and the Fur Trade of the Far West*, (Glendale, California: Arthur H. Clark Co., 1965)

Haines, F. 'The Northward Spread of Horses among the Plains Indians', *American Anthropologist*, vol. 40 (1938), pp. 429–37

Hamilton W.J. *American Mammals* (New York and London: McGraw Hill, 1939)

Hanson, C.E. Jr. 'A Paper of Vermillion', *The Museum of the Fur Trade Quarterly*, vol. 7 (1971), pp. 1–3

—— 'Castoreum', *The Museum of the Fur Trade Quarterly*, vol. 8 (1972), pp. 1–4

—— 'The Fort Pierre–Fort Laramie Trail', *The Museum of the Fur Trade Quarterly*, vol. 1 (1965), pp. 3–7

Hawgood, J.A. *America's Western Frontiers* (New York: Alfred A. Knopf, 1967)

Hermann, B. *The Lousianna Purchase* (Washington, DC: Government Printing Office, 1898)

Hewitt, J.N.B. (ed.). *The Journal of Rudolph Friederich Kurz*

(Fairfield, Washington: Viking Press, n.d.)

—— (ed.). *Indian Tribes of the Upper Missouri.* Forty-sixth Annual Report of the Bureau of American Ethnology, 1928–9 (Washington, DC: Government Printing Office, 1930)

Holder, P. 'The Fur Trade as Seen from the Indian Point of View', in McDermott, J.F. (ed.), *The Frontier Re-examined* (Urbana: University of Illinois Press, 1967), pp. 129–39

—— *The Hoe and the Horse on the Plains* (Lincoln: University of Nebraska Press, 1970)

Hunter, L.C. *Steamboats on Western Rivers* (Cambridge: Harvard University Press, 1949)

Innis, H.A. *The Fur Trade in Canada* (New Haven: Yale University Press, 1962)

Irving, W. *Astoria* (New York: The Century Co., 1909)

—— *The Adventures of Captain Bonneville* (New York: John B. Alden, 1886)

Jackson, D. and Spence, M.L. (eds.). *The Expeditions of John Charles Fremont* (Urbana: University of Illinois Press, 1970)

Jacobs, W.R. *Wilderness Policy and Indian Gifts: The Northern Colonial Frontier, 1748–63* (Lincoln: University of Nebraska Press, 1963)

—— 'The Indian and the Frontier in American History — A Need for Revision', *The Western Historical Quarterly*, vol. 4 (1973), pp. 43–56

Johansen, D.O. (ed.). *Robert Newell's Memoranda* (Portland: Champoeg Press, 1969)

Johnson, E.R. *Ocean and Inland Water Transportation.* (New York and London: D. Appleton Co., 1911)

Josephy, A.M. *The Nez Perce Indians and the Opening of the Northwest* (New Haven and London: Yale University Press 1965)

Kroeber, A.L. *Cultural and Natural Areas of Native North America* (Berkeley and Los Angeles: University of California Press, 1953)

Lass, W.E. *A History of Steamboating on the Upper Missouri River* (Lincoln: University of Nebraska Press, 1962)

Lavender, D. *Bent's Fort* (Garden City: Doubleday and Co., 1954)

Lechleitner, R.R. *Wild Mammals of Colorado* (Boulder: Pruett

Publishing Co., 1969)

Lewis, G.M. 'Three Centuries of Desert Concepts in the Cis-Rocky Mountain West', *Journal of the West,* vol. 4 (1965), pp. 457—68

—— 'The Great Plains and Its Image of Flatness', *Journal of the West,* vol. 6 (1967), pp. 11—26

Lowenthal, D. 'Past Time, Present Place: Landscape and Memory', *Geographical Review,* vol. 65 (1975), pp. 1—36

Martin, C. 'Wildlife Diseases as a Factor in the Depopulation of the North American Indian', *The Western Historical Quarterly,* vol. 7 (1976), pp. 47—62

Mattison, R.H. 'The Military Frontier on the Upper Missouri', *Nebraska History,* vol. 37 (1956), pp. 159—82

—— 'The Army Post on the Northern Plains, 1865—1885', *Nebraska History,* vol. 35 (1954), pp. 17—44

Prince Maximilian of Wied. Neuweid. *Travels in the Interior of North America, 1832—34,* vols. 22—4 of Thwaites, R.G. (ed.), *Early Western Travels* (Cleveland: Arthur H. Clark, 1904—7)

McCracken, H. and Van Cleeve H. *Trapping* (New York: A.S. Barnes and Co., 1947)

McDermott, J.F. (ed.). *Up the Missouri with Audubon: The Journal of Edward Harris* (Norman: University of Oklahoma Press, 1951)

Meinig, D.W. *The Great Columbia Plain: A Historical Geography, 1805—1910* (Seattle and London: University of Washington Press, 1968)

Merk, F. *The Oregon Question* (Cambridge: Belknap Press, 1967)

—— (ed.). *Fur Trade and Empire: George Simpson's Journal, 1824—1825* (Cambridge: Belknap Press, 1968)

Metcalf, G. 'The Bull Boat of the Plains Indians and the Fur Trade', *The Museum of the Fur Trade Quarterly,* vol. 8 (1972), pp. 1—10

Miller, C.F. 'The Excavation and Investigation of Fort Lookout II (39LM57) in the Fort Randall Reservoir, South Dakota', in Roberts, F.H.H. (ed.), *River Basin Surveys Papers* (Washington, DC: US Government Printing Office 1960), pp. 55—81

Mishkin, B. *Rank and Warfare among the Plains Indians* (New York: Monographs of the American Ethnological

Society, 1940)

Moodie, D.W. and Ray, A.J. 'Buffalo Migrations in the Canadian Plains', *Plains Anthropologist*, vol. 21 (1976), pp. 45—54

Moore, A.K. *The Frontier Mind* (New York: McGraw Hill, 1963)

Morgan, D.L. *Jedediah Smith and the Opening of the West* (Lincoln: University of Nebraska Press, 1967)

—— (ed.). *The West of William H. Ashley* (Denver: The Old West Publishing Co., 1964)

—— and Harris, E.T. (eds.). *The Rocky Mountain Journals of William Marshall Anderson* (San Marino: The Huntington Library, 1967)

Nash, R. *Wilderness and the American Mind* (New Haven and London: Yale University Press, 1973)

Nichols, R.F. 'The Louisiana Purchase: Challenge and Stimulus to American Democracy', *The Louisiana Historical Quarterly*, vol. 38 (1955), pp. 1—25

Nute, G.L. (ed.). *Calender of the American Fur Company Papers*. Annual Report of the American Historical Association, vol. 2 (Washington, DC: US Government Printing Office, 1945)

Oglesby, R.E. *Manuel Lisa and the Opening of the Missouri Fur Trade* (Norman: University of Oklahoma Press, 1963)

—— 'The Fur Trade as Business', in McDermott, J.F. (ed.), *The Frontier Re-examined* (Urbana: University of Illinois Press, 1967), pp. 111—27

Pearce, R.H. *Savagism and Civilization, A Study of the Indian and the American Mind* (Baltimore: Johns Hopkins Press, 1967)

Phillips, P.C. (ed.). *Life in the Rocky Mountains* (Denver: The Old West Publishing Co., 1940)

—— *The Fur Trade* (Norman: University of Oklahoma Press, 1961)

Porter, C.M. and Hafen, L.R. *Ruxton of the Rockies* (Norman: University of Oklahoma Press, 1950)

Porter, K.W. *John Jacob Astor* (Cambridge: Harvard University Press, 1931)

Prucha, F.D. *American Indian Policy in the Formative Years* (Cambridge: Harvard University Press, 1962)

Ray, A.J. 'Diffusion of Diseases in the Western Interior of

Canada, 1830–1850', *Geographical Review,* vol. 57 (1967), pp. 301–32
–– 'Some Conservation Schemes of the Hudson's Bay Company, 1821–50: An Examination of Resource Management in the Fur Trade', *Journal of Historical Geography,* vol. 1 (1975), pp. 49–68
Rich, E.E. (ed.). *Part of Dispatch from George Simpson, Esqr, Governor of Rupert's Land and to the Governor and Committee of the Hudson's Bay Company, London, March 1 1829, Continued and Completed March 24 and June 25, 1829* (Toronto and London: Publications of the Champlain Society, Hudson's Bay Company, 1947)
–– *The Letters of John McLoughlin, First Series, 1825–38* (Toronto: Champlain Society, 1943–4)
Roe, F.G. *The North American Buffalo* (Toronto: University of Toronto Press, 1951)
Rollins, R.A. *The Discovery of the Oregon Trail* (New York and London: Charles Scribner's Sons, 1935)
Ross, M.C. (ed.). *The West of Alfred Jacob Miller* (Norman: University of Oklahoma Press, 1968)
Russell, O.P. 'Wilderness Rendezvous Period of the American Fur Trade', *Oregon Historical Quarterly,* vol. 42 (1941), pp. 1–47
–– *Firearms, Traps, and Tools of the Mountain Man* (New York: Alfred A. Knopf, 1967)
Ruxton, G.F. *Adventures in Mexico and the Rocky Mountains* (London: John Murray, 1849)
Sage, R. *Scenes in the Rocky Mountains* (Philadelphia: Carey and Hart, 1847)
Sauer, C.O. 'Theme of Plant and Animal Destruction in Economic History', *The Journal of Farm Economics,* vol. 20 (1938), pp. 765–75. Reprinted in *The CoEvolution Quarterly,* vol. 10 (1976), pp. 48–51
Saum, L.O. *The Fur Trader and the Indian* (Seattle and London: University of Washington Press, 1965)
Schorger, A.W. 'A Brief History of the Steel Trap and its Use in North America', *Transactions of the Wisconsin Academy of Sciences, Arts and Letters,* vol. 40 (1951), pp. 171–99
Seton, E.T. *Life Histories of Northern Animals* (New York: Constable and Co., 1910)
Shaler, A.E. 'Beaver Food Utilization Studies', *Journal of*

Wildlife Management, vol. 2 (1938), pp. 215—22

Shepard, P. *Man in the Landscape* (New York: A.A. Knopf, 1967)

Smith, D.R. *The Bighorn Sheep in Idaho* (Boise: Idaho Department of Fish and Game, 1954)

Smith, G.H. *Big Bend Historical Sites* (Lincoln, Nebraska: Smithsonian Institution River Basin Surveys, Publications in Salvage Archaelogy, no. 9, 1968)

Smith, H.N. *Virgin Land: The American West as Symbol and Myth* (New York: Vintage Books, 1950)

Spicer, E.H. 'Types of Contact and Processes of Change', in Spicer, E.H. (ed.), *Perspectives in American Indian Culture Change* (Chicago: University of Chicago Press, 1961)

Steward, J.H. *Basin-Plateau Aboriginal Sociopolitical Groups.* Bureau of American Ethnology Bulletin, no. 120 (Washington, DC: Government Printing Office, 1938)

Stoddart, D.R. 'Organism and Ecosystem as Geographical Models', in Chorley, R.J. and Haggett, P. (eds.), *Integrated Models in Geography* (London: Methuen, 1970), pp. 511—48

Sunder, J.E. *Joshua Pilcher* (Norman: University of Oklahoma Press, 1968)

—— *The Fur Trade on the Upper Missouri, 1840—65* (Norman: University of Oklahoma Press, 1965)

—— *Bill Sublette: Mountain Man* (Norman: University of Oklahoma Press, 1959)

Thornbury, W.D. *Regional Geomorphology of the United States* (New York: John Wiley and Sons, 1965)

Thwaites, R.G. (ed.). *Original Journals of the Lewis and Clark Expedition, 1804—1806* (New York: Dodd, Mead and Co., 1905)

Turner, F.J. *The Significance of the Frontier in American History* (Madison: State Historical Society of Wisconsin, 1894)

Tyler, D.B. *Steam Conquers the Atlantic* (New York and London: D. Appleton-Century Co., 1939)

US Department of Agriculture. *Yearbook of Agriculture 1941: Climate and Man* (Washington, DC: Government Printing Office, 1941)

Utah Fur-Bearers Management Recommendations and Harvest Report (Boise: Utah Department of Fish and Game, 1953—4)

Vance, J.E. Jr. *The Merchant's World.* (Englewood Cliffs, New Jersey: Prentice Hall, 1970)

—— 'The Oregon Trail and the Union Pacific Railroad: A Contrast in Purpose', *Annals*, Association of American Geographers, vol. 60 (1961), pp. 357—79

Victor, F.F. (ed.). *The River of the West* (Newark: Bliss and Co., 1870)

Von Bertalanffy, L. *General System Theory* (New York: George Braziller, 1968)

Wagner, W.F. (ed.). *Leonard's Narrative* (Cleveland: The Burrows Brothers Co., 1904)

Warren, E.R. and Hall, E.R. 'A New Sub-Species of Beaver from Colorado', *Journal of Mammalology*, vol. 20 (1939), pp. 358—67

Washburn, W.E. 'Symbol, Utility, and Aesthetics in the Indian Fur Trade', in *Aspects of the Fur Trade* (St Paul: Minnesota Historical Society, 1967), pp. 50—4

Washington, H.A. (ed.). *The Writings of Thomas Jefferson* (Washington, DC: Taylor and Maury, 1854)

Weaver, J.E. and Albertson, F.W. *Grasslands of the Great Plains* (Lincoln: Johnson Publishing Co., 1957)

Weber, D.J. *The Taos Trappers: The Fur Trade in the Far Southwest, 1540—1846* (Norman: University of Oklahoma Press, 1971)

Weltfish, G. *The Lost Universe* (New York and London: Basic Books, 1965)

Wheat, C.I. *Mapping the Transmississippi West, 1540—1861* (San Francisco: The Institute of Historical Cartography, 1958)

Whittlesey, D. 'Sequent Occupance', *Annals*, Association of American Geographers, vol. 19 (1929), pp. 162—5

Will, G.F. and Hyde, G.E. *Corn Among the Indians of the Upper Missouri* (Lincoln: University of Nebraska Press, 1964)

Wilson, F.T. 'Old Fort Pierre and Its Neighbours', *South Dakota Historical Collections*, vol. 1 (1902), pp. 259—440

Wishart, D.J. 'Agriculture at the Trading Posts on the Upper Missouri Prior to 1843', *Agricultural History,* vol. 47 (1973), pp. 57—62

—— 'Images of the Northern Great Plains from the Fur Trade, 1807—1843', in B.W. Blouet and M.P. Lawson (eds.), *Images of the Plains* (Lincoln: University of Nebraska Press, 1975), pp. 45—55.

—— 'Cultures in Co-operation and Conflict: Indians in the Fur Trade on the northern Great Plains, 1807—1840', *Journal of Historical Geography,* vol. 2 (1976), pp. 311—28

—— 'The Fur Trade of the West, 1807—1840: A Geographic Synthesis', in D.H. Miller and J.O. Steffen, *The Frontier: Comparative Studies* (Norman: University of Oklahoma Press, 1977), pp. 161—200

Woolworth A.R. and Wood, W.R. 'The Archaeology of a Small Trading Post (Kipp's Post, 32MN1) in the Garrison Reservoir, South Dakota', in Roberts, F.H.H. (ed.), *River Basins Surveys Papers* (Washington, DC: US Government Printing Office, 1960), pp. 239—305

Young, F.J. (ed.). 'The Correspondence and Journals of Captain Nathaniel J. Wyeth, 1831—6', *Sources of the History of Oregon* (Eugene: University Press, 1899), vol. 1, Parts 3—6

Zelinsky, W. *The Cultural Geography of the United States* (Englewood Cliffs, New Jersey: Prentice Hall, 1973)

IV. Unpublished Sources

Cahalane, V.H. 'Wildlife, Ecology, and the Fur Trade', Paper Presented at the North American Fur Trade Conference, St Paul, 1965

Hafen, L.R. 'The Fur Trade Rendezvous of the Central Rockies', Paper Presented at the North American Fur Trade Conference, St Paul, 1965

Smith, G.H. 'The Buildings of the Fur Trade', Paper Presented at the North American Fur Trade Conference, St Paul, 1965

Index

Absaroka 29, 60, *see also* Crow
  Country
Adams-Onis Treaty 14
Adobe construction 88, 91-2
Agriculture: at trading posts
  102-4; Native American
  102-4
Alcohol: as a trade good 68-9;
  Hudson's Bay Company
  policy concerning 77n;
  impact on Native Americans
  69-70
American Fur Company: expan-
  sion onto Upper Missouri
  46-53, expansion into Rocky
  Mountains, 140, 146, 148-52,
  policies of 52; trading net-
  work on Upper Missouri
  52-73, *see also* Astor, John
  Jacob, Upper Missouri Outfit,
  Western Department
Anderson, William Marshall 34,
  128, 151, 204n
Arapahoe 19, 72
Arapooish, Chief 188-9
Arikara 20, 67, 68; attitude to
  fur trade of 51-2
Ashley, William 25, 29, 32,
  183, 190, 198; establishes the
  Rocky Mountain Trapping
  System 121-7; on the Upper
  Missouri 50-3; withdraws
  from fur trade 127
Aspen: as source of food for

beaver 28
Assiniboine 19; attitude to fur
  trade 67, 81-2
Astor, John Jacob 52, 70,
  116-19, 152, 160, *see also*
  American Fur Company
Astoria, see Pacific Fur Com-
  pany
Atkinson, General Henry 50
Atsina 19
Attitudes to Resources: Ameri-
  can 31-3, 215, 217n; British
  32-3, 130

Ball, John 195-6
Bannock 158, 185
Bean-Sinclair Party 142
Bear Lake 124
Bear River 25, 30, 124; as a ren-
  dezvous site 126, 133,
  154-5; as a winter site 184-5
Beaver: ecology 27-33; exhaus-
  tion of reserves 31-3, 65, 132,
  137, 183; methods of trap-
  ping 180-1; price of pelts
  141, 147, 160-1, 164-5; re-
  establishment 212-13; trap-
  ping seasons 175-84
Bent and St Vrain 73
Berger, Jacob 61
Berthold, Bartholomew 50
Biddle, Thomas 41, 42, 69
Bighorn River 29, 42, 146, 187; .
  as a transportation route 125,

154, 193
Big Sioux Post 54
Bison: depletion of herds 183,
    213; ecology 33-5; methods
    of hunting 95-8; robes, pro-
    duction of 109
Blackfoot 19-20, 67; annual
    regime 96-7; attitude to fur
    trade 29, 45, 48, 81-2, 115;
    treaty with 61, *see also*
    Piegan.
Blackfoot Brigades 140, 145-6,
    163-4, 175-7, 187
Blackfoot Country 29, 50, 140,
    143, 145
Black Hills 25, 50, 122
Bodmer, Carl 88-90
Bonneville, Captain Benjamin
    142, 152-6, 172n
Boston: as market for robes 107
Bourdon, Michael 129
Bridger, Jim 140, 143, 145, 163,
    177, 198, *see also* Rocky
    Mountain Fur Company
Brown's Hole 185
Buenaventura: mythical river
    132
Bullboats 71, 85-6
Burr, David: map of 133, 169n

Cabanne, Jean 41, 66, 86
Cabannes Post 59, 64, 104;
    description of 91
Cache: description of 181
Cache Valley 125, 132, 181; as a
    rendezvous site 193; as a
    winter site 185
California 133, 154, 183, 184
Campbell, Robert 62, 64, 138,
    142, 188, *see also* Sublette
    and Campbell
Camp Keepers 178
Canton Trade 116-17, 167n
Carson, Kit 146, 165
Castoreum 181, 200n
Cedar Island Post 45
Cerre, Michael Sylvestre 152,
    154
Chardon, Francis 20, 68, 101,

113n
Cheyenne 19, 63, 72
Cheyenne River 63, 122
Chittenden, Hiram Martin 214
Chouteau, August 41
Chouteau, Pierre Jr 34, 50-1,
    73-74, 108-9, 154, 161; as
    dominant force in the fur
    trade 76n, 166, *see also*
    Pratte, Chouteau and Com-
    pany
Clamorgan, Jacques 41-2
Clark, William 133, *see also*
    Lewis and Clark Expedition
Clayton, James 207
Clearwater Post 119
Colter, John 45
Columbia Fur Company 50-3
Columbia River 14, 19, 26,
    116-18, 158
Cottonwoods: as forage 124,
    188
Council Bluffs: as trading post
    site 45, 91
Cowan, J.M. 31
Craig, William 154
Crazy Bear, Chief 94
Cree 19, 65
Crooks, Ramsey 48, 52, 83,
    106-9
Crow 19, 29-30, 45, 48, 68-9;
    attitude to fur trade 60, 81-2,
    184; perception of their
    country 188; wintering
    grounds 96
Crow Country, 139, 143, 146,
    154-5, *see also* Absaroka
Culbertson, Alexander 68, 103

Dasmann, Raymond 215
Deerskins: value 37; market 107
Dakota; Teton 54, 67, 73; atti-
    tude to fur trade 19-20
Deforestation 87, 212
Denig, Edwin 18, 32, 97; descrip-
    tion of Fort Union 89-90,
    102-3; on bison migrations
    34; on the impact of alcohol
    on Native Americans 69-70;

on the return of beaver to the
Upper Missouri 212-13; on
the trading cycle 92-4
DeVoto, Bernard 23, 172n
Dougherty, John 67, 101
Douglas, James 165
Drips, Andrew 74, 140, 148-52,
163
Drouillard, George: map of 43,
74n; death of 46

Environment: effect on fur trade
27
Environmentalism 17
Epishemores 199
Epizootics 31, 39n
Erie Canal 107
Evans, Robert 158
Exploration: and the fur trade
132-3, 154, 208-9
Ewers, J.C. 190

Farm Island 103
Ferris, Warren 143, 178, 181
Fitzpatrick, Tom 35, 52, 140,
146, 156, 209, *see also*
Fontenelle, Fitzpatrick and
Co., and Rocky Mountain
Fur Company
Flathead Indians 20, 21, 68, 149
Flathead Lake 122, 137, 185
Flathead Post 26, 122, 129, 138,
144-5
Fontenelle, Lucien 34, 140,
148-52, 163, *see also* Fonte-
nelle, Fitzpatrick and Co.
Fontenelle, Fitzpatrick and Co:
formed 151-2; bought out by
Pratte, Chouteau and Co. 163
Fontenelle's Post 104
Forts *see individual forts and
posts*
Fort Atkinson 48, 122
Fort Benton 48
Fort Bonneville (Horse Creek)
152-3, 192
Fort Bonneville (Salmon River)
154
Fort Bridger 166-7

Fort Cass: establishment of 59;
fur production at 61
Fort Clark: agriculture at 101;
establishment 59; fur produc-
tion at 58-61, 100
Fort Davy Crockett 166, 185
Fort George 91
Fort Hall 158-60, 166, 185;
trading rates at 199
Fort John 63, *see also* Fort
Laramie
Fort Laramie 63; description
of 91
Fort Lisa 46
Fort Lookout 73
Fort Lupton 73
Fort McKenzie: description of
90; establishment of 59;
fur production at 62
Fort Nez Perces 129, 155, 156,
157
Fort Pierre: abandonment of
211; agriculture at 103-4;
description of 88-9; fur pro-
duction at 55-6; wood con-
sumption at 214
Fort Platte 73; description of 91
Fort Raymond 42, 45
Fort Tecumseh: establishment
of 53; fur production at 54,
56; replaced by Fort Pierre
54
Fort Uintah 166
Fort Union: description of
88-90; fur production at
57-8; head of steamboat
navigation 86
Fort Vasquez 73
Fort William (Savies Island) 159
Fort William (Upper Missouri)
71, *see also* Sublette and
Campbell
Fort William (North Platte)
149, 165, 197; fur production at 62-3; road-ranch
function 196
Four Bears, Chief 69, 77n
Fraeb, Henry 140, 143, *see also*
Rocky Mountain Fur Comp-

any
Fremont, James C. 35
French Fur Company 50-2
French Fur Trade 41-2
Fuel Shortages 105, 214
Fur Trade: as a frontier stage 18,
   205-15; a network 79-80,
   175-6; British and American
   fur trades compared 128-9;
   impact on Native Americans
   66-9, 214-15

Gantt-Blackwell Party 142
Gervais, Jean Baptiste 140, 143,
   see also Rocky Mountain
   Fur Company
Gift-Giving: implications of
   98-9
Goetzman, W.H. 205, 206, 208
Gordon, William 33, 65, 144-5
Gray, Captain Robert 14
Great American Desert 17, 37n,
   196
Great Basin 26, 126, 132, 183,
   see also Starvation Country
Great Britain: war with 46, 119;
   treaties with 14, 120
Green River 25, 122, 124, 192-3,
   see also Rendezvous
Griffin, Thomas 17
Griswold, Gaylord 17

Halsey, Jacob 68
Hamilton, Michael 103
Ham's Fork 191
Harris, Edward 101
Harris, Moses 139
Hempstead, Thomas 48
Henry, Andrew 45, 46, 102,
   117, 121-2
Henry's Fork 125, 126, 143
Herzog, Moses 205
Hidatsa 20, 45, 50, 59, 67, 214
Horses: diffusion of 20-1; price
   of 113n
Hudson's Bay Company: compe-
   tition in Rocky Mountains
   128-31, 165-6; competition
   in European markets 107-8;

competition on Upper
   Missouri 70; conservation
   policies 32; Snake River
   policy 32, 131, *see also*
   Snake River Brigades
Hunt, Wilson Price 117

Independence 156, 194
Indians *see individual groups and
   Native Americans*
Immel, Michael 29; Immell-Jones
   Massacre 48
Innis, Harold 207
Irving, Washington 155, 197

Jackson, David 136, 137, *see
   also* Smith, Jackson and
   Sublette
Jackson Hole 25, 26, 185, 202n
Jefferson, Thomas: plans for the
   fur trade 13, 17-18, 116,
   207-8

Keelboats 83-4
Kelley, Hall J.: influence on
   Wyeth 156
Kipp, James 52, 81, 103
Kipp's Post: description of 91

Laidlaw, William 64, 73, 88-9,
   103
Lamont, Daniel 34
Lampson, Curtis 107-9, 160-1
Larpenteur, Charles 101
Leipzig: as fur mart 107
Lemhi Pass 26, 129
Leonard, Zenas 99, 162, 182-3,
   198, 206
Leopold, Aldo 213
Lewis, Meriwether 46, *see also*
   Lewis and Clark Expedition
Lewis, Reuben 46
Lewis and Clark Expedition 115;
   objectives, and influence on
   fur trade 18-22
Lisa, Manuel: head of Missouri
   Fur Company 42-6; object-
   ives of 41; personality of 42;
   strategy of 42-3; Sub-Agent

for Indian Affairs 46
London: as fur mart 107
Long, Stephen 17, 124
Louisel, Regis 43
Louisiana Territory: boundaries
  of 13-14; geographic images
  of 16-17, 115; Jefferson's
  plans for 13-18; map of 15;
  purchase of 13-14
Lowenthal, David 184
Lupton, Lancaster 73

McKenzie, Donald 129
McKenzie, Kennth 61, 70, 98;
  founder of Fort Union 56;
  head of Upper Missouri
  Outfit 76n, 148; innovator
  of steamboat navigation on
  Missouri 86
Mackinaw 84-5, 105
McLoughlin, Dr John 137, 165
Mandan 43, 59-60, 66; attitude
  to fur trade 19
Marias river 20
Markets, for furs 105-7, 160-1
Meek, Joe 35, 150, 160, 165-6,
  180, 184-5, 189; in Oregon
  209
Meinig, D.W. 160
Merk, Frederick 128-9
Merle and Company (New
  Orleans) 82, 106
Military Frontier 210-11
Miller, Alfred Jacob 91, 112n,
  197
Mishkin, Bernard 20
Missionary Frontier 210-11
Missouri Fur Company 42-52
Missouri Plateau 23
Missouri River: annual regime
  83; transportation on 83-7,
  106
Montero, Antonio 155-6, 189
Muskrat: ecology 36

Native Americans: acculturation
  of 19-22, 95, 214-15; map of
  culture areas and populations
  16; role in the fur trade 21-2,

92-100; trade systems 21;
  see individual groups
Navy Yard, 105
Newell, Robert 145, 209
New Orleans 82, 107
New York: as market 79, 107-8
Nez Perce 21, 158, 185
Northwest Company 12, 119

Ogden, Peter Skene 128, 184
Ohio Canal 107
Ojibway 19
Okanagan Post 119
Omaha 20, 45, 50, 66, 96;
  impact of fur trade on 95
Oregon: claims to 14;
  competition over 128-9, 160;
  trappers settle in 209-10
Oregon Trail 125, 156, 212
Osage 23, 41
Oto 41, 45
Otter: ecology 36

Pacific Fur Company 14, 116-20
Passage to India 115
Pawnee: annual regime 95;
  attitude to fur trade 19; Skidi
  band (Loups) 124
Pemmican 101, 183
Pennysylvania Canal 107
Piegan 19-20, 32, 68; wintering
  grounds 96
Pierres Hole 25, 139, 141, 192
Pike, Zebulon 17
Pilcher, Joshua 48, 115, 138-9
Piroques 85
Pittsburgh 107, 111n
Platte Overland Route 23, 122,
  125-6, 135-6, 194-7
Ponca 20, 66-7
Ponca Post 54, 66
Popo Agie 138, 191
Portneuf River 30, 185
Powder River 29, 42; as
  wintering site 187-9
Pratte, Bernard, Sr 50, 166
Pratte, Couteau and Company
  152, 162-5, 198
Provost, Etienne 128, 149

Rendezvous: decline of 160, 164-5; evolution of 122, 190; location and functions of 190-3

Robidoux, Joseph 140

Rocky Mountain Fur Company 141-8, 158, 160

Rosebud River 29

Ross, Alexander 129-30

Russell, Osborne 97, 157-8, 183, 188, 206

Russian-American Company 116-17

Ruxton, Frederick 22, 213

Sage, Rufus 91

St. Louis: control point of fur trade 41, 47, 92, 106-9, 175; economic growth as result of fur trade 207

Salmon River 26; as wintering site 143, 145, 185

Santa Fe: as base for trappers 121; trade 140-1

Sarpy's Post 54

Sauer, Carl O. 39n, 205

Seton, E.T. 27

She-Whaps Post 119

Shoshoni 21, 99, 158; trade fair 190

Simpson, Sir George: conservation policies of 32; reorganizes Columbia Department 131; response to American settlement in Oregon 210

Sinclair, Alexander 142

Smallpox: impact on Native Americans 66-9, 109

Smith, Jedediah 26, 52, 121, 126, 141, 188; Southwest Expeditions of 133, 136-7

Smith, Jackson and Sublette 132-41, 142, 169n, 208

Smith, Willard 91

Snake River 25, 26, 32, 35, 122, 130, 137, 182, 185

Snake River Brigades 127, 130-1, 182

Snake River Plains 26, 117, 130, 137, 143

South Pass 25, 125; Euro-American discovery of 122, 167n; transportation route 193-4, 212

Spanish Fur Trade 41-2, 127-8

Spokane Post 119

Starvation Country *see* Great Basin

Steamboat: on the Upper Missouri 85-7

Stone, Bostwick and Company 48, 52

Stuart, Robert 119

Sublette, Andrew 72

Sublette, Milton 139, 140, 143

Sublette, William 52, 62, 133, 197, *see also* Sublette and Campbell

Sublette, William, and Campbell, Robert: opposition to the American Fur Company 71-4, 148-52

Subsistance: at the trading posts 100-6; in the Rocky Mountains 183, 185

Sunder, John 83

Taos: as a base for trappers 127-8, 142, 193

Temporary trading posts 54, 64-5

Teton River 53, 54, 56

Tongue River 29, 42

Trade goods: types and sources 81-3

Trading Posts: agriculture at 102-4; hierarchy 54; location factors 53-64; maintenance and industry at 105-6; morphology 87-93. *see also individual posts*

Trading Rates: in Rocky Mountains 198-9; on Upper Missouri, 94-5

Trading Rituals 93-100

TransAtlantic Transportation 79, 110n

Trappers: as pioneers 209;
mortality rates 138, 169n;
motivations 206; origins 204;
salaries 147; types of 125
Traps 180, 200n
Traverse, Lake 50
Tularemia 34, 39n
Turner, Frederick Jackson 212,
217n

Union Fur Company 74, 91
Union Pacific Railroad 212
Union Pass 122
Upper Missouri: definition of
38n
Upper Missouri Outfit 53, 61
65, 171n

Vance, James 207, 212
Vanderburgh, Henry 148-52
Vasquez, Louis 73
Vermillion: trade good 110n
Vermillion Post 54

Walker, Joseph R. 26, 152-5,
183-4
Washburn, W.E. 190
Weber, Captain John 121-2
Western Department: creation of
52-3, 164; entry into Rocky
Mountain Trapping System
148

White Earth River Post 53
Whittlesey, Derwent: concept of
sequent occupance 210
Wied-Neuwied, Prince
Maximilian of 54, 56, 87-9,
103
Williamette Post 119
Williamette Valley 136, 158,
209
Wind River 139, 191; as a
rendezvous site 166; as a
winter site 189
Winter Express: to Upper
Missouri 79-80; to Rocky
Mountains, 189-90
Winter Sites 184-90
Work, John 130
Wyeth, Nathaniel 104, 142,
147, 157-62, 183, 195

Yankton 20, 50, 54, 60, 65
Yanktonai 21, 60
Yellowstone Expedition 86
Yellowstone River 26, 42,
146; as transportation route
125, 193; as winter site
177, 187

Zelinsky, Wilbur: doctrine of
First Effective Settlement
207

Date Due